microsoft
windows xp

Visual QuickProject Guide Collection

by John Rizzo, Jan Ozer, and Tom Negrino

Peachpit Press

Microsoft Windows XP Visual QuickProject Guide Collection
John Rizzo, Jan Ozer, and Tom Negrino

Peachpit Press
1249 Eighth Street
Berkeley, CA 94710
510/524-2178
800/283-9444
510/524-2221 (fax)

Find us on the Web at: www.peachpit.com
To report errors, please send a note to errata@peachpit.com

Peachpit Press is a division of Pearson Education

ISBN 0-321-37463-0

9 8 7 6 5 4 3 2 1

Printed and bound in the United States of America

A Note About This Collection

Thank you for purchasing the Microsoft Windows XP Visual QuickProject Guide Collection. By combining three books into one, you save money and learn just what you need to get the job done.

Customizing Windows XP: Visual QuickProject Guide is the first book in this combined volume, with the index for the book following immediately after the text. This is followed by Making a Movie with Windows XP: Visual Quick-Project Guide and Managing Your Personal Finances with Quicken: Visual QuickProject Guide, with their respective indexes following immediately after each book, as well.

Full-color projects
from the folks
who bring you
Visual QuickStart
Guides...

Visual QuickProject

Customizing
Windows XP

JOHN RIZZO

customizing
windows xp

Visual QuickProject Guide

by John Rizzo

Peachpit
Press

Visual QuickProject Guide
Customizing Windows XP
John Rizzo

Peachpit Press

1249 Eighth Street
Berkeley, CA 94710
510/524-2178
800/283-9444
510/524-2221 (fax)

Find us on the World Wide Web at: www.peachpit.com
To report errors, please send a note to errata@peachpit.com
Peachpit Press is a division of Pearson Education

Copyright © 2005 by John Rizzo

Editor: Suzie Lowey Nasol
Production Editor: Lupe Edgar
Compositor: Owen Wolfson
Indexer: FireCrystal Communications
Cover design: The Visual Group with Aren Howell
Interior design: Elizabeth Castro Cover
Photo credit: PhotoDisc

Notice of Rights

Notice of Liability

Trademarks

ISBN 0-321-32124-3

Printed and bound in the United States of America

Special Thanks to...

Christine for her continuing support and tolerance of my work habits;

Sal for his patience and persistence and for his continuing interest in my work;

Suzie Lowey Nasol for being at the helm and adeptly steering this project's journey to a successful conclusion;

Cliff Colby for pointing me towards this project;

and to the folks at Peachpit Press for their superb design and production values, and for throwing a great party in a 100-year-old San Francisco bar.

contents

contents

contents

introduction

The Visual QuickProject Guide you're reading offers a unique way to learn new skills. Instead of drowning you in long text descriptions, this Visual QuickProject Guide uses color screen shots with clear, concise, step-by-step instructions to show you how to complete a customization project in a matter of minutes.

The projects in this book personalize different aspects of Windows XP, so that your computer looks and acts the way that best fits your personal style of working. We'll dig into some of the many configuration dialog boxes to expose the plethora of options available to you. In fact, one problem confronting many people is the fact that Windows XP offers so many options that it can become overwhelming. To narrow it down, we'll focus in on the settings that make Windows XP more intuitive and useful. You may not care for every customization feature presented in this book, but by following along with each project, you'll learn some of the possibilities Windows XP offers. Once you see how configuration works, you'll be able to continue to explore the other customization options available to you.

We will be working with the standard settings dialog boxes to make changes to a variety of different parts of Windows, including the Desktop and Start menu, files, folders and windows, and the way you work with the Internet.

what you'll learn

Personalize the Desktop with your own art and make other modifications.

Add different types of toolbars to the edges of your screen.

Create shortcuts to files and dialog boxes.

Add your own programs to the Quicklaunch area of the toolbar.

Add toolbars to the Taskbar for access to the Internet, your files, and other Windows XP features.

introduction

Replace Internet Explorer
with another Program as
your default Web browser.

Change static icons into
hierarchical menus.

Add your
programs and
folders to the
top of the
Start menu.

Change the
number of
recently used
program icons
displayed.

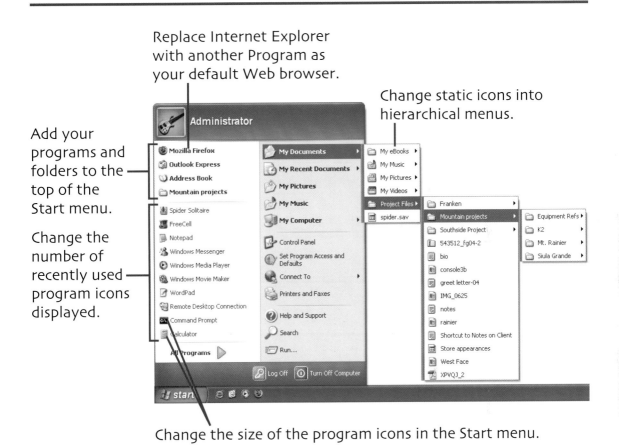

Change the size of the program icons in the Start menu.

introduction

what you'll learn (cont.)

Add new icons to the window toolbar.

Hide or display the side pane.

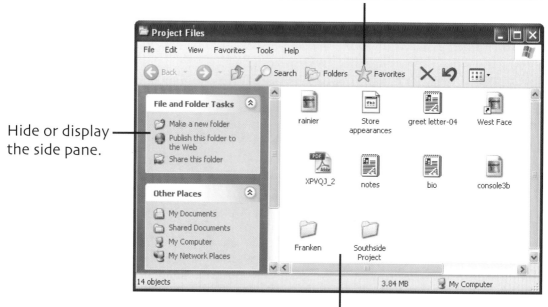

Use custom icons for files and folders.

Automatically arrange file icons in different ways.

Hide or display various window toolbars.

Add new software and remove old software.

Add new Windows features and update Windows.

Change the default programs that open certain types of files.

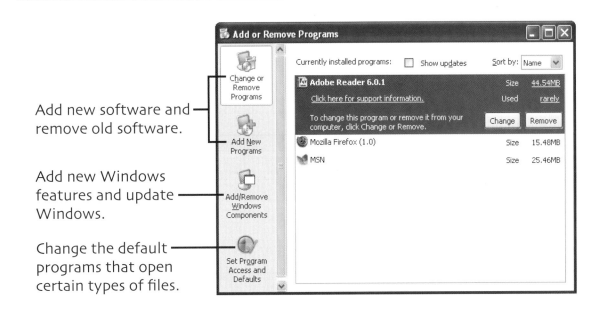

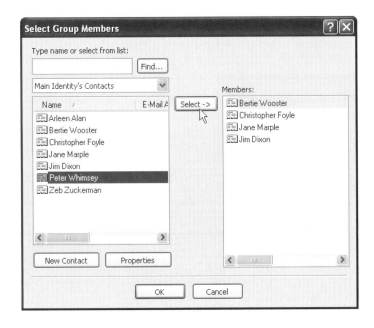

Create a high-speed Internet connection, turn off Outlook Express graphics to keep spammers at bay, and create groups in Outlook Express' address book.

how this book works

The title of each section explains what is covered on that page.

add player to taskbar

Ordinarily, when you click the Taskbar's Windows Media Player icon, the Player's window appears. You can add a smaller version of the Media Player right in the Taskbar that will be available to you while other programs are open.

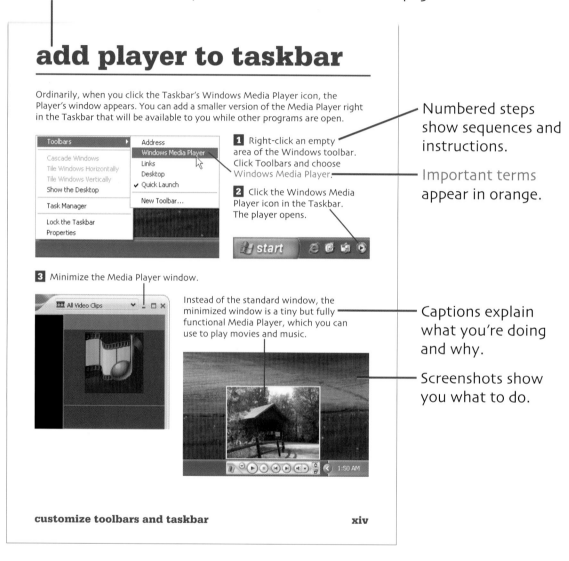

1 Right-click an empty area of the Windows toolbar. Click Toolbars and choose Windows Media Player.

2 Click the Windows Media Player icon in the Taskbar. The player opens.

Numbered steps show sequences and instructions.

Important terms appear in orange.

3 Minimize the Media Player window.

Instead of the standard window, the minimized window is a tiny but fully functional Media Player, which you can use to play movies and music.

Captions explain what you're doing and why.

Screenshots show you what to do.

customize toolbars and taskbar   **xiv**

The extra bits section at the end of each chapter contains additional tips and tricks that you might like to know—but that aren't absolutely necessary.

extra bits

place files and folders p. 48

- Did you know that the documents and shortcut files on the Desktop actually sit inside a folder called, well, Desktop?

  It's in the Documents and Settings folder, inside a folder named after your user name.

  Add an item to the Desktop folder and it appears on the Desktop.

- Have you ever wanted easy access to a small portion of a file? You don't have to create a new document—just create a scrap.

  To create a scrap, simply select some text—a paragraph, sentence, or phrase—and drag it from the document window to the Desktop. A new file is created that has an icon with a jagged bottom.

WordPad
Document Scrap
'winter of our...'

cleanup desktop p. 52

- Another way to quickly access your Desktop icons is with a key command. You can press Windows-D to minimize all of the open windows at the same time.

  This technique will even minimize windows that don't have a minimize button, such as dialog boxes and the Control Panel.

  Pressing Windows-D again will restore all of the windows you just minimized—unless you've opened, minimized, or restored any windows since hitting the command. If that's the case, Windows-D will only work on the last window you worked with.

The heading for each group of tips matches the section title.

The page number next to the heading makes it easy to refer back to the main content.

the next step

While this Visual QuickProject Guide will give you a foundation In customizing the way your computer looks and acts, there's much more to learn about Windows XP.

If you want to dive into the details of using and configuring Windows XP, try Windows XP: Visual QuickStart Guide, also published by Peachpit Press, as an in-depth, handy reference.

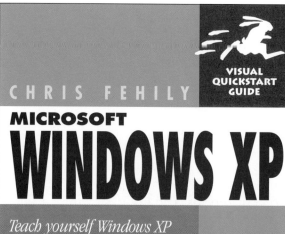

CHRIS FEHILY

MICROSOFT

WINDOWS XP

Teach yourself Windows XP the quick and easy way! This Visual QuickStart Guide uses ...tures rather than lengthy ...lanations. You'll be up ...d running in no time!

VISUAL QUICKSTART GUIDE

COVERS HOME AND PROFESSIONAL EDITIONS

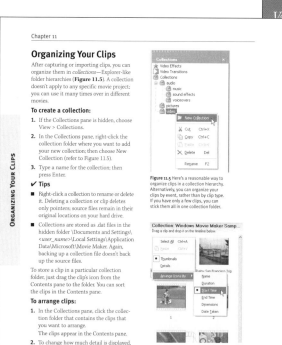

Chapter 11

Organizing Your Clips

After capturing or importing clips, you can organize them in *collections*—Explorer-like folder hierarchies (**Figure 11.5**). A collection doesn't apply to any specific movie project; you can use it many times over in different movies.

To create a collection:

1. If the Collections pane is hidden, choose View > Collections.

2. In the Collections pane, right-click the collection folder where you want to add your new collection; then choose New Collection (refer to Figure 11.5).

3. Type a name for the collection; then press Enter.

✔ Tips

■ Right-click a collection to rename or delete it. Deleting a collection or clip deletes only pointers; source files remain in their original locations on your hard drive.

■ Collections are stored as .dat files in the hidden folder \Documents and Settings\ *<user_name>*\Local Settings\Application Data\Microsoft\Movie Maker. Again, backing up a collection file doesn't back up the source files.

To store a clip in a particular collection folder, just drag the clip's icon from the Contents pane to the folder. You can sort the clips in the Contents pane.

To arrange clips:

1. In the Collections pane, click the collection folder that contains the clips that you want to arrange.
   The clips appear in the Contents pane.

2. To change how much detail is displayed, choose View > Details or View > Thumbnails.

3. Choose View > Arrange Icons By; then choose a property to display (**Figure 11.6**).

Figure 11.5 Here's a reasonable way to organize clips in a collection hierarchy. Alternatively, you can organize your clips by event, rather than by clip type. If you have only a few clips, you can stick them all in one collection folder.

Figure 11.6 You also can arrange clips via the shortcut menu; just right-click an empty area of the Contents pane.

296

ORGANIZING YOUR CLIPS

The Windows XP VQS features clear examples, concise, step-by-step instructions, hundreds of illustrations, and lots of helpful tips that will help you master Windows XP.

1. explore windows xp customization

Where do I start?

That's the first question that comes to mind when seeking to personalize Windows XP. The answer can be found all over Windows. You can start with shortcut menus, the Start menu, the taskbar and toolbars, and other menus.

Your destination can be a properties dialog box, items in the Control Panel, or other dialog boxes. There are often different ways to get to a particular settings dialog box which may have buttons and tabs to get where you need to be, and other times Windows will launch wizards to guide you through a set up process.

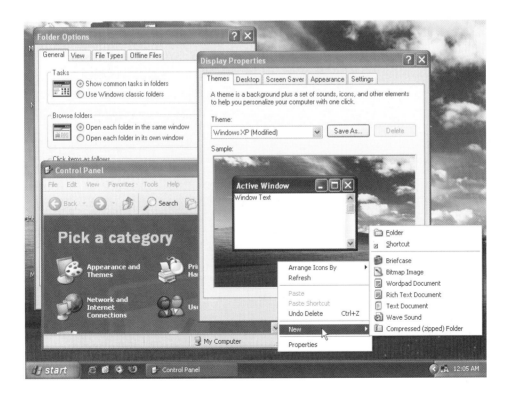

open shortcut menus

In Windows XP, pressing the right mouse button (known as right-clicking) will open a menu known as a shortcut menu. Many customizations in this book begin by bringing up a shortcut menu.

Not all shortcut menus are the same, however. What the shortcut menu looks like depends on what the cursor is pointing to when you right-click.

Try right-clicking on different objects: files, the Taskbar, items in the Start menu, title bars of windows, and even empty space on the Desktop. The shortcut menu that appears will have options specific to the object you are pointing to.

Shortcut menus present options that you can also get to from various menus and toolbars throughout Windows. The shortcut menu is usually the quickest way to access these options.

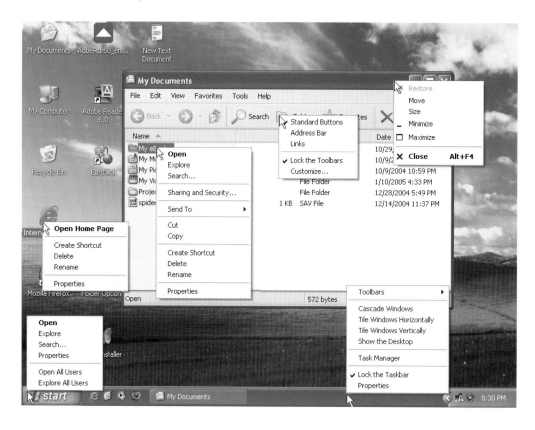

properties windows

Many of the shortcut menus contain a Properties command. This brings up a properties dialog box that has settings specific to the item you right-clicked.

Much of the personalizing you'll do in Windows XP will take place in these properties dialog boxes, which are as varied as shortcut menus. Some, such as file properties dialog boxes, are simple, offering only a few settings options.

Others are more complex, with multiple tabs, each containing numerous settings options.

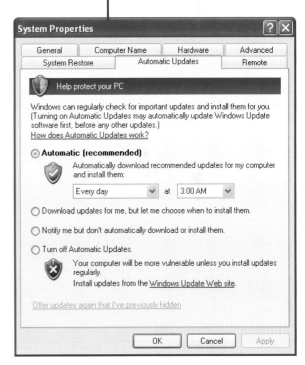

use the control panel

The Control Panel is a repository for all kinds of settings dialog boxes. If you're not sure where to find certain properties dialog boxes or other settings, you can click around in the Control Panel. The Control Panel is also handy if you're accessing multiple settings dialog boxes.

There are two main ways to view the Control Panel. The default is the category view, which displays icons that represent categories of settings dialog boxes. Click an icon here and you'll be presented with a number of choices.

You can get to the Control Panel from the Start menu.

If you know what you're looking for, try clicking Switch to Classic View.

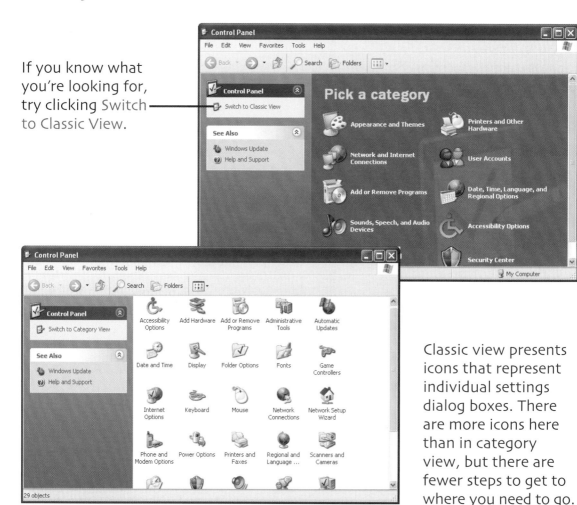

Classic view presents icons that represent individual settings dialog boxes. There are more icons here than in category view, but there are fewer steps to get to where you need to go.

　　　explore windows xp customization

run wizards

A wizard is a program that gives you step-by-step instructions for setting up a specific feature. Windows XP contains dozens of wizards that guide you through tasks such as creating an Internet connection, setting up a printer, and creating a network of PCs.

A wizard will present a series of screens, each asking you to select options or to type in information.

You don't have to go looking for the right wizard to accomplish a task. Windows XP presents the correct wizard the first time you set up a new function or piece of hardware.

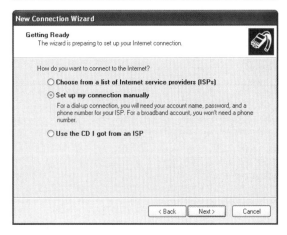

get dialog box help

Windows XP offers several different ways to get answers to your questions about what the commands in dialog boxes do. Of course, you can search the main help system by going to the Start menu and selecting Help and Support. This is the hard way, as it requires you to search the Help system

There is a better way to find out specifically what an option or button in a dialog box does.

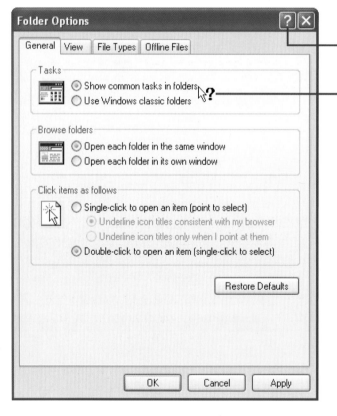

1 Click the question mark at the top-right of a dialog box.

2 A question mark appears next to the cursor arrow. Move the cursor/question mark over a command or button that you want to know about and click.

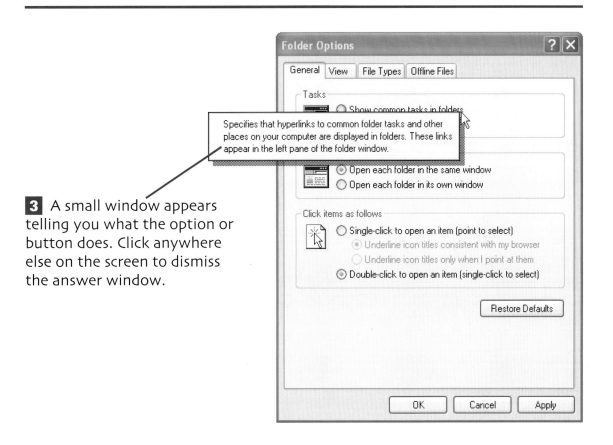

3 A small window appears telling you what the option or button does. Click anywhere else on the screen to dismiss the answer window.

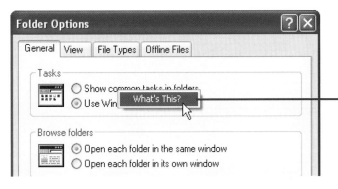

Another way to bring up the same pop-up window is to right-click a command or button in the dialog box. This brings up a small shortcut menu with a single item in it: What's This?. Click on What's This? and the answer appears.

extra bits

properties windows p. 3

- In any dialog box, the OK button enacts the changes you just made to the settings and closes the dialog box.

- The Apply button also makes the change, but keeps the dialog box open.

use the control panel p. 4

- When the Control Panel is in classic view, you can rearrange and change the size of icons just as you can documents in a folder window. Just go to the View menu and select an option.

get dialog box help p. 6

- Sometimes the help you get in a dialog box is so specific that you can't tell what it means. If you can't find what you're looking for in the Help and Support Center in the Start menu, you can look online. Click the Support icon at the top of the Help and Support Center window. Your Web browser will launch and take you to Microsoft's support Web site.

2. personalize the desktop

The Desktop is what's on your monitor when you've opened Windows but don't have any programs open. In this chapter you'll learn how to change Microsoft's default Desktop to make it your own.

Working with the Display Properties dialog box, you can replace the standard Desktop picture with a favorite family photo, a solid color, or an abstract pattern. In the Display Properties dialog box you can also make the Desktop icons bigger or smaller, or change the size of everything on your computer screen.

replace desktop photo

Sick of the grassy hill? Have a nice picture you'd rather look at? You can replace the standard desktop picture with your own digital photo (such as a JPEG file) from your hard disk. Use a horizontally oriented photo to have it automatically fit to the Desktop.

1 Right-click on the desktop and select Properties from the shortcut list.

2 Click the Desktop tab.

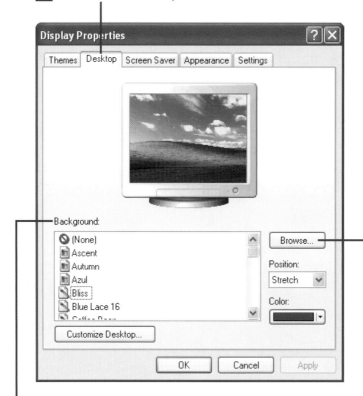

3 Click the Browse button to bring up the Browser window.

If you don't have your own photo, Windows XP has many pictures and patterns to choose from in the Background field. You'll find the grassy hill listed here, going by the name of Bliss.

personalize the desktop

4 Navigate through your folders to find the picture you'd like to use.

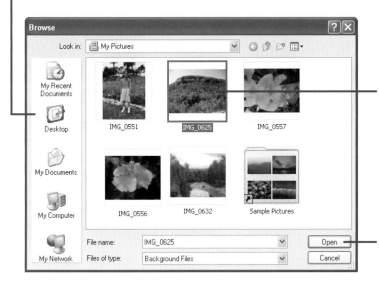

5 When you find your photo, click on it to select it.

6 Click the Open button. The Browse window will close, bringing you back to the Properties window.

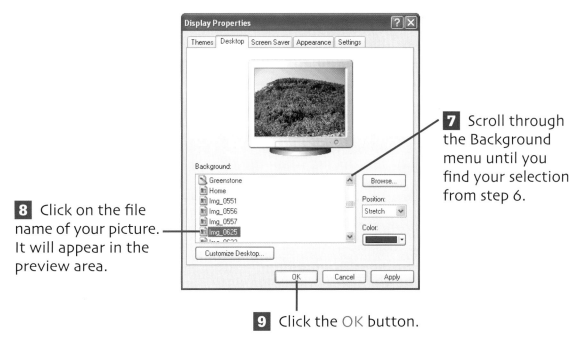

7 Scroll through the Background menu until you find your selection from step 6.

8 Click on the file name of your picture. It will appear in the preview area.

9 Click the OK button.

replace desktop photo

After the Display Properties window closes, you'll see your photo where the standard desktop picture used to be.

Windows will shrink or stretch your photo to fit the screen if your image doesn't fit exactly. If your picture is too small you can tell Windows to simply center the picture at full size.

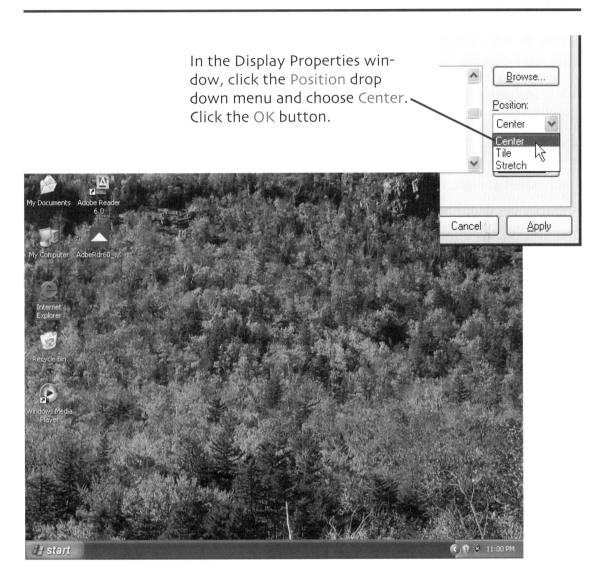

In the Display Properties window, click the Position drop down menu and choose Center. Click the OK button.

You can see that the desktop picture here is larger than on the facing page, with the outside edges cut off. In this case, it's a pleasing effect, but might not be with other photos.

personalize the desktop

change desktop size

If your Desktop is getting crowded with icons that you don't want to remove, making them smaller will help make your Desktop appear less cluttered and create more space. We can do this by adjusting the the display resolution.

For instance, this screen, set at 640x480 pixels, barely has enough room for the Start menu.

When you increase the resolution (to 1152x768 pixels), everything shrinks, giving you more room on the Desktop for icons, windows, and other objects.

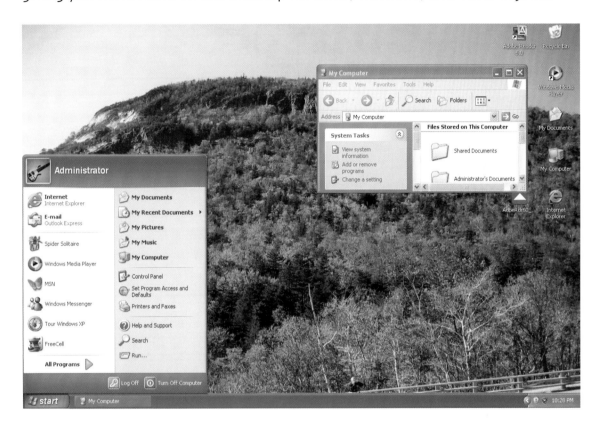

1 Right-click on the Desktop and select Properties from the shortcut menu.

change desktop size (cont.)

2 Click the Settings tab.

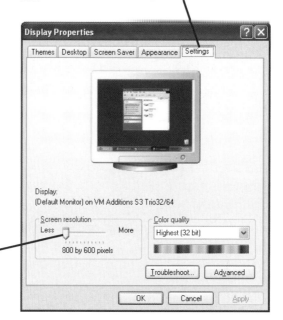

3 Drag the Screen resolution slider bar to change the pixel resolution.

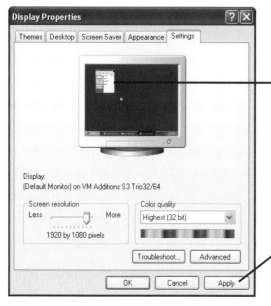

4 Watch the sample area as you move the slider back and forth. You'll see the sample window and Desktop icon shrink as you increase the screen resolution, and grow as you decrease the resolution.

5 Click the Apply button to see what your selection will look like on your full Desktop.

personalize the desktop

6 Your Desktop resolution changes, but only temporarily. The Monitor Settings dialog box appears telling you that it will revert to the previous setting in a few seconds. If you do nothing, your Desktop will revert to the previous resolution when the count down reaches zero seconds. By clicking the No button you'll cancel the change without waiting for the countdown.

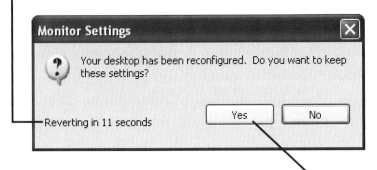

7 To accept the new resolution, click Yes before the countdown ends.

8 Click OK to close the Display Properties dialog box.

switch themes

Switching themes is the easiest way to change the way Windows XP looks. In the Themes tab, you can change the look of windows, menus, and buttons, and select new fonts and colors. If you prefer the way previous versions of Windows looked, no problem. Just switch to the Classic theme.

1 Right-click on the Desktop and select Properties from the shortcut list.

2 In the Display Properties dialog box, click the Themes tab.

3 From the Theme drop-down menu, select Windows Classic.

The Sample area displays the look of the current theme. Here, the Windows XP theme is displayed. The window called Active Window isn't a real window; It's just a sample of what a window looks like in the current theme.

personalize the desktop

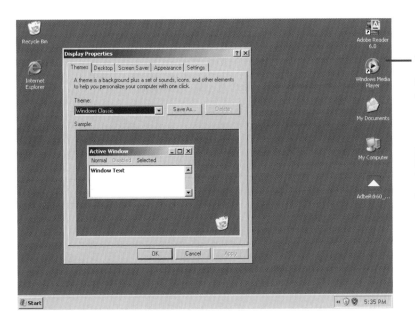

The Sample area displays the look of the Classic Windows theme that you just chose. However, your Desktop still shows the Windows XP theme.

4 To set Windows to the new theme, click the Apply button.

The Desktop now sports the Classic Windows theme.

5 Click OK to close the Display Properties dialog box.

personalize the desktop

enlarge desktop items

You don't have to be satisfied with the themes provided. Within a theme, you can change the look and feel of icons, the size and types of fonts, and the way windows and buttons look. You can also change the color scheme of a theme. Here, we're going to change the look of the Desktop icons.

1 Right-click on the Desktop and select Properties from the shortcut list.

2 In the Display Properties dialog box, click the Appearance tab.

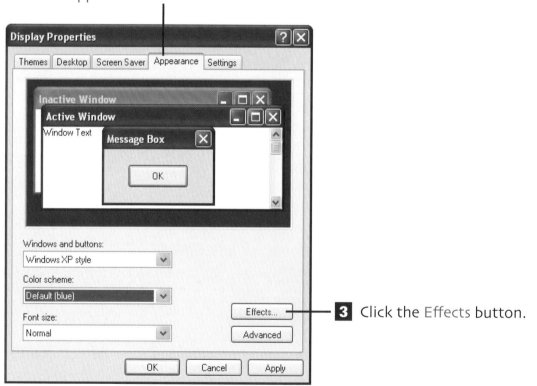

3 Click the Effects button.

personalize the desktop

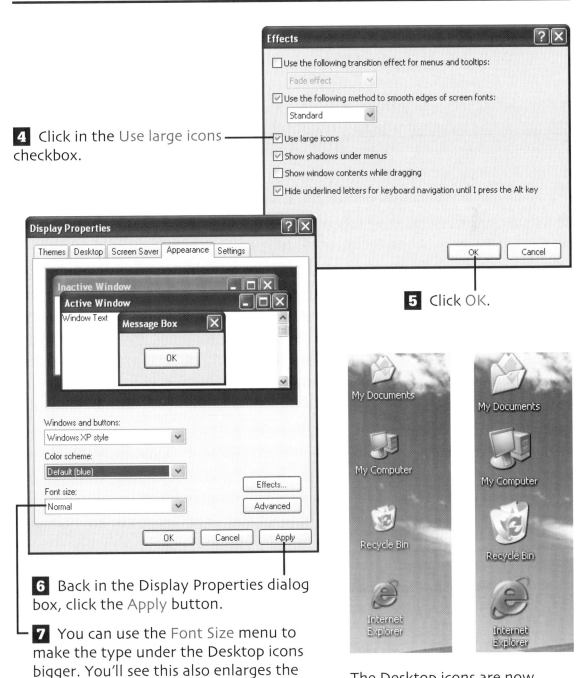

Effects

☐ Use the following transition effect for menus and tooltips:

Fade effect ▾

☑ Use the following method to smooth edges of screen fonts:

Standard ▾

4 Click in the Use large icons checkbox.

☑ Use large icons

☑ Show shadows under menus

☐ Show window contents while dragging

☑ Hide underlined letters for keyboard navigation until I press the Alt key

OK   Cancel

Display Properties

Themes | Desktop | Screen Saver | Appearance | Settings

Inactive Window

Active Window

Window Text

Message Box ☒

OK

Windows and buttons:

Windows XP style ▾

Color scheme:

Default (blue) ▾

Font size:

Normal ▾

Effects...

Advanced

OK   Cancel   Apply

5 Click OK.

6 Back in the Display Properties dialog box, click the Apply button.

7 You can use the Font Size menu to make the type under the Desktop icons bigger. You'll see this also enlarges the text in title bars and in the Start menu.

The Desktop icons are now enlarged, as shown on the right.

personalize the desktop

extra bits

replace desktop photo p. 10

- If you don't know the pixel resolution of a photo, it's easy to find out. Right-click it and choose Properties from the shortcut menu. Next, click the Summary tab, then the Advanced button. The dialog box will show the height and width of the photo in pixels.

- You don't need to switch to the Windows Classic theme in order to set the Desktop to a solid color. Right-click the Desktop and select Properties. Click the Desktop tab. Under background, select None. Now choose a color from the Color menu. Click the Apply button to see your color on the Desktop.

switch themes p. 18

- I have to admit, switching between Windows XP and Classic Windows themes isn't the most exciting way to customize your desktop. However, you can add more themes that will give you a variety of new looks for Windows.

There are many sites you can visit to buy themes and even download free themes. PC World magazine has a good selection of free themes at http://www.pcworld.com/downloads/.

Microsoft will sell you new themes as part of its $30 Microsoft Plus Pack. To get to Microsoft's Web page, right click your desktop to open the Display Properties dialog box, click the Themes tab, and select More Themes online.

3. customize toolbars and taskbar

The Taskbar is a jumping off point for opening folders and files. It includes the Start button and a few icons that open programs. You can add more icons to have one-click access to the programs you need. There are also toolbars hidden away in the Taskbar that give you access to even more of your files and folders.

Microsoft stretches the meaning of toolbar beyond that of a horizontal strip with icons on it. Windows XP toolbars can also exist as vertical strips or even as menus on the Taskbar or floating windows.

add new toolbar

Desktop toolbars can take several forms. In addition to the traditional icon-studded horizontal, Desktop toolbars can appear as items on the Taskbar, and as stand-alone windows. You can add one or more of the toolbars that come with Windows XP. You can also create your own customized toolbar containing the contents of one of your folders.

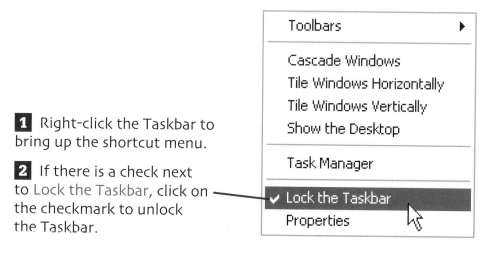

1 Right-click the Taskbar to bring up the shortcut menu.

2 If there is a check next to Lock the Taskbar, click on the checkmark to unlock the Taskbar.

This is a locked Taskbar.

This is an unlocked Taskbar, which sports these double dotted lines. An unlocked Taskbar is also a little taller.

3 In the shortcut menu that you just opened, move the cursor to Toolbars at the top of the menu.

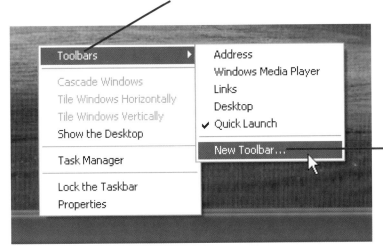

4 In the submenu that opens, click on New Toolbar.

5 In the New Toolbar dialog box, navigate to the folder that you would like to put in the toolbar. Here, we are choosing the folder called Project Files.

New Toolbar

Choose a folder, or type an Internet address

- 🗀 My Documents
    - 🗀 My eBooks
    - 🗀 My Music
    - 🗀 My Pictures
    - 🗀 Project Files
        - 🗀 Franken
        - 🗀 Mountain projects
        - 🗀 Southside Project

Folder: Project Files

Make New Folder | OK | Cancel

6 Click the OK button.

customize toolbars and taskbar

add new toolbar (cont.)

7 A toolbar will appear in the Taskbar with the name of the folder you choose, which is Project Files in this example. Click the double arrows to open the toolbar's menu.

8 You can now navigate through the hierarchical menus to the folder or file you'd like to open.

rearrange the toolbar

Once you activate a toolbar, you can move it off of the Taskbar to anywhere on the Desktop.

1 Drag your toolbar from the Taskbar and drop it onto the Desktop. Your toolbar transforms into a window known as a floating toolbar. —

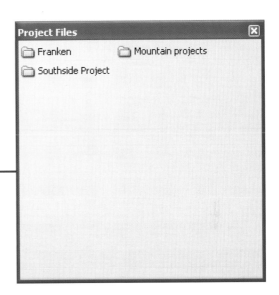

2 Drag the floating toolbar to the top or sides of the screen. The window transforms into a fixed toolbar. This fixed toolbar is on the right side of the screen. —

If you change your mind, you can change the fixed toolbar back into a floating toolbar by dragging from these └ dotted lines.

rearrange the toolbar

3 The folder icons are a bit small, but you can enlarge them. Right-click on a blank spot on the toolbar (not on one of the icons). Click View and then Large Icons.

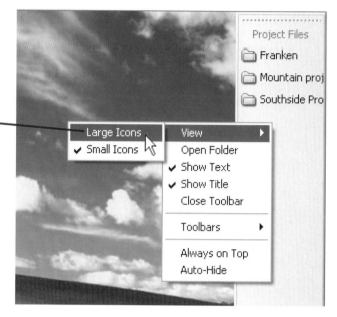

The toolbar's icons are now bigger. Each icon is a button; click and it will open the folder or file depicted.

customize toolbars and taskbar

4 You can add file and folder shortcuts by dragging them to the toolbar. You can even drag the My Computer icon here to make a shortcut.

The files that you drag to the toolbar will have filenames that begin with "Shortcut to," which isn't very helpful.

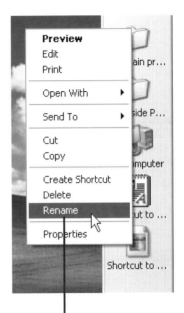

5 You can change the name of the shortcut by right-clicking the icon and selecting Rename.

6 Delete Shortcut to from the file name.

The shortcut in the toolbar now has a name that you can recognize.

add taskbar icons

In addition to the Start menu and minimized windows, the Taskbar holds icons that let you quickly open programs. You can add programs to the Taskbar for easy access.

The Quick Launch toolbar, the area next to the Start menu on the left side of the Taskbar, contains icons for certain programs. Click one, and the program opens. You can easily add another program by dragging it to the Quick Launch toolbar. In this example, we'll add Outlook Express.

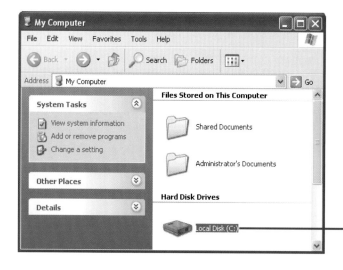

1 To find your program, open My Computer and double-click Local Disk.

2 Double-click Program Files.

3 Scroll through the list of programs, find the folder with your program, and open it.

4 Drag the program file to the middle of the Quick Launch toolbar on the Taskbar.

customize toolbars and taskbar

add taskbar icons (cont.)

The program's icon is now on the Taskbar. You can click it to open your program whenever you need it.

Notice that the Windows Media Player icon has been pushed off of the Taskbar. You'll find it in the pop-up menu if you click the double arrow.

Fortunately, you can get the Windows Media Player icon back on the Taskbar by widening the Quick Launch area.

5 Right-click an empty space on the Taskbar and select Lock the Taskbar to remove the checkmark. The Taskbar is now unlocked.

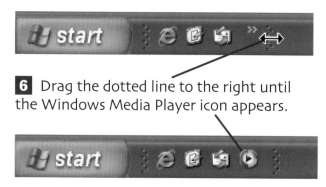

6 Drag the dotted line to the right until the Windows Media Player icon appears.

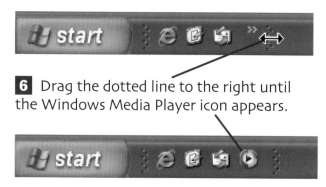

add player to taskbar

Ordinarily, when you click the Taskbar's Windows Media Player icon, the Player's window appears. You can add a smaller version of the Media Player right in the Taskbar that will be available to you while other programs are open.

1 Right-click an empty area of the Windows toolbar. Click Toolbars and choose Windows Media Player.

2 Click the Windows Media Player icon in the Taskbar. The player opens.

3 Minimize the Media Player window.

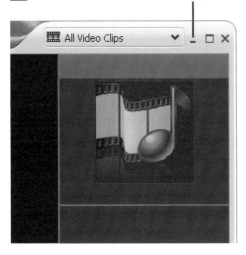

Instead of the standard window, the minimized window is a tiny but fully functional Media Player, which you can use to play movies and music.

extra bits

add new toolbars p. 24

- You can remove a toolbar from the Taskbar or from the side of the screen by dragging it to the middle of the Desktop.

    The toolbar turns into a floating toolbar window. To dismiss it, just click the X button in its upper right corner.

add taskbar icons p. 30

- The Taskbar doesn't have to sit on the bottom of the screen. You can move to the top or sides of your screen simply by unlocking it and dragging it.

    When you move the Taskbar, everything on it goes with it, including the Start menu and any items you've installed.

4. customize the start menu

The Start menu is the chief method of getting to your programs and files. There are a number of ways to customize the Start menu to better suit your needs.

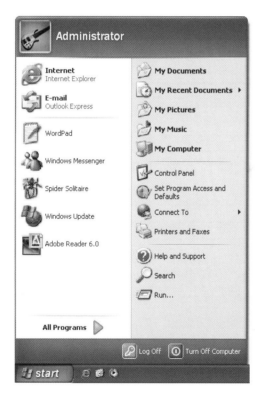

The left side of the Start menu contains icons representing programs. The top left icons are always present. The bottom left area lists programs you've recently used. In this chapter, you'll change the way these icons look and act.

The right side of the Start menu gives you access to your files, settings, the Help system, and other features of Windows XP. In this chapter, you'll convert some of these icons into menus. You'll also remove and add items to the Start menu.

restyle the start menu

There are lots of ways you can change the look of the Start menu. Here, we're going to shrink the size of the left-side icons and allow Windows to display more of them.

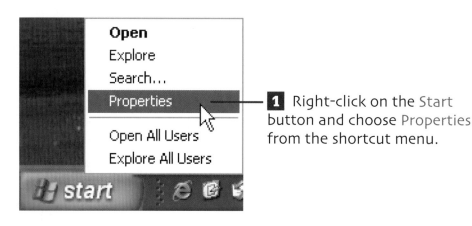

1 Right-click on the Start button and choose Properties from the shortcut menu.

2 Click the Customize button in the Properties dialog box.

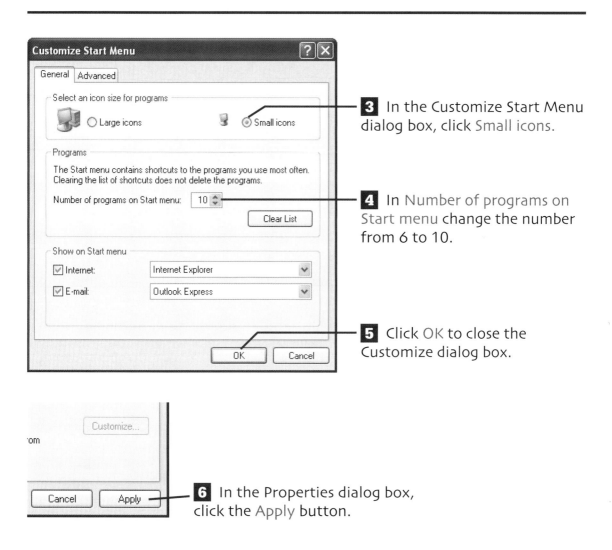

3 In the Customize Start Menu dialog box, click Small icons.

4 In Number of programs on Start menu change the number from 6 to 10.

5 Click OK to close the Customize dialog box.

6 In the Properties dialog box, click the Apply button.

restyle the start menu

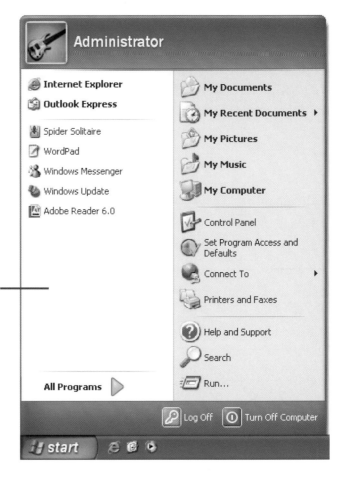

7 Go back to the start menu to see the result of your changes. You'll see that there is now space on the left side of the Start menu to hold more program icons.

8 If you are satisfied with the result, click OK in the Properties dialog box to close the dialog.

convert links to menus

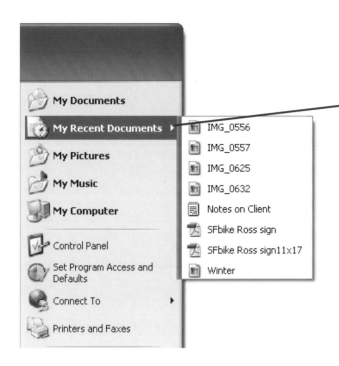

Most of the icons on the right side of the Start menu open a new window when you click on them. Items that have an arrow next them are hierarchical menus that let you delve into the contents.

Next, we're going to change the My Document and My Computer links into hierarchical menus.

1 Right-click on the Start button and choose Properties from the shortcut menu.

2 Click the Customize button in the Properties dialog box.

3 In the Customize dialog, click the Advanced tab.

Customize Start Menu

General | Advanced

Select an icon size for programs

○ Large icons   ⊙ Small icons

Programs

The Start menu contains shortcuts to the programs you use most often. Clearing the list of shortcuts does not delete the programs.

Number of programs on Start menu: 10

Clear List

Show on Start menu

☑ Internet: Internet Explorer
☑ E-mail: Outlook Express

OK   Cancel

convert links to menus

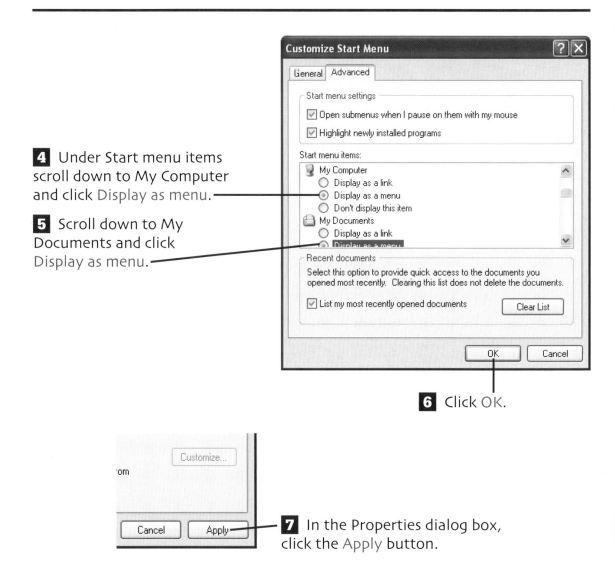

4 Under Start menu items scroll down to My Computer and click Display as menu.

5 Scroll down to My Documents and click Display as menu.

6 Click OK.

7 In the Properties dialog box, click the Apply button.

customize the start menu

8 Go back to the Start menu to see the result of your changes. You can now click on My Computer and My Documents to select an item several levels down.

9 If you are satisfied with the result, click OK in the Properties dialog box to close the dialog.

add a program

The left side of the Start menu is handy for opening programs with a single click. The icons on the upper left are always there for your use, while the icons below are programs you recently opened. For other programs, you have to dig through the Programs submenu.

Here you'll add a program to the top left of the menu. Windows calls this "pinning" a program to the Start menu. There are two ways to do this.

If the program is already in the recently opened portion of the Start menu, simply drag it up to the top left area of the Start menu.

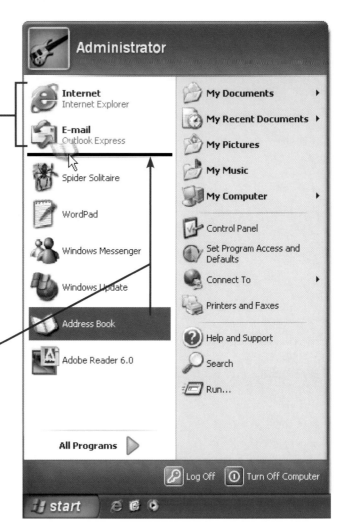

If the program is not in the Start menu, you can use the All Programs menu.

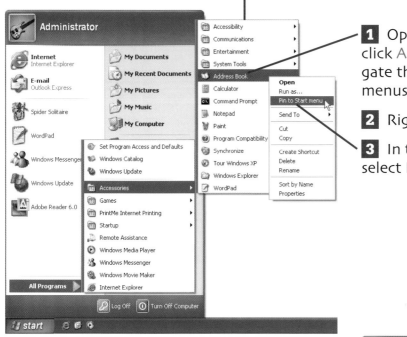

1 Open the Start menu, click All Programs, and navigate through the hierarchical menus to your program.

2 Right-click your program.

3 In the shortcut menu, select Pin to Start menu.

With either method, the result is the same: your program is pinned to the top of the Start menu.

customize the start menu 43

add a folder

Programs aren't the only items you can pin to the left side of the Start menu. You can place a shortcut to a folder on the Start menu.

You can drag a folder from the Desktop, from a window, or from a hierarchical menu in the Start menu. Here, you're going to drag your folder from Windows Explorer.

1 Right-click the Start menu and choose Explore from shortcut menu.

2 Windows Explorer will open. Locate your folder and drag it onto the Start menu button.

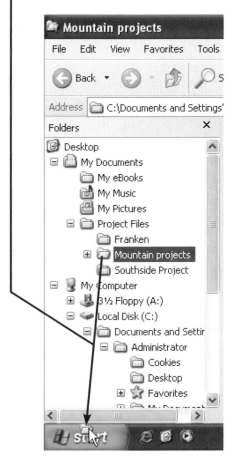

The Start menu now includes your folder at the top left. If you click the folder icon its window will open.

customize the start menu

delete a menu item

Of course, nothing is forever, including decisions you make in Windows XP. If you no longer need an item that is pinned to the top left of the Start menu, you can remove it.

Right-click the item in the Start menu and select Remove from This List. The item will disappear from the Start menu, but the original folder or program is still in your PC.

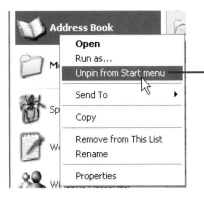

When you right-click on a program at the top left of the Start menu, you get an additional choice, Unpin from Start menu. When you select this, the program icon will move to the list of recent programs below the line.

extra bits

restyle the start menu p. 36

- You may have noticed that the Start menu's Properties dialog box gives you a Classic Windows Start menu option.

  This option doesn't just serve as nostalgia for Windows past. It offers a more stream-lined Start menu, one that takes less screen space.

  The classic Start menu has its own customization dialog box with customization features that are different from those of the standard Start menu.

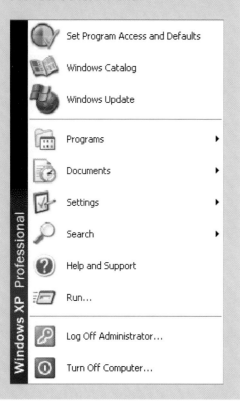

	Set Program Access and Defaults
	Windows Catalog
	Windows Update
	Programs ▶
	Documents ▶
	Settings ▶
	Search ▶
	Help and Support
	Run...
	Log Off Administrator...
	Turn Off Computer...

convert links to menus p. 40

- You may have noticed throughout this chapter that the Start menu has a submenu called My Recent Documents. In Windows XP Professional, this is always turned on. In Windows XP Home Edition, you'll have to turn on My Recent Documents to see it in the Start menu. Just right-click Start and click Properties. Then click Customize and select List my most recently opened documents. (Windows XP Professional doesn't give you the option to turn off My Recent Documents.)

add a folder p. 44

- Another way to bring up Windows Explorer is to press Windows-E.

customize the start menu

5. rearrange desktop items

The previous chapters have been focused in and around the Desktop—how to personalize the Desktop, the Taskbar, and the Start menu. In this chapter, you'll learn how to place different types of items on the Desktop, and how to remove others.

The Desktop is another place to put files and folders for easy access. Windows XP gives you special techniques for adding different types of items to the Desktop. You'll also learn how to put Desktop items in the Taskbar.

With this ability to add items, the Desktop can easily become cluttered. You'll learn how to clean up the Desktop with the tools of Windows XP.

place files and folders

You know from previous versions of Windows that you can drag and drop folders from a window to the Desktop. Windows XP offers several other ways of bringing your work out onto the Desktop.

First, let's look at another kind of drag-and-drop called a right drag.

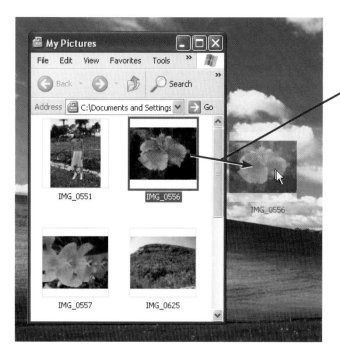

1 Open a folder containing a file or folder that you want to place on the Desktop.

2 Click on the file with the right mouse button and drag it to the Desktop. As long as you hold the right mouse button down, it looks like an ordinary drag-and-drop.

3 Release the right mouse button. Instead of the usual file icon on the Desktop, you'll see a shortcut menu.

4 Select one of the options.

Move Here is just like an ordinary drag-and-drop; the file moves out of the folder onto the Desktop.

Copy Here creates a new file on the Desktop while keeping your original file in its place.

Create Shortcuts Here is the best of both worlds: it keeps your original file in its original location, but creates a small pointer file, the shortcut, that takes up a fraction of the hard drive's space that a copy of a big graphic file might take.

Shortcuts have the same icon as the original file except for an arrow in the lower-left corner.

You don't need the words Shortcut to in the file name. You can change the name of the original file or of the shortcut. Double-clicking the shortcut will open the original file or folder.

rearrange desktop items

hide standard icons

There are serveral places you can access My Computer, Internet Explorer, and My Documents, so you may not need them cluttering up the Desktop. You can choose to hide some or all of these standard Desktop icons.

1 Right-click on a blank spot on the Desktop and choose Properties from the pop-up menu.

2 In the Display properties dialog box, click the Desktop tab.

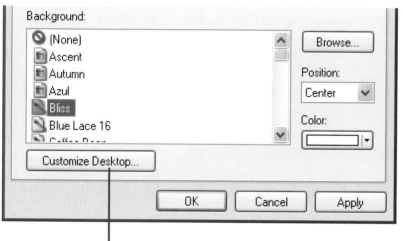

3 Click the Customize Desktop button.

rearrange desktop items

4 In the Desktop Items dialog box you'll find four standard Windows Desktop icons listed. If you want to hide the icon, make sure there is no checkmark next to it. If you want the icon to appear on the Desktop, make sure there is a checkmark next to it.

5 Click OK to close the Desktop Items dialog box.

6 Click OK to close the Display Properties dialog box.

If you removed all the checkmarks in Step 4, the four standard Windows icons will now be gone from the Desktop.

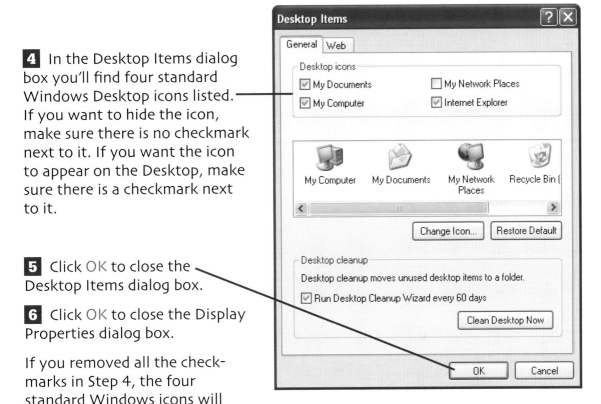

cleanup the desktop

Your new PC probably came with demostration software that included annoying Desktop shortcut icons. In addition, programs that you install often create shortcuts you don't need.

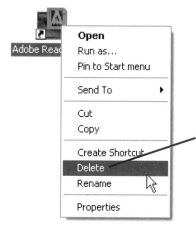

One way you can deal with these nuisance icons is to command-click them and choose Delete.

The problem with this is that you'd have to repeat this for every one of the icons you want to get rid of.

A better method is to have Windows move icons that you haven't been using recently off of your Desktop and into a folder called Unused Desktop Shortcuts.

1 Right-click on a blank spot on the Desktop and choose Properties from the shortcut menu.

2 In the Display Properties dialog box, click the Desktop tab.

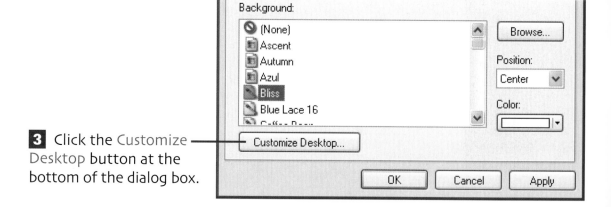

3 Click the Customize Desktop button at the bottom of the dialog box.

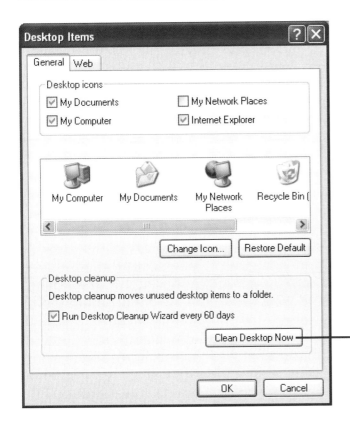

4 In the Desktop Items dialog box, click the Clean Desktop Now button.

5 The Desktop Cleanup Wizard will appear. Click the Next button.

rearrange desktop items 53

cleanup the desktop (cont.)

6 The Wizard will now list the shortcuts on your Desktop. Those that you haven't used recently will have a checkmark next to them. These will be moved off of the Desktop. Shortcuts that you have used recently will not have a check mark and will be left on the Desktop. If you want to make any changes, you can check and uncheck any item in the list.

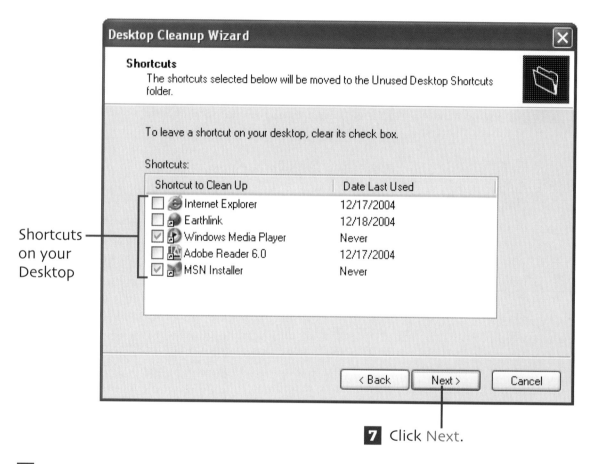

Shortcuts on your Desktop

7 Click Next.

8 A final screen will appear listing the shortcut files you want to remove. If this is correct, click Finish. If not, click Back.

You'll notice back in step 4 that there was an option called Desktop Cleanup Wizard every 60 days. If you aren't adding a lot of new shortcuts, it might be worthwhile to uncheck it.

rearrange desktop items

add icons to taskbar

Having items on the Desktop can be very handy—unless you have a bunch of windows open. Instead, you can add a Desktop toolbar to the Taskbar to give you access to Desktop icons, whether they represent programs, documents, or folders.

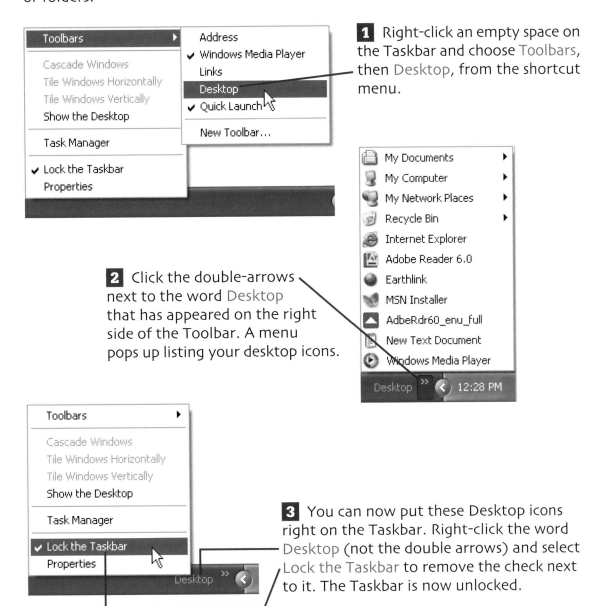

1 Right-click an empty space on the Taskbar and choose Toolbars, then Desktop, from the shortcut menu.

2 Click the double-arrows next to the word Desktop that has appeared on the right side of the Toolbar. A menu pops up listing your desktop icons.

3 You can now put these Desktop icons right on the Taskbar. Right-click the word Desktop (not the double arrows) and select Lock the Taskbar to remove the check next to it. The Taskbar is now unlocked.

rearrange desktop items

add icons to taskbar (cont.)

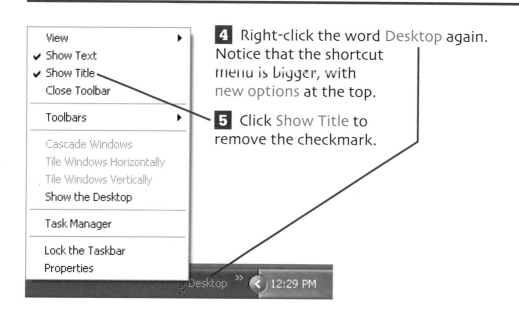

4 Right-click the word Desktop again. Notice that the shortcut menu is bigger, with new options at the top.

5 Click Show Title to remove the checkmark.

The word Desktop has disappeared. Your Taskbar will now hold as many of your items that fit.

The rest are displayed in the double-arrow menu.

6 If you want all of your Desktop icons to fit on the Taskbar, you'll have to get rid of the text next to the icons. Right-click on the area on the Taskbar where the word Desktop used to be and click Show Text to remove the checkmark.

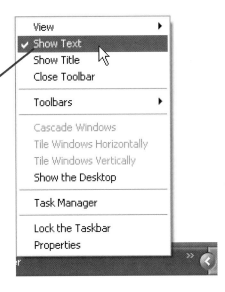

Now all of your Desktop icons can fit on the Taskbar (unless you really have a lot of Desktop items).

The double-arrows have disappeared.

Hold the cursor arrow over an icon, a description of the item will appear.

extra bits

place files and folders p. 48

- Did you know that the documents and shortcut files on the Desktop actually sit inside a folder called, well, Desktop?

  It's in the Documents and Settings folder, inside a folder named after your user name.

  Add an item to the Desktop folder and it appears on the Desktop.

- Have you ever wanted easy access to a small portion of a file? You don't have to create a new document—just create a scrap.

  To create a scrap, simply select some text—a paragraph, sentence, or phrase—and drag it from the document window to the Desktop. A new file is created that has an icon with a jagged bottom.

WordPad
Document Scrap
'winter of our...'

cleanup the desktop p. 52

- Another way to quickly access your Desktop icons is with a key command. You can press Windows-D to minimize all of the open windows at the same time.

  This technique will even minimize windows that don't have a minimize button, such as dialog boxes and the Control Panel.

  Pressing Windows-D again will restore all of the windows you just minimized—unless you've opened, minimized, or restored any windows since hitting the command. If that's the case, Windows-D will only work on the last window you worked with.

rearrange desktop items

6. customize folders and windows

Windows XP offers plenty of options for customizing the look and function of your windows and folders in order to better fit the way you work. You can remove interface elements that you don't use, change the way icons look and work, and display information about files in a folder window. Here are some examples of the changes you can make:

You can add pictures to folder icons.

You can hide or modify Window toolbars.

You can hide the pane on the left side of the window and bring it back when you need it.

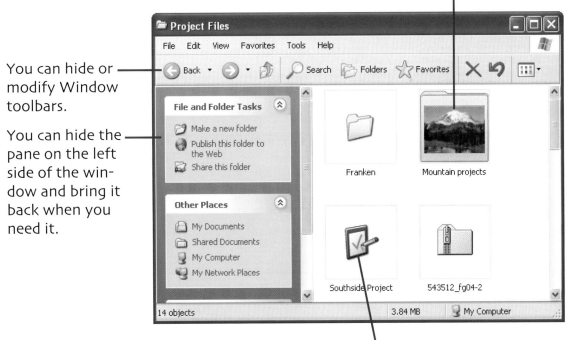

You can view the file and folder icons in different sizes and sort them in different ways.

You can also replace a folder icon with something new.

In this chapter, you'll be making all of these changes. We'll begin with changing the look of the windows. Then we'll change the look of the folder contents.

hide the left pane

The links pane on the left side of the folder windows provides links to related places and tasks. But you might not always need it. You might want to use the space to show files instead. To do this, you can temporarily turn off the left pane.

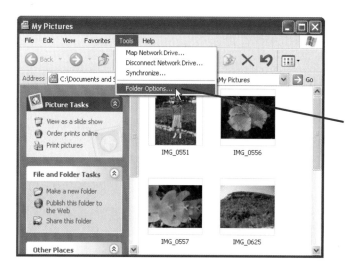

1 Go to the Tools menu of the folder you want to change and select Folder Options.

2 On the General Tab, under Tasks, click Use Windows classic folders.

The links pane on the left has now disappeared from all folders.

customize folders and windows

create a shortcut

You may not want the side pane hidden all of the time; you may need it for viewing some folders and not for others. While you can't specify this setting for different folders, you can make it easy to open the Folder Options dialog. You'll create a shortcut.

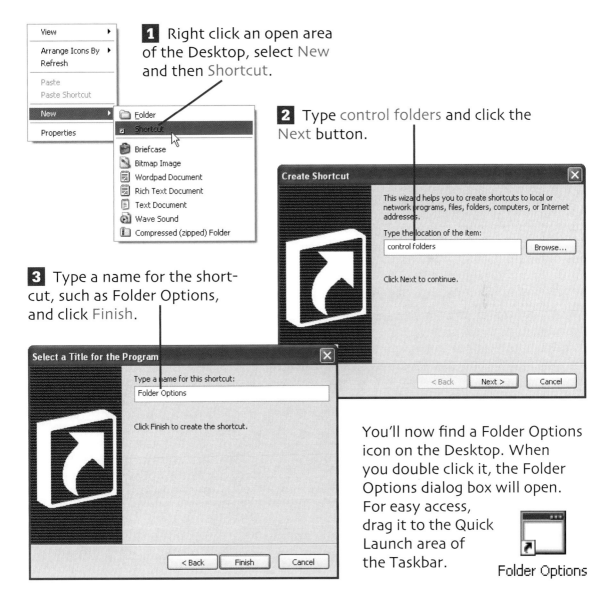

1 Right click an open area of the Desktop, select New and then Shortcut.

2 Type control folders and click the Next button.

3 Type a name for the shortcut, such as Folder Options, and click Finish.

You'll now find a Folder Options icon on the Desktop. When you double click it, the Folder Options dialog box will open. For easy access, drag it to the Quick Launch area of the Taskbar.

Folder Options

modify folder toolbars

Folder windows have several toolbars that you can hide or modify. Each toolbar has a different set of functions that can often be found in the related menus, making the toolbar unnecessary.

The Address toolbar. You use the Address bar to type the path of a folder to go directly to that folder or to the Internet. If you don't type folder paths, you can hide the Address bar without missing much.

The Buttons toolbar. Similar to a Web browser toolbar, the Buttons toolbar lets you navigate between folders on your PC. The Buttons toolbar is completely customizable.

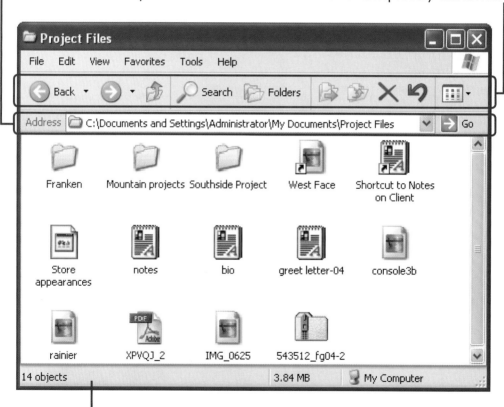

The Status bar. This gives you information on the open folder, or of a selected file or folder, in the open folder window.

First, we'll hide the Address bar.

Go to the View menu, move the mouse to Toolbars, and click Address bar. The Address bar will disapear.

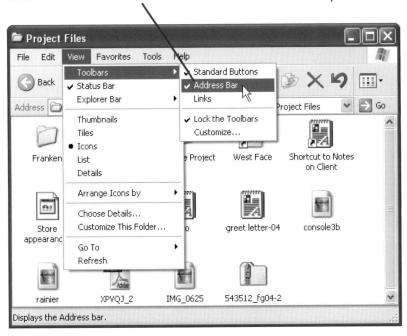

We're now going to modify the icon toolbar, remove some icons, add some new ones, and move things around a bit.

1 In the View menu, move the mouse to Toolbars and then click Customize.

customize folders and windows

modify folder toolbars

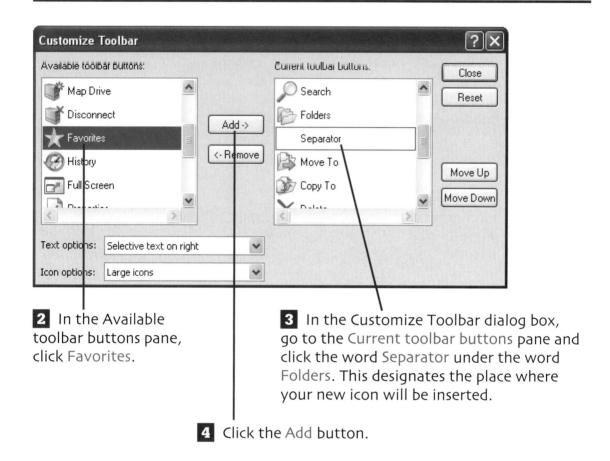

2 In the Available toolbar buttons pane, click Favorites.

3 In the Customize Toolbar dialog box, go to the Current toolbar buttons pane and click the word Separator under the word Folders. This designates the place where your new icon will be inserted.

4 Click the Add button.

customize folders and windows

The Favorites icon has been added above the separator.

5 Now click Move To below it and click Remove. Do the same for Copy to.

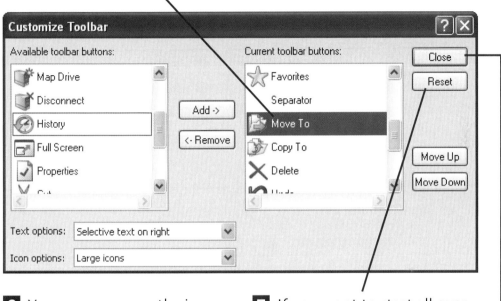

6 You can rearrange the icons and separators on the toolbar by dragging them up and down in the Current toolbar buttons pane. Items at the top of the list will be located on the left of the toolbar; bottom items are on the right of the toolbar.

7 If you want to start all over again, click the Reset button.

8 Click the Close button when you're finished customizing the toolbar.

The toolbar now sports a new Favorites icon, and the Move To and Copy To icons are gone.

customize folders and windows   **85**

sort & organize files

The View menu of a folder window lists five different ways to see the file and folder icons inside. Thumbnails gives you the largest icons, followed by Tiles and then Icons. List and Details give you the smallest icons. In any of these views, you can sort the content. You'll now sort in a few different ways in different views.

In the Thumbnails, Tiles, and Icons views, you can move icons around. To get them back in a sorted order go to the View menu, move the mouse to Arrange Icons by, and click on a sorting criteria. Here we'll use Name to sort alphabetically.

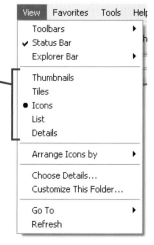

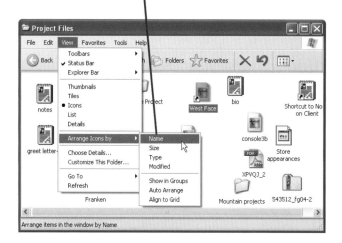

The icons are now sorted alphabetically; folders first, then files.

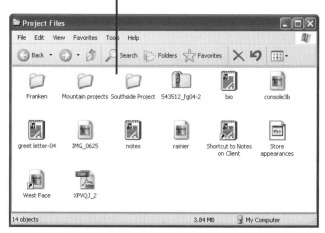

customize folders and windows

You'll notice that one of the choices for sorting was Modified. This is short for date modified. This can be a useful way to sort files, though it is more useful in Details view than in icon view.

1 Go to the View menu and select Details to bring the Details view forward.

2 The Details view defaults to alphabetical order, again with folders first, then files. You can sort by a particular criterion by clicking on its column head. To sort by date, click the Date Modified column head.

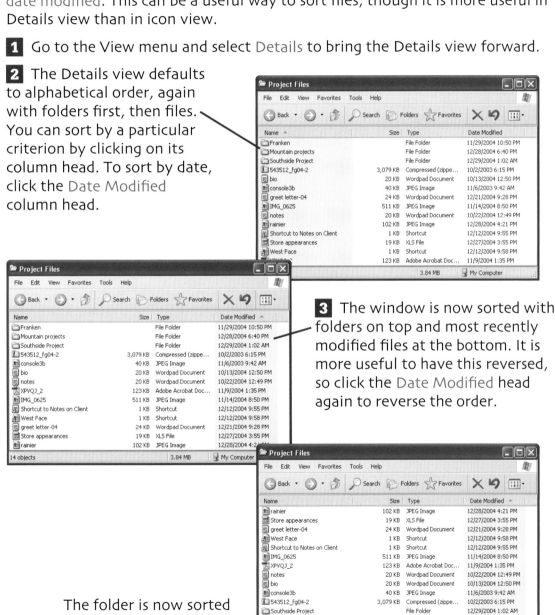

3 The window is now sorted with folders on top and most recently modified files at the bottom. It is more useful to have this reversed, so click the Date Modified head again to reverse the order.

The folder is now sorted with the most recently modified files at the top.

modify details view

You can add more sorting criteria to the Details view by displaying more details. One way to do this is to select Choose Details from the View menu, make your selections in the Choose Details dialog box, then click OK. There is, however, an easier way—the shortcut menu.

1 Right click on any of the column headings.

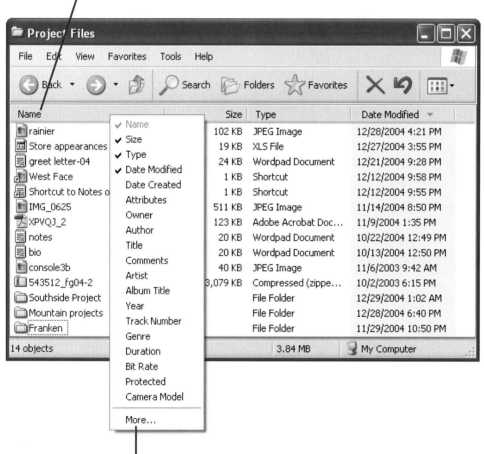

2 A shortcut menu appears with a list of possible column headings. The criteria that are currently displayed have checkmarks next to them. Clicking one of these to remove the checkmark would hide that column from the window. Here, however, you're going to click Date Created to add it to the window.

customize folders and windows

3 Newly added columns always appear on the far right of the window, sometimes out of view. To make room for it, narrow the Name, Size, and Type columns by dragging the line to the right of the column header on the left.

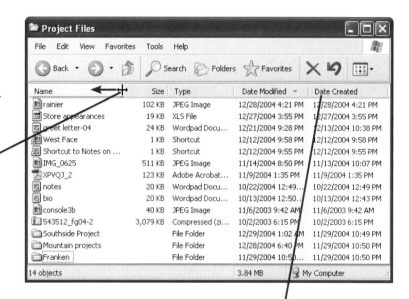

4 We now want to move the columns around. Grab the Date Created column head and drag it to the left, next to Name.

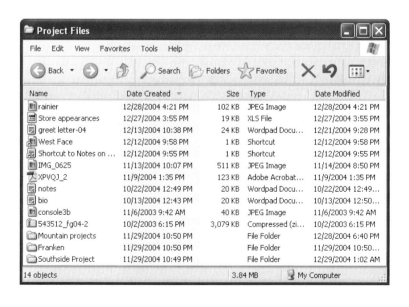

5 Click Date Created to sort by date. Click again to reverse the sort, putting most recently created files at the top. The result will look like this.

customize folder icons

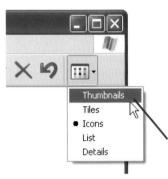

All folder icons don't have to look alike. You can add a picture to a folder icon that Windows will display in Thumbnails view.

1 Open a window containing the folder you want to customize. If the folder view is not already in thumbnails, click the views icon on the folder toolbar and select Thumbnails.

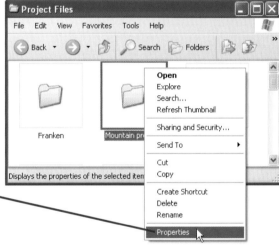

2 Right-click the folder you want to customize and select Properties.

3 Click the Customize tab in the properties dialog box.

The middle of the dialog box is a section called Folder pictures. If the current folder contains image files, the sample folder will display up to two of them. If not, this area will be blank.

4 Click the Choose Picture button.

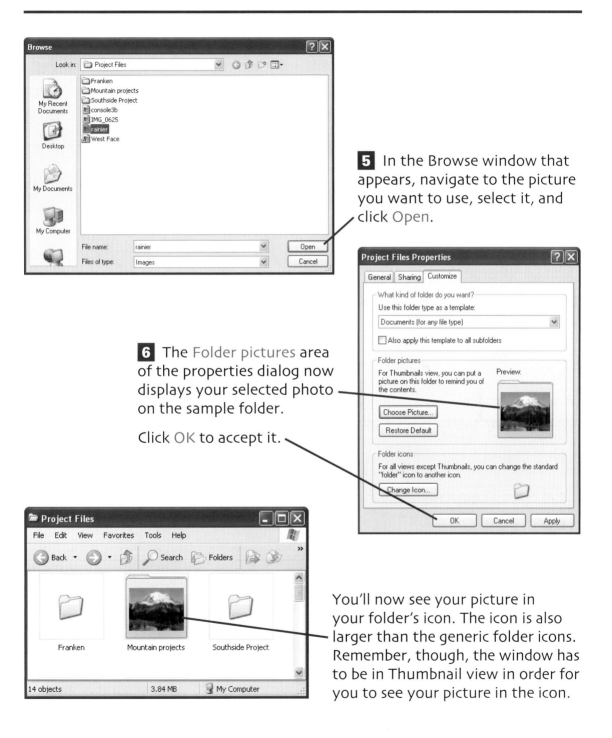

5 In the Browse window that appears, navigate to the picture you want to use, select it, and click Open.

6 The Folder pictures area of the properties dialog now displays your selected photo on the sample folder.

Click OK to accept it.

You'll now see your picture in your folder's icon. The icon is also larger than the generic folder icons. Remember, though, the window has to be in Thumbnail view in order for you to see your picture in the icon.

replace a folder icon

For other views, you can make a folder stand out by replacing its generic icon with one of dozens of special icons supplied by Windows.

1 Right-click the folder you want to customize and select Properties. Then choose the Customize tab.

2 Click the Change Icon button at the bottom of the properties dialog box.

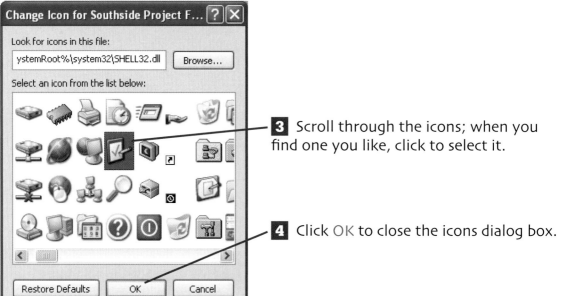

3 Scroll through the icons; when you find one you like, click to select it.

4 Click OK to close the icons dialog box.

5 Click OK to close the Properties dialog box.

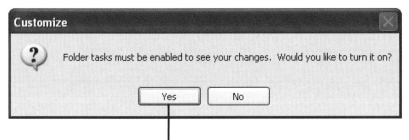

6 You may get a dialog asking if you would like to turn on Folder Tasks. Click Yes.

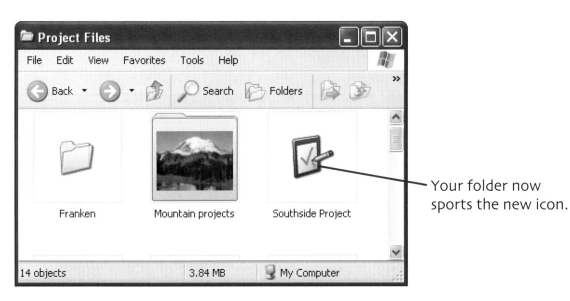

Your folder now sports the new icon.

extra bits

sort & organize files p. 66

- In addition to sorting, you can organize files by renaming them in a more orderly way. For instance, if the files all start with the same characters, they'll be easier to scan when sorted by name, for example: Murry Analysis, Murry Analysis (1), Murry Analysis (2), etc.. Windows gives you an easy way to rename a group of files with the same name followed by a number.

  Select the files that you want to rename. Right-click one of the selected files and select Rename from the shortcut menu.

  Now type a name for the group of files. Hit Enter, and the files will be renamed.

customize folder icons p. 70

- If Windows' extra folder icons don't excite you, you can add more. Pear Software's Folder Icon XP (http://www.pear-viewer. com/) is a $20 utility that gives you thousands of great-looking icons to choose for your folders. It's easy to use, too.

7. install software and features

In some respects, adding and removing software and software features is the ultimate act of customization you can do to your computer. In this chapter, you'll install programs as well as software features of Windows XP itself. You'll also tell Windows which of these you want to be the default programs.

You'll do most of this in the Add or Remove Programs dialog box.

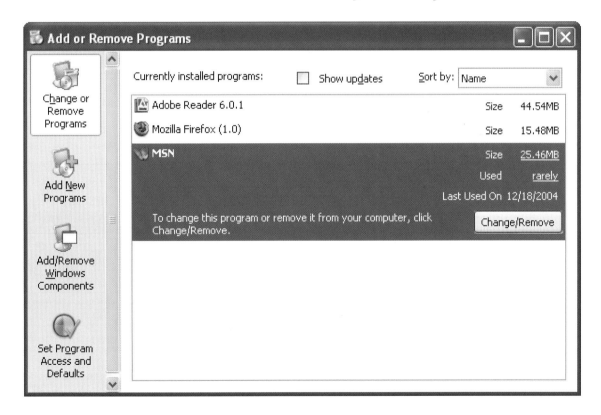

install a program

You can install a program you download from the Internet or from a CD. In either case, there is usually an installer program called setup.exe or install.exe that is run. Sometimes this is run in the background, and you don't have to do anything. Just download the software or insert the CD, and the installer program takes over. With some programs, you'll see a dialog asking you to install it only after you choose the program from the Start menu.

For other programs, you may insert a CD and nothing will happen. When this occurs, you can tell Windows to install the program.

1 Go to the Start menu and choose Control Panel.

2 Double-click the Add or Remove Programs icon.

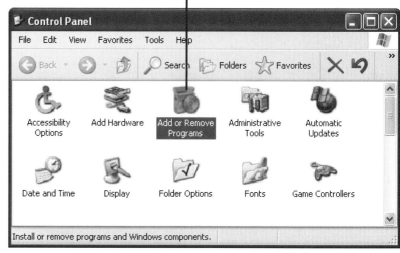

install software and features

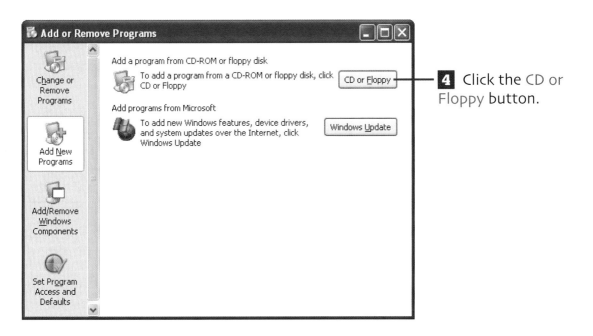

3 A dialog appears showing programs you've previously installed. Click the Add New Programs button.

Add or Remove Programs

Currently installed programs: ☐ Show updates   Sort by: [Name ▼]

Change or Remove Programs

Add New Programs

Add/Remove Windows Components

Set Program Access and Defaults

Adobe Reader 6.0.1   Size   44.54MB
    Click here for support information.   Used   rarely
    To change this program or remove it from your   [Change] [Remove]
    computer, click Change or Remove.

Mozilla Firefox (1.0)   Size   15.48MB
MSN   Size   25.46MB

Add or Remove Programs

Change or Remove Programs

Add New Programs

Add/Remove Windows Components

Set Program Access and Defaults

Add a program from CD-ROM or floppy disk
    To add a program from a CD-ROM or floppy disk, click   [CD or Floppy]
    CD or Floppy

Add programs from Microsoft
    To add new Windows features, device drivers,   [Windows Update]
    and system updates over the Internet, click
    Windows Update

4 Click the CD or Floppy button.

install software and features   **77**

install a program (cont.)

5 Insert the program's installation CD and click the Next button.

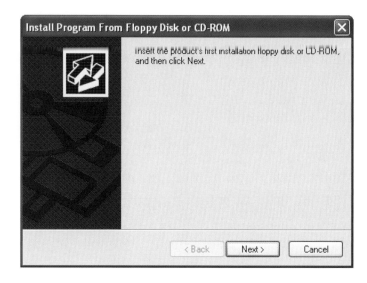

6 At this point, a dialog box called Run Installation Program will appear.

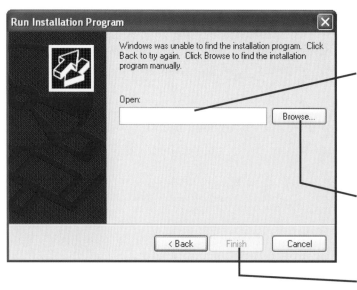

If Windows found the installation program on the CD, it will list it here (something like D:\SETUP.EXE), and you can click the Finish button.

If Windows can't find the installation program, as is the case here, click the Browse button to locate the installer program on the CD.

After you find it and it is listed in the Open field, click Finish.

install software and features

set default program

Windows XP designates certain programs to be the default program.

There are two types of default programs. The first type of default program is related to the Internet: your email, Web browser, instant messaging, and music/video player. The other type of default program is the program that opens when you double-click a certain type of document file.

Often when you install a new program it will ask you if you want it to become the default. If it doesn't, or if you said no, you can still tell Windows XP that you want it to be the default.

First, we'll assign Firefox as the default Web browser. (Firefox is a free Web browser you can download from http://www.mozilla.org.)

1 Go to the Start menu and choose Control Panel.

2 In the Control Panel, double-click the Add or Remove Programs icon.

3 A dialog appears showing programs you've previously installed.

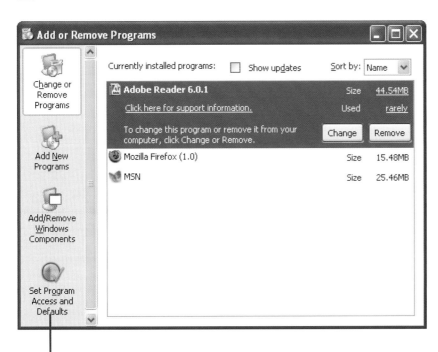

Click the Set Program Access and Defaults button.

set default program (cont.)

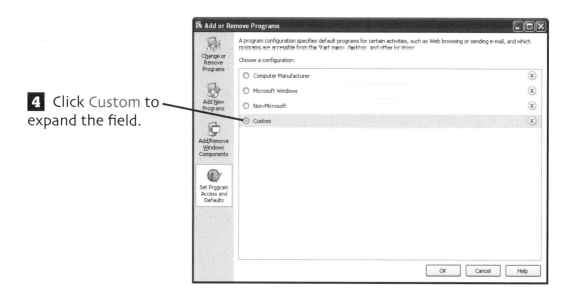

4 Click Custom to expand the field.

5 Under each listed category, the dialog box will list the programs that are installed on your computer. In this example, select Mozilla Firefox under the Web browser category.

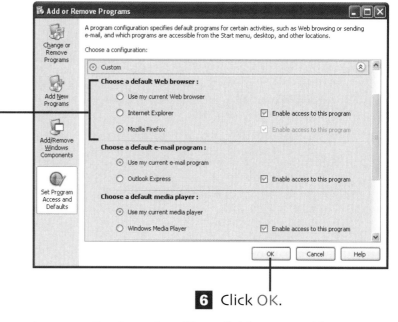

6 Click OK.

Internet Explorer is still available to you if you want to use it. However, when Windows or another program calls for a Web browser, Firefox will launch.

install software and features

reset a file opener

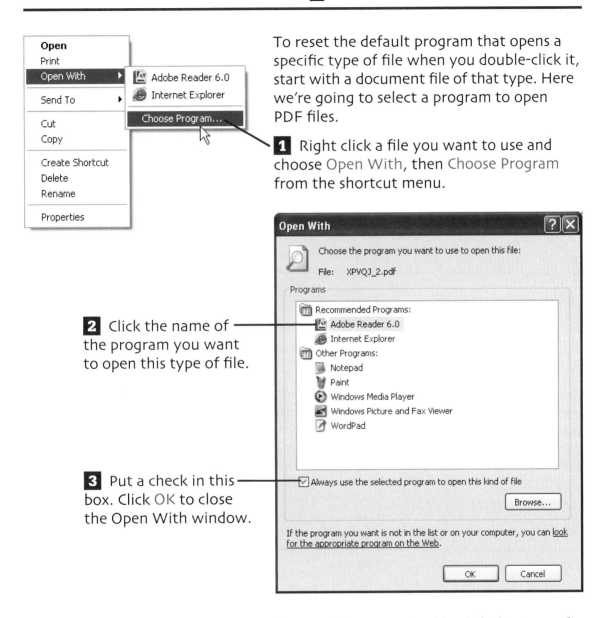

To reset the default program that opens a specific type of file when you double-click it, start with a document file of that type. Here we're going to select a program to open PDF files.

1 Right click a file you want to use and choose Open With, then Choose Program from the shortcut menu.

2 Click the name of the program you want to open this type of file.

3 Put a check in this box. Click OK to close the Open With window.

The next time you double-click this type of file, the program you specified will launch and open the file.

add/remove features

Whether Windows XP came pre-installed on your PC or you installed it yourself, there are features that may not be installed. Windows calls these extra features components.

There may also be components installed that you aren't using. For instance, if you don't subscribe to Microsoft's MSN Internet services, then you don't need MSN Explorer.

You can easily add new components or remove components you aren't using.

1 Go to the Start menu and choose Control Panel.

2 Double-click the Add or Remove Programs icon.

3 A dialog appears listing the programs and updates that are installed. Click Add/Remove Windows Components to bring up the Windows Component Wizard.

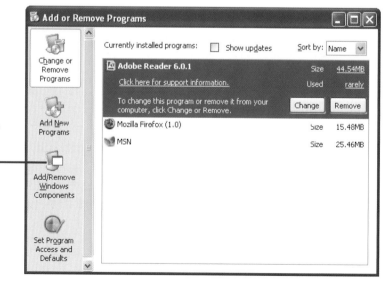

install software and features

4 Put a check next to the feature you want to add. (Or uncheck an item you wish to remove.)

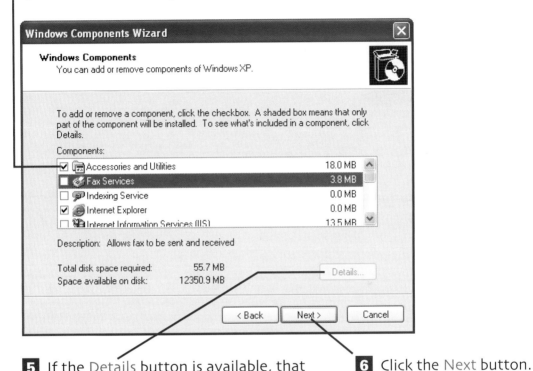

5 If the Details button is available, that means that the item selected contains subcomponents that you can add or remove separately. You do this by clicking the Details button and checking or unchecking items from a list. If the Details button is grayed out (as it is here), the selected item does not contain subcomponents.

6 Click the Next button.

7 Wait while Windows does the installation (or the removal), and then click Finish. If you are installing a component, Windows may ask you to insert your Windows XP CD depending on how your computer is set up and what you are installing.

install software and features

update windows xp

Microsoft regularly releases updates to Windows XP that fix problems and add security from Internet intruders. By default, Windows XP is set to update automatically at 3 am. If you don't have your computer on and connected to the Internet at the time, it won't update. However, you can update any time, as long as you're connected to the Internet.

1 Go to the Start menu and choose Control Panel.

2 Double-click the Add or Remove Programs icon.

3 Click Add New Programs.

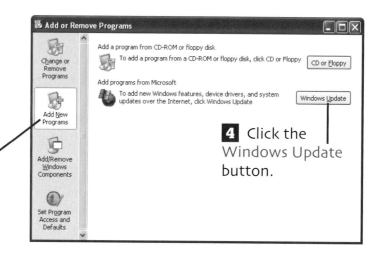

4 Click the Windows Update button.

5 Your web browser will launch and connect to a Microsoft Web site. Click Express Install.

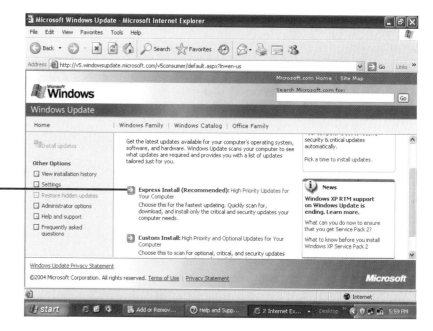

install software and features

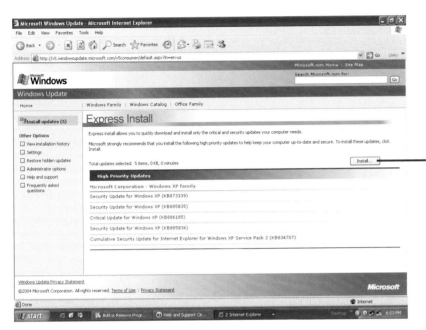

6 After a few minutes you'll see a list of updates that are not installed on your computer. Click the Install button.

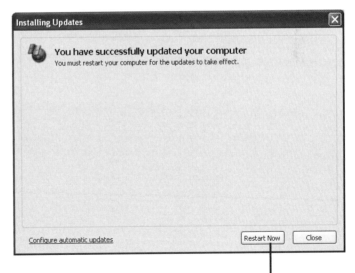

7 Wait for installation. Click the Restart Now button.

Your computer will restart.

extra bits

install a program p. 76

- Some software programs require you to have a certain version of Windows or a service pack installed on your computer. Fortunately, this kind of technical information is available at your fingertips.

  Open My Computer and select About Windows under the Help menu. A dialog box will display the Windows version and build number and service pack installed.

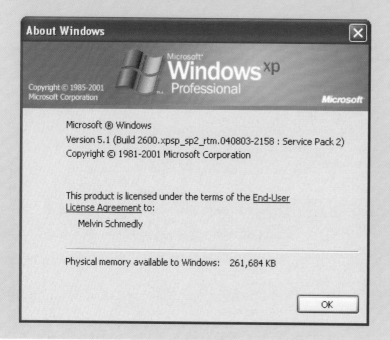

install software and features

8. customize internet access

Most people who use a computer also use the Internet. Windows XP offers many ways to set up Internet access so that it works the way you want it to.

This chapter contains assorted tips for accessing the Internet. You'll set up a high-speed Internet connection, customize aspects of sending and receiving email, and make it easier to access Web sites.

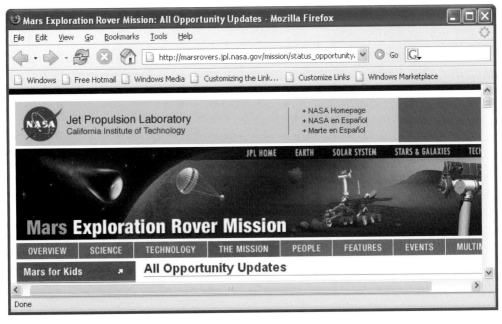

create a connection

To create an Internet connection, we'll use Windows XP's New Connection Wizard. Be sure you have the account Information given to you by your Internet service provider at hand. Creating a dial-up connection is easy, but creating a high-speed connection, such as DSL or cable modem, is much less obvious; windows refers to DSL as a broadband modem connection.

Here you'll create the most common type of DSL connection, one that requires a username and password.

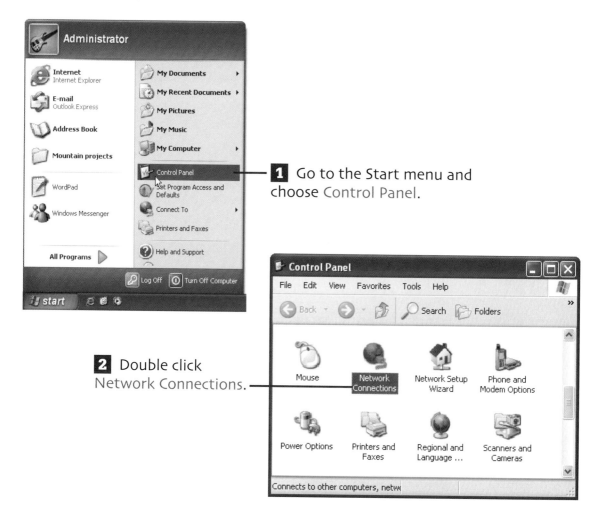

1 Go to the Start menu and choose Control Panel.

2 Double click Network Connections.

customize internet access

3 Under Network Tasks, click Create a New Connection.

The New Connection Wizard will appear.

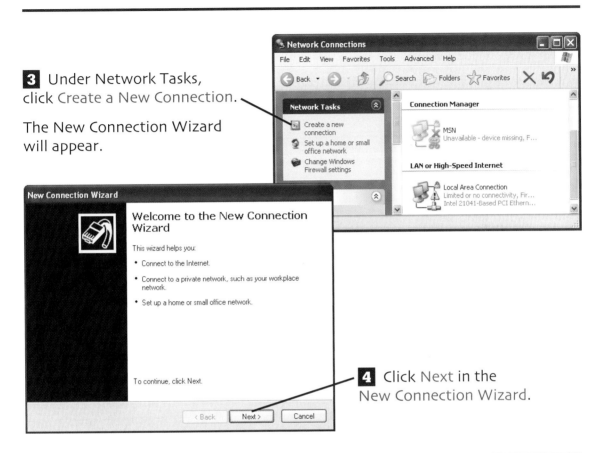

4 Click Next in the New Connection Wizard.

5 Select Connect to the Internet.

6 Click Next.

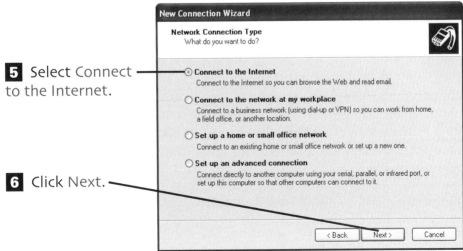

create a connection (cont.)

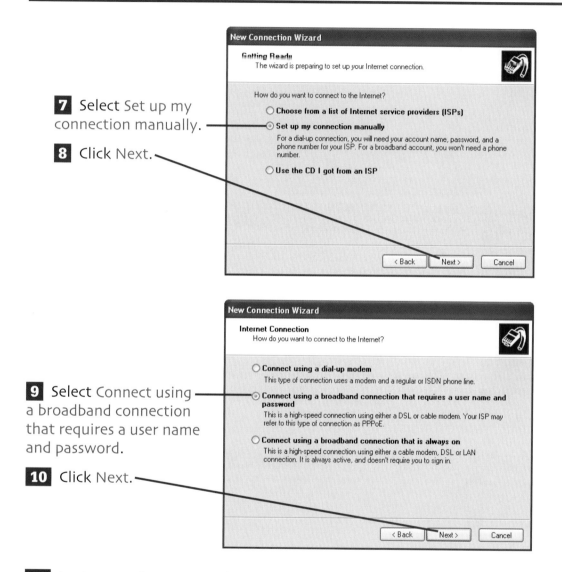

7 Select Set up my connection manually.

8 Click Next.

9 Select Connect using a broadband connection that requires a user name and password.

10 Click Next.

11 In the next few screens that appear, type in your account information from your Internet service provider. Click Next after each dialog box, and click Finish in the last dialog.

When you click Finish, the wizard disappears and your Internet connection is complete. You're now ready to hook up to the Internet.

connect to the net

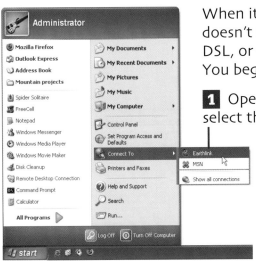

When it comes to connecting to the Internet, it doesn't matter if you're using a dialup modem, DSL, or cable modem. The procedure is the same. You begin with the Start menu.

1 Open the Start menu, click Connect To, and select the name of the connection you set up.

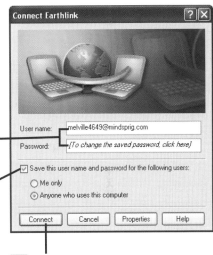

2 A Connect window opens. Your user name and password should be automatically entered. If not, type them in here.

3 If you always want your account information automatically entered, make sure the box is checked next to Save this user name and password for the following users.

4 Click the Connect button.

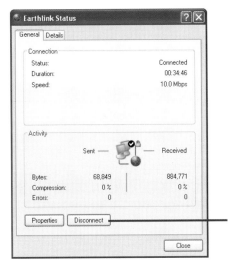

5 A Status window replaces the Connect window; you're now connected to the Internet. You can browse the web and check email. To close the Internet connection, click the Disconnect button.

add outlook accounts

In Outlook Express, a wizard launches and asks you for your email account information. If you give the wizard everything it needs, it will set up the connection for you. You can also add a second email account in Outlook Express. This could be for your work email address on a home computer, or an email account for another person.

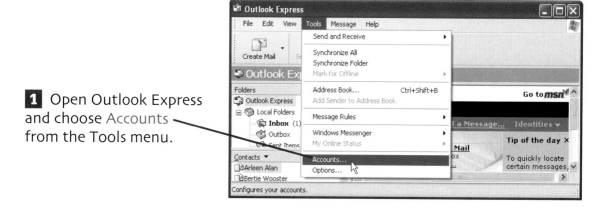

1 Open Outlook Express and choose Accounts from the Tools menu.

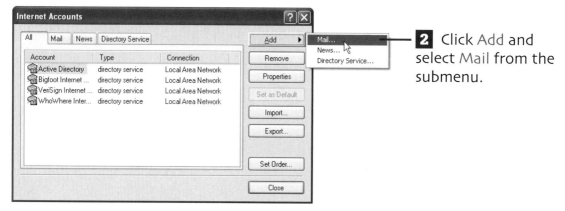

2 Click Add and select Mail from the submenu.

3 The Internet Connection Wizard appears, just as it did the first time you opened Outlook Express. In each screen, enter information about your email account from your Internet service provider. Click the Next button to move to the next screen. The last wizard screen has a Finish button. Click it and your email account is ready to use.

turn off email graphics

One of the best customization features in Outlook Express is to turn off graphics in email messages that you receive. Not only will you no longer have to see pictures from advertising that you didn't ask for, but you can prevent spammers from verifying your email address.

When you open an email message from a spammer, your email software tells the spammer's server to send you the picture, which notifies the spammer that your email address is valid. Turn the graphics off, and your email software will not try to contact the spammer.

1 Go to the Start menu and open Outlook Express.

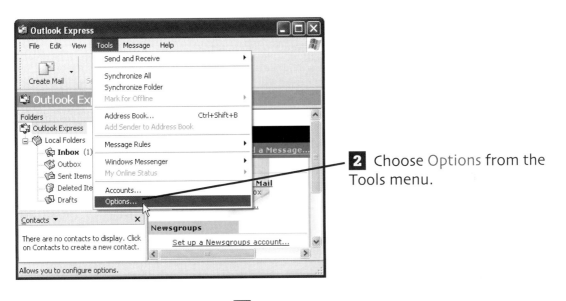

2 Choose Options from the Tools menu.

3 In the Options dialog box click the Security tab.

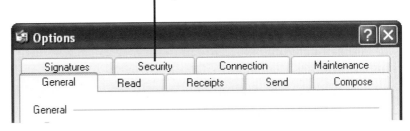

turn off email graphics

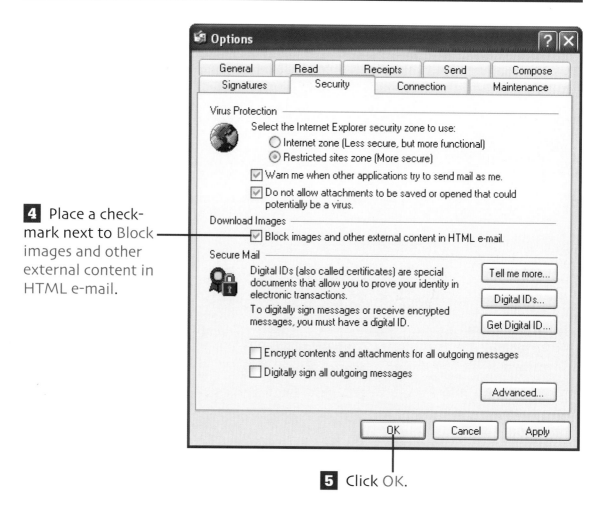

4 Place a check-mark next to Block images and other external content in HTML e-mail.

5 Click OK.

When you receive messages, Outlook will tell you if it has blocked pictures. If the message is from someone you know, you can click a link in the email message called Click here to download pictures.

customize internet access

create email groups

If you frequently send email to the same group of people, you can save yourself a lot of typing by creating a list of these addresses, known as a group. You can then send a message to everyone in the group simply by typing the name of the group. Here's how to create a group in Outlook Express.

1 Click the Addresses icon.

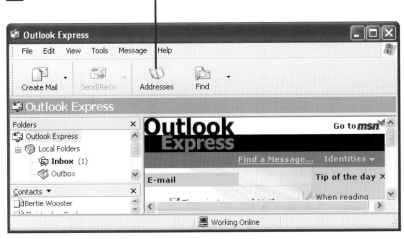

2 Click and hold the New button and choose New Group from the menu.

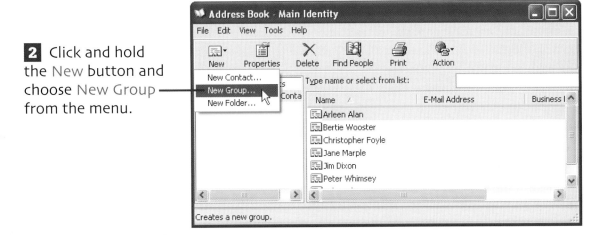

create email groups (cont.)

3 Type a group name here.

4 Click the Select Members button.

5 From your contacts list, click a name that you want in the group then click the Select button. The name will move to the right column. Do this for each contact you want in the group.

6 Click OK.

7 Click OK in the Properities dialog box and close the Address Book dialog box.

Now, when you create a new message, you can type the name

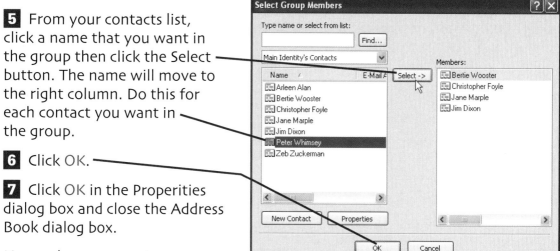

of the group, in this case Book Club, in the To field. After you send the message, if you look at the message in the Sent Items folder, you'll find each group member listed.

add links toolbar

The Links toolbar is an area on the Taskbar that contains icons representing Web pages. Click an icon there, and your browser opens to its Web page.

1 Right-click the Taskbar to bring up the shortcut menu. Move the cursor to Toolbars at the top of the menu and click Links.

2 The Links toolbar will appear on the right side of the Taskbar.

3 Click the double arrows to the reveal a menu containing links to a few Web sites.

Now we're going to expand the Links toolbar. This will place the Web link icons right on the Taskbar and allow you to add your own links as well.

4 You won't be able to expand the Links toolbar until you unlock the Taskbar. Right-click the Taskbar and click on the checkmark next to Lock the Taskbar.

5 Double-click the word Links on the Taskbar.

6 The Links bar expands, placing the Web links on the Taskbar. Any links that don't fit are available in the menu that appears when you click the double arrows at right.

add a link

Now that you have the Links toolbar spread out on the Taskbar, you'll want to add your own Web links. Here, we'll add a Web link and do some editing of the Links toolbar to make it more convenient to access your new link.

1 Drag your Web link icon from the Address field of your Web browser to the Links toolbar. You can also drag any link on a Web page to the Links toolbar.

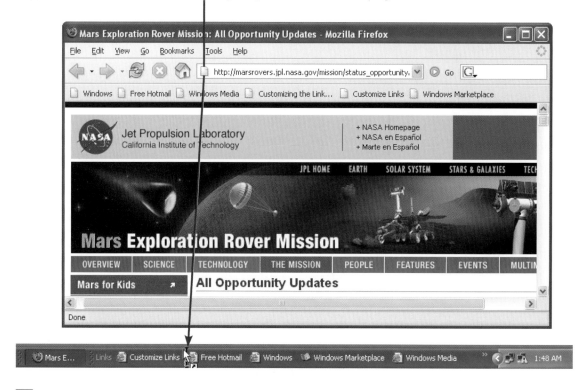

2 Here you don't see the new link on the Taskbar because there isn't room. Instead, if you click the double arrows, you'll find it in the menu.

3 To make room on the Taskbar for your new link, grab the top of the Taskbar and drag it upwards.

4 The Taskbar is now tall enough to fit all of the Web link icons. Now you need to shorten the name of your new link.

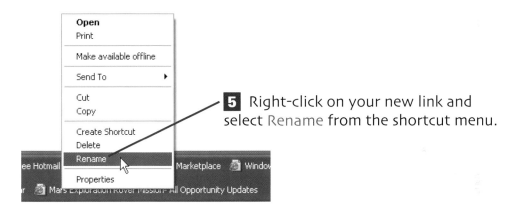

5 Right-click on your new link and select Rename from the shortcut menu.

6 Type the new name of the Web link in the Rename dialog box.

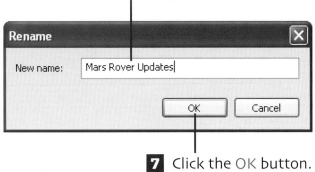

7 Click the OK button.

add a link (cont.)

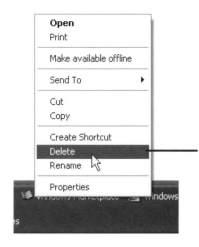

8 The Web link now takes less space. To enable it to fit in the first row of links, you need to delete some of the links that you don't use. To delete a link, right-click it and select Delete from the shortcut menu.

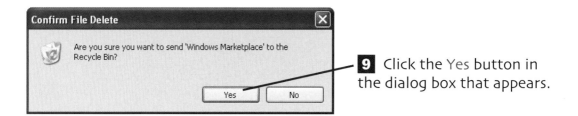

9 Click the Yes button in the dialog box that appears.

10 Finally, drag the Taskbar back down to its original size, with your new link visible.

You can lock the Taskbar if you wish by right-clicking an empty space on the Taskbar and choosing Lock the Taskbar.

add address toolbar

The Address toolbar can give you quick access to your favorite Web sites by providing a field where you can type a Web address—directly from the Taskbar.

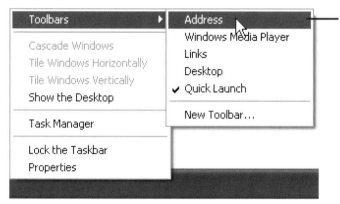

1 Right-click the Taskbar to bring up the shortcut menu. Choose Toolbars at the top of the menu and then click Address.

2 The Address toolbar will appear on the right side of the Taskbar.

3 You won't be able to open the Address toolbar until you unlock the Taskbar. Right-click the Taskbar and select Lock the Taskbar to remove its checkmark.

add address toolbar (cont.)

4 Double-click the word Address on the Taskbar.

5 The Address bar opens. You can now type in a Web address.

6 Click the Go button. Your Web browser will open to the Web page you specified.

7 The Address toolbar remembers the last few Web addresses you typed into it. To see them, click the down arrow on the Address toolbar.

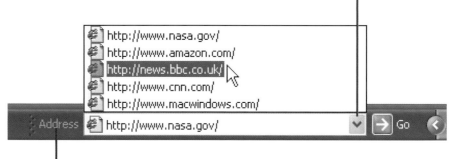

You can double-click the word Address on the Taskbar to close the Address toolbar. If you'd like to keep it open, you can lock the Taskbar by repeating step 3 on the previous page.

customize internet access

extra bits

create a connection p. 88

- If you have a constant Internet connection that a DSL or cable modem gives you, your computer will automatically update the time by connecting to a time server on the Internet.

  The automatic time updating may not occur with a dial-up modem connection, but you can manually update the time once you are connected.

  Double-click the time display on the right side of the Taskbar to open the Date and Time Properties dialog box.

  Click the Internet Time tab and place a checkmark next to Automatically synchronize with an Internet time server.

  Click Update Now. Windows will contact the time server and set the correct time on your computer. Click OK to close the dialog box.

connect to the net p. 91

- You may have noticed that the Internet status window doesn't have a minimize button. Fortunately, you don't need to keep it open while you're logged in to the Internet—you may close it at any time. If you need to bring it up again, go to the right side of the Taskbar and click the double-computer icon. This will open the Internet status window.

add address toolbar p. 101

- You can use the Address toolbar to access files and folders on your hard drive. Type a path to open the file or folder.

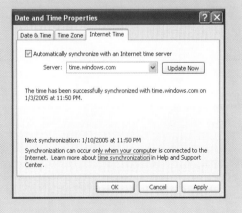

9. customize hardware

Got mouse? Of course you do. One way to customize a mouse would be to paint racing stripes on it. A better way is to tweak how Windows interacts with the mouse so that it performs better for you. The other piece of hardware that is just about as common as a mouse is a printer.

In this chapter, you'll learn how to customize your mouse settings and what to do if Windows doesn't recognize your printer after you plug it in.

The starting place for fiddling with hardware settings in Windows XP is the Control Panel.

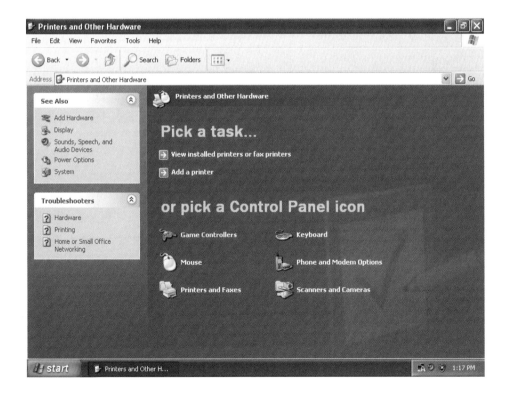

adjust mouse clicking

The computer mouse is the most personal of your PC's peripherals. Mice come in different sizes and shapes in order to fit different sized hands. But it's also true that not everyone clicks and drags at the same speed. You can change the way the mouse feels by adjusting the clicking and dragging behavior in Windows.

First, you'll adjust how fast you need to double-click your mouse to open a file or folder.

1 Go to the Start menu and select Control Panel.

2 In the left side panel, click Switch to Classic View if the Control Panel is not already in Classic mode.

The Control Panel's classic view shows each settings dialog box as an individual icon.

3 Double-click the Mouse icon.

customize hardware

4 The Mouse Properties window opens with the Buttons tab selected. Try dragging the Speed slider. Dragging to the left will allow a slower double-click to open a folder or file. Sliding it to the right requires a faster double-click.

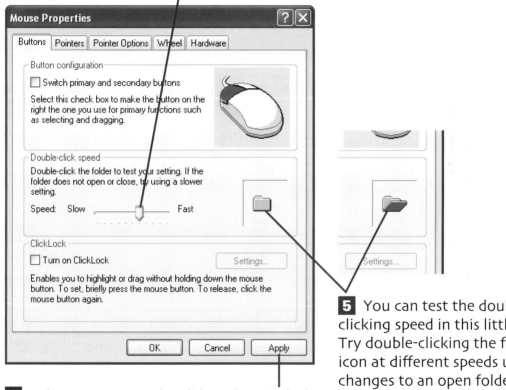

5 You can test the double-clicking speed in this little box. Try double-clicking the folder icon at different speeds until it changes to an open folder icon.

6 When you've got the slider where it feels the best, click the Apply button.

adjust mouse speed

Now we'll adjust the speed of the mouse pointer itself as it moves across the screen.

1 Click the Pointer Options tab.

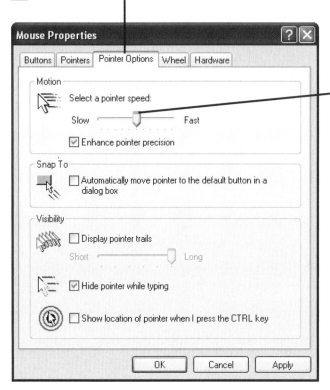

2 Under Select a pointer speed, drag the slider bar left or right. Move the mouse around to see how the change feels.

Moving the pointer toward Fast will make the mouse pointer move a long distance across the screen with small movements of the mouse. A faster setting is useful if you don't have a lot of desk space on which to navigate the mouse.

Moving the pointer toward Slow will shorten the distance the pointer travels on screen as you move the mouse. A slower setting is useful if you feel you are overshooting objects on screen.

When you have found an adjustment that feels the most comfortable, click the OK button to close the Mouse Properties window.

set up a printer

If Windows XP doesn't recognize your printer when you connect it to your computer, you may have to change some settings to get it working. If a CD came with your printer, run the installer program. If the printer still doesn't work, or you don't have an installer CD, you can run the Add Printer Wizard.

1 Turn on your printer.

2 Go to the Start menu, choose Control Panel. Switch to classic view if not already there.

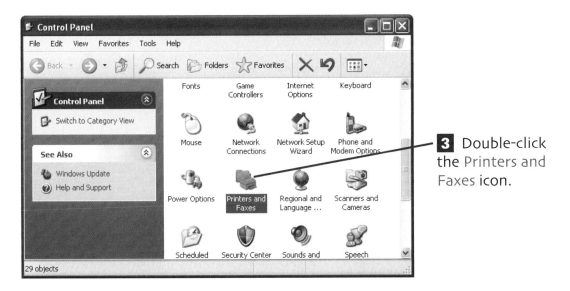

3 Double-click the Printers and Faxes icon.

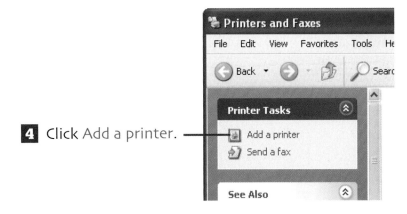

4 Click Add a printer.

set up a printer (cont.)

5 The Add Printer Wizard will launch, offering advice and asking questions. When you get to this screen, make sure these two items are checked.

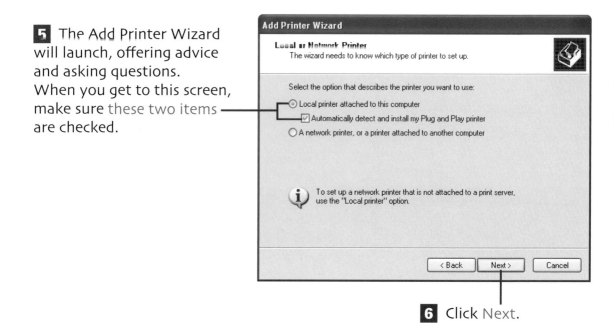

6 Click Next.

7 If Windows finds your printer, then you're set. If a window appears telling you it didn't find the printer, click the Next button, which will bring up the Select a Printer Port screen.

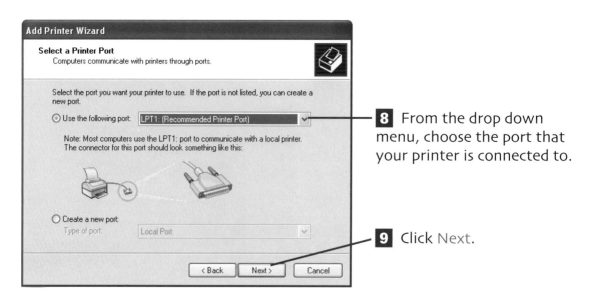

8 From the drop down menu, choose the port that your printer is connected to.

9 Click Next.

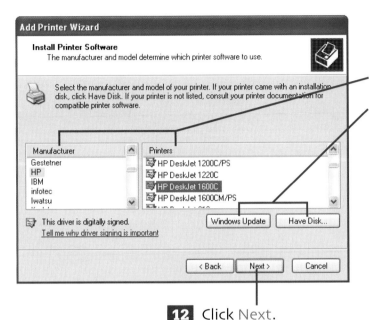

10 The wizard now asks you for your printer manufacturer and model. Select them from the lists.

11 If you've download installation files from the Internet, or have a disk, click the Have Disk button. If you have files, click the Browse button that will appear to locate them. Or, click Windows Update to download printer's installation files automatically.

12 Click Next.

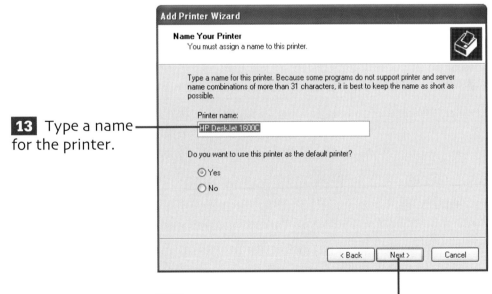

13 Type a name for the printer.

14 Click Next, and answer the questions on the next few screens. Click Finish at the last screen.

extra bits

adjust mouse speed p. 108

- If you have a mouse with a scroll wheel, you can adjust the speed of scrolling. Click the Wheel tab of Mouse Properties dialog box to get to the settings.

set up a printer p. 109

- If you have some other piece of hardware connected to your computer that Windows isn't recognizing, try running the Add Hardware Wizard. With the Control Panel in classic view, double-click Add Hardware. Click through the Wizard's screens and choose the type of device.

  If the wizard detects the hardware device, double-click it to see if the wizard offers any advice. Then complete the wizard with the Next and Finish buttons.

  If the wizard doesn't detect your device, click Search for and Install the Hardware Automatically. In the next screen, choose the manufacturer and model of the device. If you have a disk or files that you downloaded for the device, click the Have Disk button. For files, use the Browse button to locate them. Finally, complete the wizard.

  If you still can't get a printer working, open the Printers and Faxes icon in Control Panel and click Troubleshoot Printing in the left column. A dialog box will appear asking you questions about your problem and offer suggestions on how to fix it.

10. set up multiple users

So now you've gone through this book, fiddled with various settings in different parts of your computer, and adapted Windows XP to just the way you want it to look and act.

Then your spouse comes along and finds that things don't look the way they're supposed to. Worse yet, your kids get at your PC and do their own customization that is beyond your recognition.

It's time to give each person who uses the PC his or her own user account. Each user can then log in to the computer with their own user name and make their own customizations without affecting the way Windows looks to the other users. Each user will have their own individually customized Windows XP.

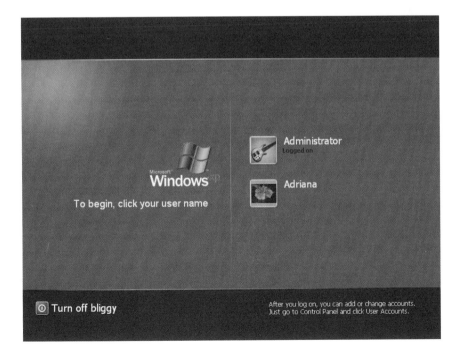

add a user account

You create user accounts one at a time, each with an individual user name.
Here's what to do to create your next user account

1 Go to the Start menu and choose Control Panel.

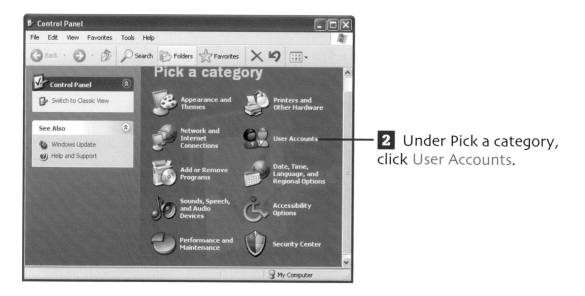

2 Under Pick a category,
click User Accounts.

3 Under Pick a task click
Create a new account.

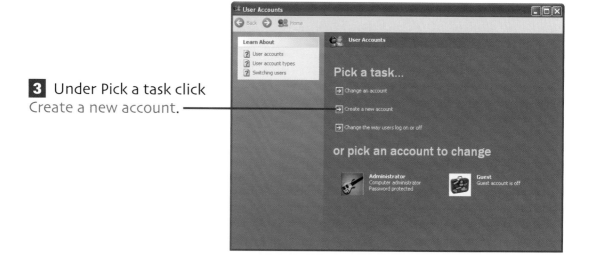

set up multiple users

4 Type in a name for the account.
A person's first name works just fine.

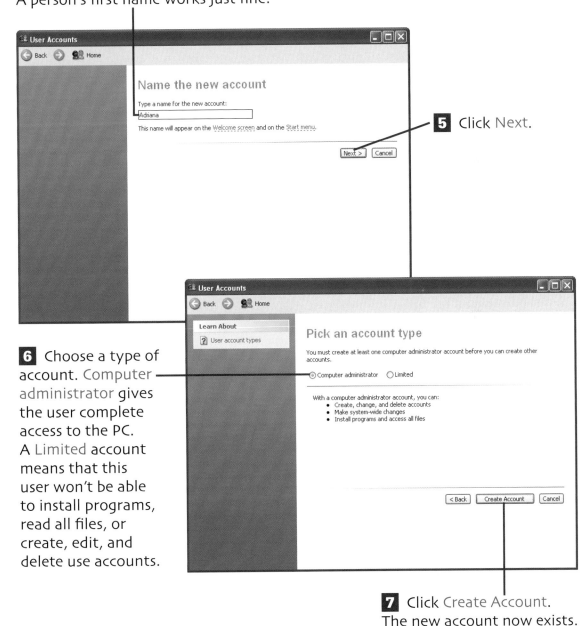

Name the new account

Type a name for the new account:

Adriana

This name will appear on the Welcome screen and on the Start menu.

5 Click Next.

Learn About
[?] User account types

Pick an account type

You must create at least one computer administrator account before you can create other accounts.

○ Computer administrator   ○ Limited

With a computer administrator account, you can:
• Create, change, and delete accounts
• Make system-wide changes
• Install programs and access all files

6 Choose a type of account. Computer administrator gives the user complete access to the PC. A Limited account means that this user won't be able to install programs, read all files, or create, edit, and delete use accounts.

7 Click Create Account. The new account now exists.

add a user password

After you create a new user account, the main User Accounts window reappears displaying it. Initially, the new account has the same icon as your account and has no password for log in. A password isn't necessary, but if you want the user to have one, here's how to create it.

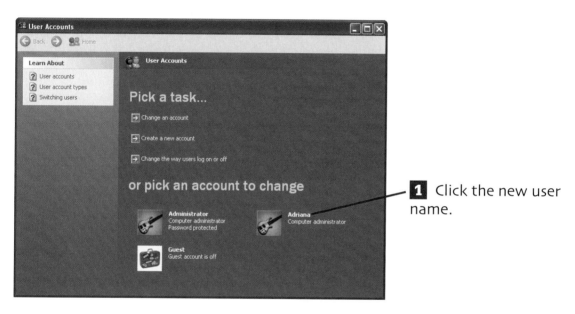

1 Click the new user name.

2 A new screen appears giving you some options to change. Click Create a password.

set up multiple users

The next screen appears with a warning that the user will lose stored passwords and other info. If this is a brand new user account, there won't be any information to lose.

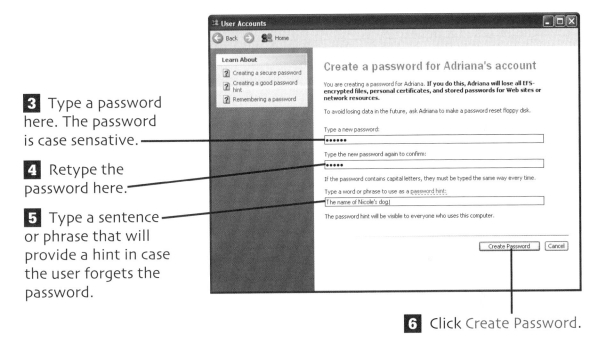

3 Type a password here. The password is case sensative.

4 Retype the password here.

5 Type a sentence or phrase that will provide a hint in case the user forgets the password.

6 Click Create Password.

The screen from step 2 reappears asking you what you want to change. Let's change the user icon this time.

change the user icon

Now that you're back at the main User Accounts dialog box, lets assign a new icon to the user account.

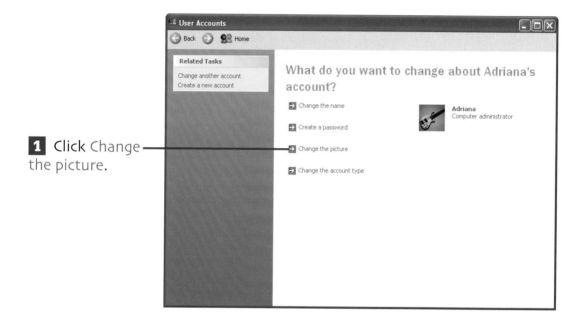

1 Click Change the picture.

2 Choose a picture from the selection Windows provides or use an image of your own. To use your own image, click Browse for more pictures.

3 A window opens to My Pictures. Find the picture you want to use and click to select it, or navigate to the picture in another location.

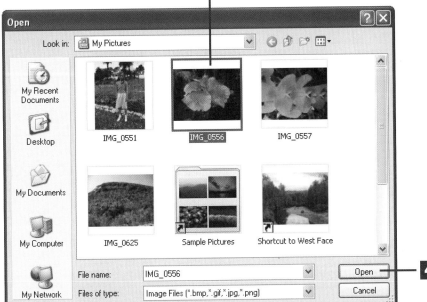

4 Click Open.

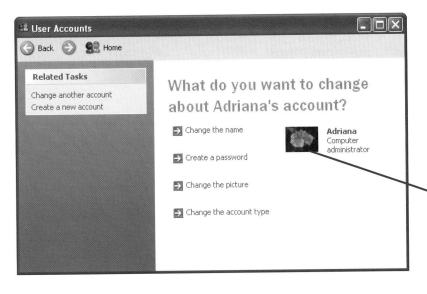

Back in the User Accounts dialog box, you'll now see your picture as the user icon. Close this window by clicking the X box in the upper right.

switch between users

Windows XP allows you to switch between users at any time without having to close your programs. This enables another user to log in. Then, when you log back in, you'll find everything right where you left it.

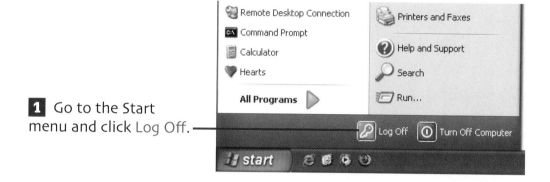

1 Go to the Start menu and click Log Off.

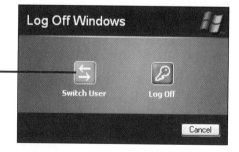

2 In the Log Off Windows dialog, click the Switch User button.

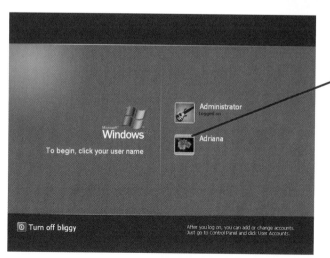

3 A screen appears showing all of the user accounts set up on the computer. Click the account button for the new user you set up.

Windows XP will now launch for the new user, bringing up a completely standard Desktop, Start menu, Taskbar, and other interface elements and basic programs.

120

extra bits

switch between users p. 120

- The reason you can switch from one user to another without closing your programs is that a feature called fast user switching is turned on by default when you create new user accounts. This works great for a home or small office PC. However, if you are concerned about security, you can turn off fast user switching, which would require that all programs close and Windows shut down before allowing another user to log on.

- To disable fast user switching, go to the Start menu, click Control Panel, and open the User Accounts category. Now click Change the Way Users Log On and Off. You can now uncheck Use Fast User Switching.

set up multiple users

index

index

index

index

O

OK button, 8
Open With option, 81
Outlook Express, 92–96
  creating email groups in,
    95–96
  opening, 93
  setting up email accounts in,
    92
  turning off email graphics in,
    93–94

P

passwords, 113, 116–117
PC World magazine, 22
Pear Software, 74
photos
  adding to folder icons, 70–71
  adding to user-account icons,
    118–119
  displaying resolution of, 22
  replacing Desktop, 10–13, 22
  setting Outlook Express to
    block, 93–94
  for user-account icons,
    118–119
pinning, 42–43, 44
Player, Windows Media, 32–33
Pointer Options tab, 108
pointer speed, 108
printer settings, 109–111, 112
Printers and Faxes icon, 109, 112
Professional, Windows XP, 46
programs
  adding to Start menu, 42–43
  adding to Taskbar, 30–32
  installing, 75–78, 86
  opening, 32, 42
  removing from Start menu,
    45
  setting default, 79–80
  switching users without
    closing, 120, 121
  viewing installed, 80

Properties command, 3
properties dialog boxes, 3, 8

Q

question mark, 6
Quick Launch toolbar, 30–32, 61

R

Recent Documents submenu, 46
Remove from This List
  command, 45
Rename command, 74, 99
Reset button, 65
resolution, 14–17, 22
Restart Now button, 85
right-clicking, 2
right-dragging, 48
Run Installation Program dialog
  box, 78

S

screen resolution, 14–17
scroll wheel, mouse, 112
Security tab, 93
security updates, 84
Select Members button, 96
separators, toolbar, 64–65
service packs, 86
Set Program Access and Defaults
  button, 79
settings dialog boxes, 4
setup.exe, 76, 78
shortcut menus, 2
shortcuts
  creating, 29, 49, 61
  deleting, 52–54
  renaming, 29
Show Text option, 57
Size column head, 69
Slow pointer option, 108

software. See programs
spammers, 93
Speed slider, 107
Start menu, 35–46
  adding folders to, 44
  adding programs to, 42–43
  changing number of
    programs on, 37
  classic vs. standard, 46
  converting links to menus in,
    39–41
  purpose of, 35
  removing items from, 45
  resizing icons in, 36–38
  ways of customizing, 35
Status bar, 62
Support icon, 8
Switch to Classic View option, 4
Switch User button, 120

T

Taskbar, 23–34
  adding icons to, 55–57
  adding programs to, 30–32
  adding toolbars to, 24–26
  adding Web links to, 97–100
  adding Windows Media
    player to, 32–33
  locking/unlocking, 24, 32,
    34, 55, 100, 101
  moving, 34
  moving toolbars to Desktop
    from, 27
  purpose of, 23
  removing toolbars from, 34
  widening Quick Launch area
    in, 32
themes, 18–21, 22
Themes tab, 18, 22
Thumbnails view, 66, 70
Tiles view, 66
time server, 103

index

Visual QuickProject

Making a Movie
with Windows XP

JAN OZER

making a movie
with windows xp

Visual QuickProject Guide

by Jan Ozer

Peachpit
Press

Visual QuickProject Guide
Making a Movie with Windows XP
Jan Ozer

Peachpit Press

1249 Eighth Street
Berkeley, CA 94710
510/524-2178
800/283-9444
510/524-2221 (fax)

Find us on the World Wide Web at: www.peachpit.com
To report errors, please send a note to errata@peachpit.com
Peachpit Press is a division of Pearson Education

Editor: Judy Ziajka
Production: Lisa Brazieal, Myrna Vladic
Compositor: Owen Wolfson
Cover design: The Visual Group with Aren Howell
Cover production: Aren Howell
Cover photo credit: Getty One
Interior design: Elizabeth Castro
Indexer: Julie Bess

ISBN 0-321-27845-3

Printed and bound in the United States of America

To Barbara, Whatley, and
Rose, the inspiration for all
my creative endeavors.

Acknowledgments

Wow, my first four-color book—
I am jazzed. Thanks to Nancy Davis
and Marjorie Baer for inviting me to
join the debut of this new series, and
to Judy Ziajka, who pretty much
whipped this book into shape single-
handedly. Thanks to moto-girl Lisa
Brazieal for all her assistance and
design encouragement (it really
helped), to Myrna Vladic for her end-
of-the-process aid, and to Owen
Wolfson, compositor for this book.

I couldn't write these books without the computers from Dell and
Hewlett-Packard that I exclusively
work on (and recommend highly) or
the software from Microsoft (Word,
PowerPoint, Windows XP, and Movie
Maker), Adobe (InDesign), and Ulead
(PhotoImpact). Special thanks to
Michael Patten and David Caulton
from Microsoft for answering my
frequent, frantic inquiries.

I appreciate the support of those
who came before me, especially
Papa John Buechler, Mr. Movie
Maker himself. Let's hope a rising
tide raises all boats in the harbor.

Once again, thanks to Pat Tracy
for technical and other assistance.

contents

contents

contents

introduction

The Visual QuickProject Guide you're reading offers a unique way to learn new skills. Instead of drowning you in long text descriptions, this Visual QuickProject Guide uses color screen shots with clear, concise step-by-step instructions to show you how to complete a project in a matter of hours.

In this book, I'll be creating a movie from the video and digital pictures my wife and I shot of my eldest daughter's last birthday. You'll be working with your own video, which may be a birthday video, but could be video from a vacation, graduation, or any other occasion. However, though the events may be different, the process of editing the video footage and digital pictures into a finished movie will be almost identical. Thus, you can apply the principles you learn here to your own movies—just replace "birthday movie" with the occasion of your choice.

We'll be working with Microsoft's video editor, Microsoft Windows Movie Maker 2. Why Movie Maker? Because it has all the features you need to build an exciting, fun-to-watch movie, and it's free with Windows XP.

what you will learn

You will learn to create a movie using Movie Maker.

You'll start by capturing video from your DV camcorder, which Movie Maker simplifies with its Video Capture wizard.

Movie Maker stores all captured video in the Contents pane.

I'll show you how to drag your clips to the Storyboard and arrange them in the proper order.

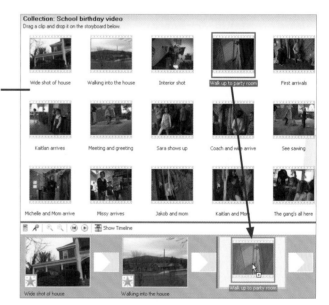

Transitions are visual effects that smooth the flow from one scene to another. Movie Maker provides dozens to tickle your creativity; here I'm using the Heart transition. I'll show you how and where to effectively use transitions and special effects.

Time to go (sniff, sniff)

Titles help your viewers understand what's going on in the movie. I'll show you how to choose among Movie Maker's extensive style options and how to change fonts and colors to your liking.

Microphone

Movie Maker makes it easy to add background music and narration (it's her birthday, so she's telling the story).

You'll learn how to add these audio elements and how to make them work smoothly with the audio captured with your camcorder.

what you will learn (cont.)

My wife is a digital camera fanatic, and I like adding her pictures to the movie, which is a snap in Movie Maker. Here I'm creating a slide show from my wife's digital pictures with my daughter narrating in the background. You'll learn how to create a slide show and set options, such as picture and transition duration, to your liking.

Here's Movie Maker in Timeline view, which, by the way, is a great view for synchronizing titles, audio, and transitions to pictures or video on the top track.

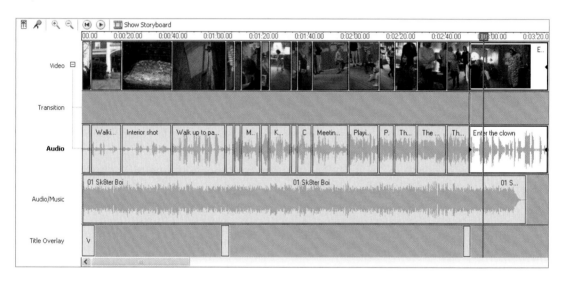

One of Movie Maker's strongest features is AutoMovie, which takes your video and synchronizes it with a song you select to create a music video. You'll learn how and when to create AutoMovies and how they integrate into larger projects.

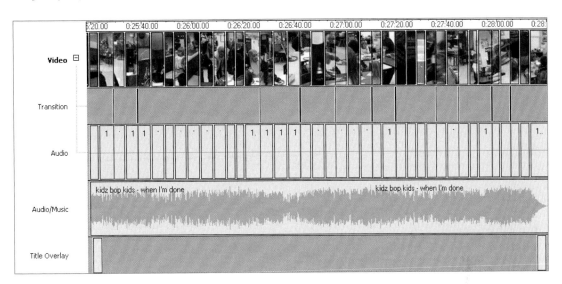

3. Finish Movie

Save to my computer
Save to CD
Send in e-mail
Send to the Web
Send to DV camera

Producing movies is fun, but sending them out to be watched by others is even more fun. You'll learn how to save a video file for viewing on your computer, save your project to a CD, send your movie via e-mail, upload your movie to a Web site, and send your movie back to your DV camera.

You'll also learn how to produce a video file you can use to create a DVD with any number of third-party programs.

how this book works

The title of each section explains what is covered on that page.

fade audio out and in

You just inserted a video transition. Now you'll work on the audio. You'll fade out the audio on the clip before the transition—from 100% volume to 0%—and fade it back in on the clip after the transition—from 0% volume to 100%.

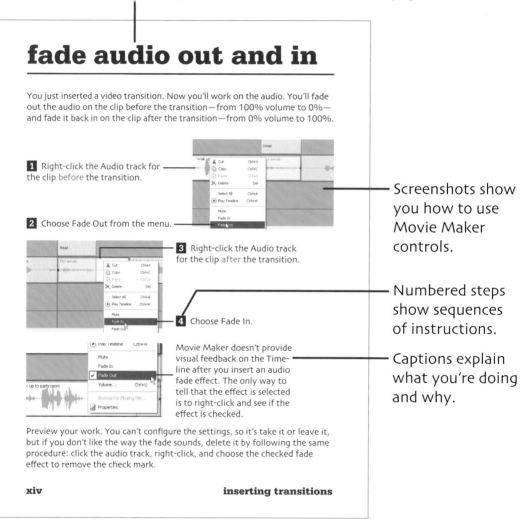

1 Right-click the Audio track for the clip before the transition.

2 Choose Fade Out from the menu.

3 Right-click the Audio track for the clip after the transition.

4 Choose Fade In.

Movie Maker doesn't provide visual feedback on the Timeline after you insert an audio fade effect. The only way to tell that the effect is selected is to right-click and see if the effect is checked.

Screenshots show you how to use Movie Maker controls.

Numbered steps show sequences of instructions.

Captions explain what you're doing and why.

Preview your work. You can't configure the settings, so it's take it or leave it, but if you don't like the way the fade sounds, delete it by following the same procedure: click the audio track, right-click, and choose the checked fade effect to remove the check mark.

xiv   **inserting transitions**

The extra bits section at the end of each chapter contains tips and tricks that you might like to know, but which aren't absolutely necessary for creating a movie.

extra bits

add background music p. 92

- I use Windows Media Player to copy audio tracks from a CD-ROM so I can include them in a movie. It's very simple to use, but if you want step-by-step guidance, see Microsoft Windows Movie Maker 2: Visual QuickStart Guide from Peachpit Press for details.

- You can also add sound effects to your videos on the Audio/Music track. Although Movie Maker doesn't come with any sound effects or background music, Microsoft offers two free sources of both. The Creativity Fun Pack (http://www.microsoft.com/windowsxp/moviemaker/downloads/create.asp) comes with 53 sound effects in five categories: animal, fun random, graduation, party and sports, and background music. Microsoft's Windows Movie Maker 2 Winter Fun Pack 2003 (http://www.microsoft.com/windowsxp/moviemaker/downloads/winterfun.asp), also free, includes 92 sound effects and 7 music tracks.

set up for narration p. 102

- There's a big difference between the microphone port and the line-in port available on some computers. The line-in port is used for the output from stereo systems and other independently powered devices and requires a significantly stronger signal than you get with the typical computer microphone. Line-in ports won't work with a microphone, so be sure you connect your microphone to the microphone port.

The heading for each group of tips matches the section title.

The page number next to the heading makes it easy to find the section the tips belong to.

using audio

tools you will need

Here's what you need to complete the project in this book:

At least 20 GB of free disk space for each hour-long project and a CD-Recordable or CD-Rewritable drive for producing recordable CDs.

A computer running Microsoft Windows XP Professional or Home Edition with a 600-MHz processor, 128 MB of RAM, a sound card, a FireWire card (to capture video from a DV camera), a microphone for narration, and an Internet connection (for sending movies via e-mail or uploading movies to a Web site).

If you produce lots of movies, you'll run out of disk space quickly. If you think you may not have enough space, consider adding another drive to your computer; contact your local computer dealer to find out how.

A digital camcorder with miniDV tapes for shooting video footage and transferring video to and from the computer.

You'll also need some interesting video to work with and some digital photographs and songs.

(Used with permission of Sony Electronics, Inc.)

A FireWire cable to connect the camcorder to the computer.

Blank CD-R discs (if you have a CD recorder and want to burn your movies to CD-R/RW).

(Used with permission of Verbatim Corporation)

Movie Maker 2 downloaded and installed.

You'll use Microsoft Windows Media Player to play your movies once they're produced, but that's installed on every Windows XP computer.

movie maker terms

To make your work in Movie Maker easier, I've defined some of the key terms you'll encounter as you work in the program. We'll be using these terms throughout this book.

- **Video:** The footage you shoot with your camcorder. It includes both images and audio.

- **Movie:** The final result that Movie Maker produces when you've finished editing and are ready to share your production.

- **Capture:** The process of transferring video from your camera to your computer.

- **Import:** The process of inserting an audio, video, or picture file already on your hard drive into Movie Maker.

- **Render:** The process Movie Maker goes through in producing a movie.

- **Video clip:** Video captured or imported into Movie Maker. Video clips include the audio originally shot with the video.

- **Audio clip:** Separate audio files (usually music) imported into Movie Maker.

- **Picture:** A still image you shoot with your digital camera and import into Movie Maker.

- **Project:** The file where Movie Maker stores your work while you're working on a movie. The project file references the video clips, audio clips, and pictures (often collectively referred to as content or assets) you're including in your movie, but Movie Maker doesn't actually copy them into the project file. This keeps the project file small, but it also means that you must be sure not to delete the captured files until after you produce your final movie.

- **AutoMovie:** A series of video clips that Movie Maker automatically assembles and synchronizes to a background audio clip. You can edit AutoMovies after Movie Maker creates them, and you can add them as components of longer productions or create them as stand-alone movies.

the next step

While this Visual QuickProject Guide will give you an excellent start, there's a lot more to learn about the art of movie making and working with Movie Maker and the excellent suite of additional media creation tools that Microsoft offers. If you're curious, check out my Microsoft Windows Movie Maker 2: Visual QuickStart Guide, also published by Peachpit Press.

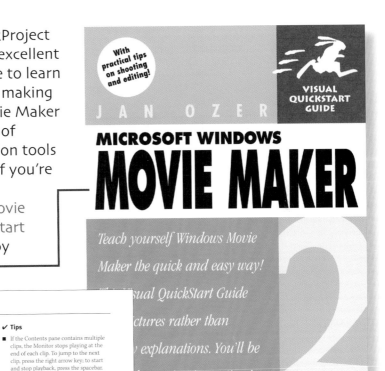

The Visual QuickStart Guide features clear examples, concise step-by-step instructions, and lots of helpful tips. It covers every aspect of shooting and capturing video and editing and producing compelling, fun-to-watch movies.

1. welcome to movie maker

Movie Maker is easy to learn, and for the most part, you can use it without having to fiddle with its options or do any elaborate set up. But just as with any new tool you use, it's a good idea to take a quick look around to familiarize yourself with the basic operations. That's what you'll do in this chapter. Then you'll be ready to jump right in and start bringing your video footage into Movie Maker and begin making movies.

So Launch Movie Maker, and let's get underway.

Movie Maker 2 in all its glory.

Producing family videos is fun and rewarding (plus you get to make sure that you're included).

Here's me with Whatley, whose birthday party video will be your model throughout this book.

movie maker tour

You can switch this window between the Collections pane, which houses all your content—your video footage, audio recordings, and still pictures (together known as your project assets)—and the Movie Tasks pane (shown), where you launch Movie Maker functions such as Capture Video and Finish Movie.

The Contents pane contains imported audio, video, and pictures and Movie Maker's libraries of transitions and video effects. Click any item in the Contents pane to preview it in the Monitor.

The Monitor displays your content and previews your project.

Use the Seek bar to scroll through your clips.

This is Movie Maker's Storyboard view, which displays each clip in the project in a separate window. Storyboard view is great for arranging your content in the desired order. Once you've arranged your clips, you switch to Timeline view to add titles, transitions, effects, and other audio.

You can control playback with the VCR-like controls at the bottom.

The window now shows the Collections pane with the first imported content (assets) and Movie Maker's Video Effects and Video Transitions collections. Click any collection to view its assets in the Contents pane.

Click the appropriate button to view the Collections pane or Movie Tasks pane. Spend a few moments clicking back and forth between these views to familiarize yourself with them.

The Contents pane showing Movie Maker's Video Transitions collection. Again, click any item to preview it in the Monitor.

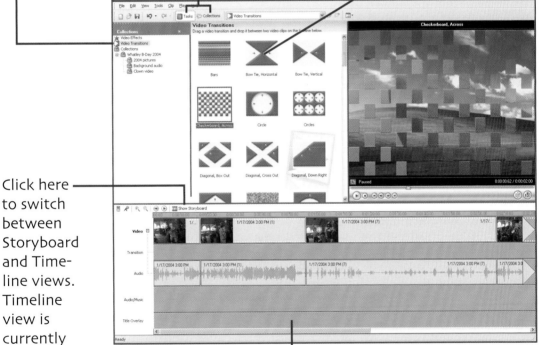

Click here to switch between Storyboard and Timeline views. Timeline view is currently displayed.

This is Movie Maker's Timeline view, a longitudinal view with separate tracks for video, transitions, audio, audio/music (background music or narration), and title overlays (titles).

movie maker tour (cont.)

Now take a quick look at the main toolbar. Once you're familiar with how to view your collections and access Movie Maker's tools, you'll be in great shape to start editing. Don't worry about becoming an expert right away; you'll learn a lot more about working with collections in Chapter 2.

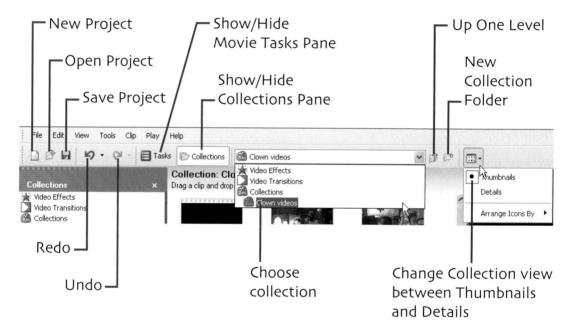

New Project

Open Project

Save Project

Show/Hide
Movie Tasks Pane

Show/Hide
Collections Pane

Up One Level

New
Collection
Folder

Redo

Undo

Choose
collection

Change Collection view
between Thumbnails
and Details

welcome to movie maker

resize the work area

You can resize Movie Maker's windows to suit your needs. Simply hover the pointer over any solid blue line until the pointer changes to a two-headed arrow. Click and then drag the line until that window is sized to your liking. You can use this feature to maximize the size of whatever window you're working in. If you think Whatley's smiling now, wait until she watches this movie I'm making!

set project options

Choose Tools > Options to access Movie Maker's project default options.

Most of these options are self-explanatory, but a few bear some comment.

For convenience, store your content and project files in the same folder. That way, you can always find the files to use them again, and you can easily delete them when the project is complete. I usually create the folder on my capture drive, which is a separate disk drive used solely for video editing. Even on my laptop, which has only one drive, I always create a separate folder for each project.

Select the Save Auto-R ecover option to have Movie Maker save your project file automatically so if your computer crashes, you won't lose all of your work. Try a setting of 10 minutes. No matter what autorecover setting you use, also save your project frequently, just to be safe.

Codecs are the compression technologies used to render and output your project. It's a good idea to keep them current, so keep this option checked.

You'll use passwords in Chapter 10 when uploading files to the Web. If multiple users access your computer and you're concerned that they may upload files to your Web site, here's an easy way to delete your passwords.

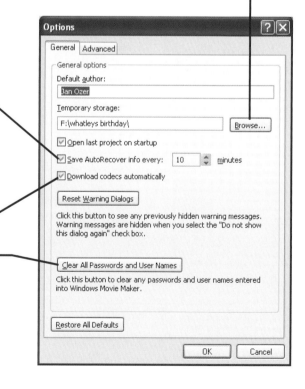

Click the Advanced tab to
access these functions.

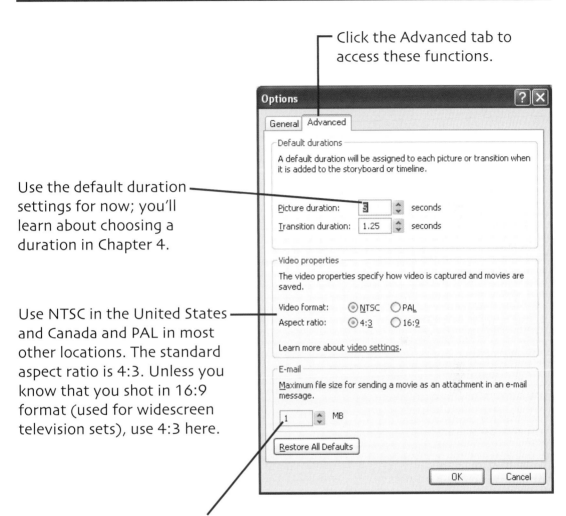

Use the default duration
settings for now; you'll
learn about choosing a
duration in Chapter 4.

Use NTSC in the United States
and Canada and PAL in most
other locations. The standard
aspect ratio is 4:3. Unless you
know that you shot in 16:9
format (used for widescreen
television sets), use 4:3 here.

Movie Maker automatically limits the size of videos produced for e-mail dis-
tribution to the size set here. Check with your Internet service provider (ISP)
to learn what your sending limit is, and recognize that most recipients have a
receiving limit as well. For example, my Hotmail account limits these attach-
ments to 1 MB. Be sure to consider both your limits and your recipients' when
setting this default. If you don't know the limits set by your ISP or those of
your recipient, use 1 MB.

extra bits

movie maker tour p. 2

- This book describes Movie Maker 2, which is available for free download at http://www. microsoft.com/windowsxp/ moviemaker/|downloads/ moviemaker2.asp.

set project options p. 6

- Changing the Picture Duration setting affects pictures and transitions inserted after you make the change (not those previously inserted into the project).

2. collecting project assets

I like collecting all of my audio and video clips and pictures—the project assets, or content—before I start serious editing, and that's what you'll do here. You'll set up and capture—or transfer—some video from a DV camera and import some audio files and still pictures, such as those shot with a digital camera. You'll also learn to manage these collections in Movie Maker's Collections pane.

I'm assuming that you've already shot your video and that you may have some digital photographs and music files already stored on your computer that you want to use to create a slide show to include with your video footage. You'll be getting these assets into Movie Maker in this chapter and then working with them to create your project in the rest of this book.

Here's a collection of digital pictures.

Movie Maker 2 stores all content in Collections located here.

You can build movies from video and digital pictures and add your own background music tracks or narration.

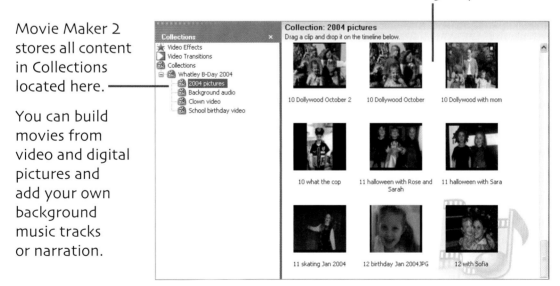

9

set up for dv capture

Find the DV output port on your DV camera. It's usually marked DV, as shown here.

Not this one—it's for analog audio-video you watch on your TV.

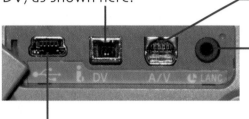

Not this one—LANC is a little-used standard for controlling your camera with external devices.

Not this one—it's the universal serial bus (USB) port used to send still pictures to the computer.

6-pin FireWire port on the computer. You can connect the cable to any FireWire port on the bracket.

4-pin to 6-pin DV cable. This end goes into your camera.

This end goes into the DV card in your computer. Note that some laptops have 4-pin ports, like the DV camera shown here, instead of 6-pin ports. If this is the case for your computer, make sure you buy a 4-pin to 4-pin DV cable.

Power up your camera and set it to VTR or Play mode.

capture dv

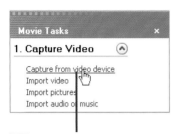

1 With your video camera connected to your computer, click here to start the capture process. If the Movie Tasks pane isn't visible, click the Show Movie Tasks Pane button on the main toolbar.

2 Click the Browse button to choose a folder for the captured video and enter a file name. Click Next at the bottom of the screen to continue (not shown).

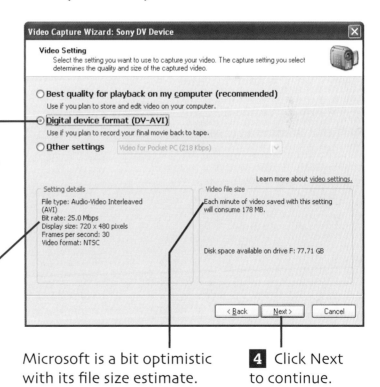

3 The best approach is to work in DV-AVI format since that's the highest-quality format. You can always render your final movie in a different format, as you'll see in Chapter 10.

These are the parameters for the captured video. There's nothing here you really need to know about at this point. You'll learn a bit more about these in Chapter 10.

Microsoft is a bit optimistic with its file size estimate. DV-AVI video actually uses 216 MB per second.

4 Click Next to continue.

capture dv (cont.)

Capture Method

Select whether to capture the entire tape automatically or specific parts manually.

○ **Capture the entire tape automatically**

The video tape rewinds to the beginning and the video is then captured automatically.

◉ **Capture parts of the tape manually**

Cue the video tape to the part of the video you want to capture and start the capture process manually. You can capture more than one part of the video tape without restarting the wizard.

☑ **Show preview during capture**

On some computers, displaying the Preview window during the video capture can affect the quality of the captured video. If you find that your captured video files do not play back smoothly, clear this checkbox.

5 Capturing the entire tape is easy—just select the top option and on the next screen click Start Capture. But often, you'll want to capture only a portion of the tape for your video. You'll do this here. To start, select Capture Parts of the Tape Manually.

If you're working on a slow computer (Pentium III or slower), I recommend that you uncheck the Show Preview During Capture check box, which lets the computer concentrate solely on capturing the video. Most modern computers are fast enough to capture and show the preview at the same time.

6 Click Next to continue (not shown).

7 Watch the preview window and use these player controls to move the tape to the desired start position and then stop the tape.

8 Click Start Capture, and Movie Maker will start the tape rolling and start capturing. The Stop Capture button becomes active; click it if you want to stop capturing. Repeat step 7 and this step until you've captured all necessary video.

Select the Create Clips check box to have Movie Maker create a separate clip for each time you started and stopped the camera during shooting. This can be a real time saver, especially when you shot the tape over a few days or longer, since it breaks the video into the scenes as you shot them. Otherwise, Movie Maker will show just one clip in the Contents pane, and you'll have to identify the scenes yourself.

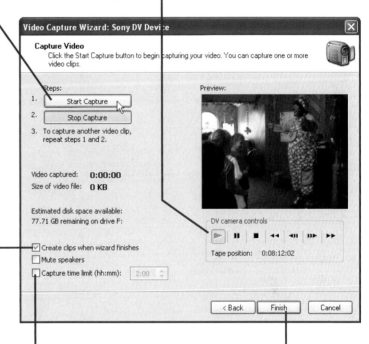

Video Capture Wizard: Sony DV Device

Capture Video
Click the Start Capture button to begin capturing your video. You can capture one or more video clips.

Steps:
1. Start Capture
2. Stop Capture
3. To capture another video clip, repeat steps 1 and 2.

Video captured: **0:00:00**
Size of video file: **0 KB**

Estimated disk space available:
77.71 GB remaining on drive F:

☑ Create clips when wizard finishes
☐ Mute speakers
☐ Capture time limit (hh:mm): 2:00

Preview:

DV camera controls

Tape position: 0:08:12:02

< Back   Finish   Cancel

You can set the capture time limit to capture a specific duration of tape (for instance, the last 20 minutes of a tape). Then you can walk away and let Movie Maker stop the capture for you.

9 Click Finish when you've finished capturing all your video clips.

collecting project assets   **13**

capture dv (cont.)

After you click Finish, if you checked Create Clips, Movie Maker scans the captured video for scene breaks (where you stopped and started the camera during shooting) and imports each scene into the collection as a separate video clip.

Note, however, that Movie Maker actually stores only one file on your hard disk for each capture session.

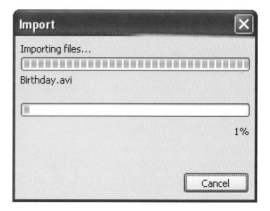

Movie Maker stores each capture session as a separate collection.

Click the collection name to display the collection in the Contents pane.

Movie Maker displays the captured video in the Contents pane. Double-click any thumbnail image, and Movie Maker will play the video in the Monitor.

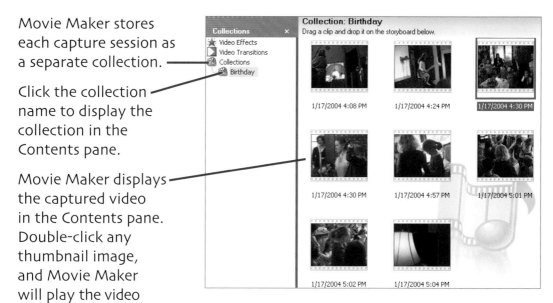

set up collections

Each time you capture or import video, Movie Maker stores it in a separate collection. In contrast, when you import digital pictures or audio, Movie Maker includes those files in the currently selected collection. I like to create one project collection, under which I store all other collections that contain video, audio, or still images. To keep my audio and still image assets separate, first I create a collection for each type, and then I import the assets into that collection. Start by creating your own project collection.

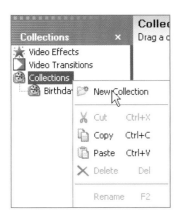

1 Click the Collections folder. Then right-click and choose New Collection.

Collections work like folders in Winows Explorer.

2 Here's your new collection. Type the desired name.

This descriptive name should make this collection easy to find. Now move all collections containing content for this project under the collection you just created.

set up collections (cont.)

3 To arrange your collections, simply drag them onto the target collection. When the target collection is highlighted, release the mouse, and Movie Maker will insert your dragged collection under the collection you selected. I dragged my collection under the Whatley B-Day 2004 collection.

4 Oops—calling the video collection Birthday was a bit too general. I need to change the name to something more specific. To change the name of a collection, click the collection; then right-click and choose Rename.

Enter a new name. Yes—Clown Video is much more descriptive.

5 Now add collections for your digital pictures and audio files, using the New Collection right-click menu option, as I did here. In a moment, you'll import those assets directly into these collections.

import pictures

1 Click the collection in which you want to store your pictures.

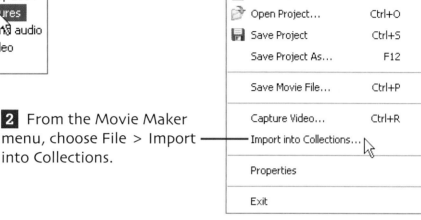

2 From the Movie Maker menu, choose File > Import into Collections.

3 In the Import File dialog box that appears, navigate to the folder that contains your pictures and select all of the pictures you want to import.

4 Click Import.

import pictures (cont.)

Here are my pictures, perfect slide show material.

Click the collection name
in the Collections pane...

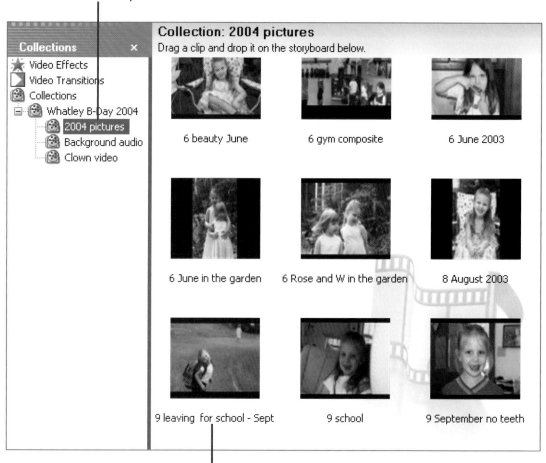

...to display the collection contents
in the Contents pane.

Click any image, and Movie Maker
will display it in the Monitor.

collecting project assets

import audio

Importing music is very similar to importing pictures. You can use the Movie Maker menu as you did to import pictures. Or if you like working with the Movie Tasks pane open, you can choose your collection in the Collections drop-down box. You'll use that approach now.

1 Click the target collection.

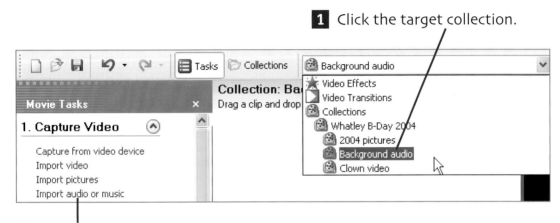

2 Click Import Audio or Music.

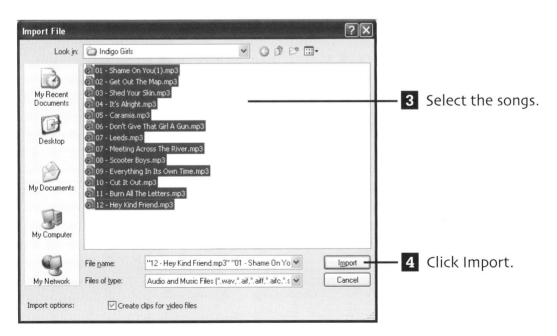

3 Select the songs.

4 Click Import.

import audio (cont.)

Click here to display the contents in Details view, to view the song name and duration.

My wife loves the Indigo Girls, so they're a safe choice as background music for slide shows. As I've learned, Springsteen is a tough sell to mommy and the girlies, despite my singing the girlies to sleep with "Thunder Road" and "Jungleland" innumerable times during their infant years.

import video

1 If your video footage is already on your computer, you need to import it. Click Import Video.

Movie Maker always inserts captured and imported video in a separate collection located below the Collections root folder, so don't bother to click the target collection first.

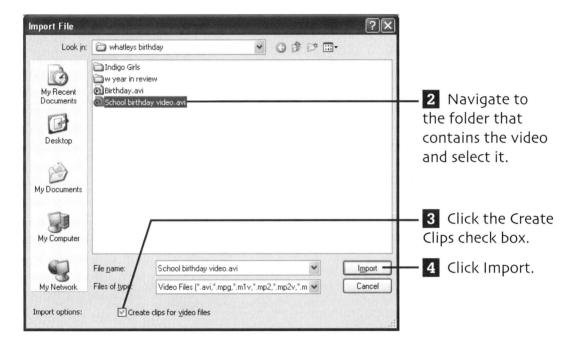

2 Navigate to the folder that contains the video and select it.

3 Click the Create Clips check box.

4 Click Import.

Because you selected Create Clips, Movie Maker breaks the video into separate clips at scene breaks, where you stopped and started the camera during shooting.

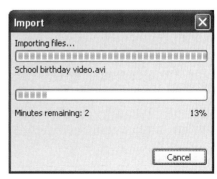

import video (cont.)

Here are the video clips, but the collection—in my case, School Birthday Video—is in the Collections root folder. Let's move it into the project folder for me, the Whatley B-Day 2004 collection.

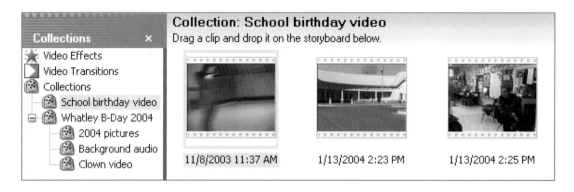

Click, drag the collection down, and release.

Now all assets are right where they can easily be found. Time to start editing—head on to Chapter 3.

extra bits

set up collections p. 15

- Collections are not project specific. Once you create a collection in Movie Maker, it stays in the program until you delete it.

- To name each captured and imported video clip, Movie Maker inserts the time and date of the shot. This naming convention is a great feature when you have three months' worth of videos on a single tape, and you're trying to figure out when you shot each one. For instance, so when exactly did little Sally start walking? Just check the date!

import pictures p. 17

- Movie Maker can import .bmp, .dib, .gif, .jpeg, .jpg, .png, .tif, .tiff, and .wmf image formats.

- Movie Maker can't edit pictures after you import them, so if you need to rotate, remove red eye, or otherwise adjust your images, do so before importing.

import audio p. 19

- Movie Maker can import .aif, .aifc, .aiff, asf, .au, .mp2, .mp3, .mpa, .snd, .wav, and .wma audio files. The only noteworthy omission is files produced with RealNetworks technology, which usually have the .rn extension.

import video p. 21

- Movie Maker can import .asf, .avi, .m1v, .mp2, .mp2v, .mpe, .mpeg, .mpg, .mpv2, .wm, and .wmv video files.

- Movie Maker can't import QuickTime videos, with the .mov extension.

collecting project assets   **23**

3. preparing your clips

When creating a birthday or other similar video, I try to accomplish two things. First, I try to tell a story, with a beginning, middle, and end. This helps keep the viewer's attention. Second, I try to chronicle the event, primarily by making sure I include all key shots inherent to the occasion, like a shot of everyone singing "Happy Birthday," and all key participants, typically family and important friends. Then I chop off the rest, aggressively and relentlessly, typically in the Contents pane, because it's a great place to isolate the key clips and delete the rest. When I'm done, I move to the Storyboard and Timeline to finish the work.

At this point, if you opted to allow Movie Maker to create clips as described in Chapter 2, you're probably staring at a bunch of video clips in the Contents pane: one for each time you started and stopped recording on your DV camera. Having these clips broken out is helpful, but to provide the necessary pace, you'll usually need to split these clips—that is, break the clips into smaller clips, each containing a shot you want to include in the final movie.

Movie Maker's Contents pane is a great place to identify the clips you'll include in your movie.

Isolating all the clips you'll include in your movie may be time consuming, but building the movie from these clips will now take no time at all.

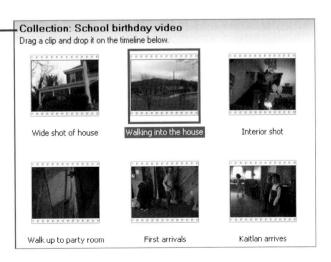

Collection: School birthday video
Drag a clip and drop it on the timeline below.

Wide shot of house   Walking into the house   Interior shot

Walk up to party room   First arrivals   Kaitlan arrives

delete video clips

Collection: School birthday video
Drag a clip and drop it on the timeline below.

11/8/2003 1		1/13/2004 2:25 PM
1/13/2004 2		1/13/2004 2:36 PM
1/13/2004 2:40 PM	1/13/2004 2:44 PM	1/17/2004 2:11 PM

Context menu:
- Add to Timeline Ctrl+D
- ▶ Play Clip Spacebar
- ✂ Cut Ctrl+X
- ⧉ Copy Ctrl+C
- 📋 Paste Ctrl+V
- **Delete Del**
- Rename F2
- Create Clips
- Combine Ctrl+M
- Browse for Missing File...
- ✓ Properties

Begin by deleting unneeded clips in the Contents pane. For the birthday movie, the first clip I'll use is the one of my house. I'll delete all the clips before it.

1 Hold down the Shift key and select the clips you want to delete.

2 Right-click.

3 Choose Delete.

split clips

Next, split the clips—that is, break them into multiple clips—so each shot you later drag to the Timeline is a separate clip.

1 Click the clip that you want to split.

Movie Maker loads it into the Monitor.

2 Drag the Seek bar to a position a few seconds after a usable shot in the clip.

3 Click the Split the Clip button.

Movie Maker splits the clip into two clips, adding another clip to the Contents pane.

Initial clip, up to the split point.

New clip.

Continue to scroll through this and other clips in the Contents pane and split the clips as necessary.

rename clips

Now rename your clips so they're easier to find when you're editing.

1 Click the clip that you want to rename.

2 Right-click.

3 Choose Rename.

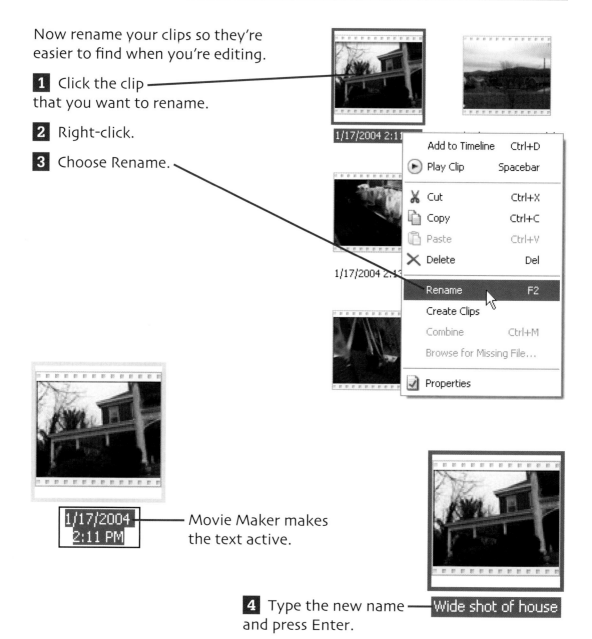

1/17/2004 2:11

Add to Timeline	Ctrl+D
▶ Play Clip	Spacebar
✂ Cut	Ctrl+X
📋 Copy	Ctrl+C
📋 Paste	Ctrl+V
✕ Delete	Del
Rename	F2
Create Clips	
Combine	Ctrl+M
Browse for Missing File...	
☑ Properties	

1/17/2004
2:11 PM — Movie Maker makes the text active.

4 Type the new name — Wide shot of house
and press Enter.

preparing your clips

tell the story

Before you get too far in the splitting process, plan the visual flow of your movie to tell your story. Then use the procedures discussed earlier in this chapter—deleting, splitting, and renaming—to isolate the shots in the Contents pane. Here are the key shots I'll include in the birthday movie.

Wide shot of house

I start with a shot of the house—technically called an establishing shot, because it establishes the location in the viewer's mind.

Interior shot

Since the party is taking place indoors, I add an interior shot to provide more visual context.

First arrivals

Folks are coming! I try to find shots of all key friends and relatives as they arrive.

The gang's all here

Next come shots of pre-entertainment meeting and greeting (multiple shots of key guests).

Enter the clown

The clown arrives and performs.

Balloon fight 1

The entertainment concludes with balloon swords and helmets for all, creating general havoc (multiple clips of key guests).

tell the story (cont.)

Time for cake

That lasts until it's time for the cake. The crowd comes down the stairs.

Happy Birthday Son

Everyone sings "Happy Birthday."

Cake and food

Then everyone starts chowing down (multiple clips of key guests).

Finally! Presents

Finally it's time to open presents (multiple clips of key guests).

Parting is such swee

Then it's time for hugs and air kisses (multiple clips of key guests).

Now, with your key clips isolated, you're ready to move to the Storyboard and Timeline.

preparing your clips

extra bits

split clips p. 27

- To understand the process of splitting a clip, you need to understand the difference between a clip and a shot. Briefly, clip is the technical term used by Movie Maker to describe what's represented as a thumbnail in the Contents pane. In contrast, a shot is a segment of video within that clip that you may or may not want to use in the final movie. For example, when shooting at the party, I left the camera running for 2 or 3 minutes at a time. When Movie Maker creates clips, it will leave me with clips of that length. Within each clip are many shorter shots that I'll want to include in the movie—say 5 seconds here of one daughter, 6 seconds there of a friend, and 3 seconds of my other daughter. The only way for me to access these shots within Movie Maker is to isolate them each in a separate clip.

- When splitting clips in the Contents pane, don't worry about starting and stopping on the exact target frame. The editing tools in the Timeline are much more precise and efficient—you can make your final adjustments there. In fact, try to split clips a few seconds before the first frame you want to appear in the final movie and a few seconds after the last frame. This will give you flexibility if you want to fade into or out of the clip or insert a transition (see Chapter 5) before or after the clip.

- Some clips, like the Happy Birthday Song clip in my birthday video, will obviously have to be long enough to cover the entire event. Most other clips, however, such as those shot just to make sure that all relevant friends and family make it into the video, should be as short as possible, under 5 seconds if possible.

- Note that all these gyrations don't affect the files on your hard drive one bit; they remain totally unchanged.

extra bits (cont.)

tell the story p. 29

- Obviously, you can't include clips in your projects that you haven't first shot with your video camera. When I shoot an event, be it a wedding, concert, birthday, or family outing, I make a short list of required shots for that event before I leave for the shoot. It's typically pretty easy to formulate the list if you think about it in advance, but if you try to get all the shots without planning, you're bound to miss one or two.

4. assembling
your clips

So far, you've collected all your project assets—video, audio, and still images—and created and named all the clips to be included in the final project. In this chapter, you're going to drag everything to the Storyboard and/or Timeline, trim away unnecessary frames, create a slide show segment of the movie composed of digital pictures, and add background audio. In other words, you're building the movie. Sure, you'll be adding lots of polish in subsequent chapters, but that will only embellish the building blocks laid in this chapter.

You'll start here in Storyboard view, which is great for sequencing your clips.

Trimming your video clips into the shortest possible segments is the best way to keep your viewers interested in the content. Just click and drag.

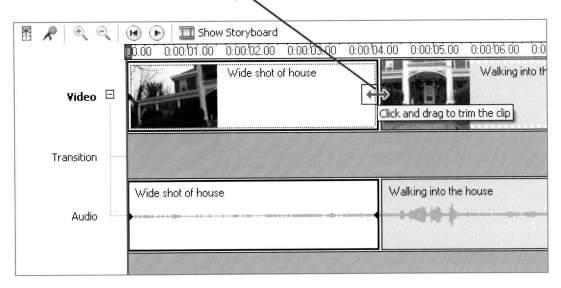

drag to storyboard

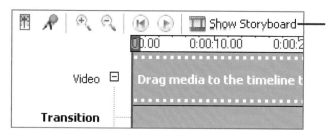

If you've worked with Movie Maker before, you may be in Timeline view. Click Show Storyboard at the top left of the Timeline to return to Storyboard view.

1 Click a clip in your collection to select the clip.

2 Hold down the mouse button and drag the clip to the first open frame on the Storyboard (you'll see a faint image of the thumbnail as you drag).

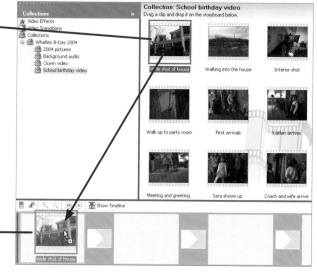

3 Release the mouse button. You've now added a clip to the Storyboard.

Movie Maker inserts the clip in the frame. Music Maker also drags down the audio portion of the video file, so you never have to worry about losing sound synchronization.

assembling your clips

drag between clips

After you've dragged down some clips, you may want to add a clip between two clips.

1 Select a clip in your collection.

2 Hold down the mouse button and drag the clip to the desired location. The ghosted image shows where you are dragging the clip.

3 Release the mouse button.

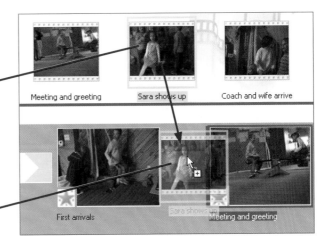

Meeting and greeting   Sara shows up   Coach and wife arrive

First arrivals   Sara shows up   Meeting and greeting

Here's the inserted clip.

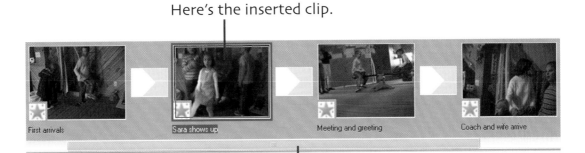

First arrivals   Sara shows up   Meeting and greeting   Coach and wife arrive

Drag this slider bar in either direction to move around the Storyboard.

rearrange clips

Oh, goodness. That last screen reminded me that I want all arrival shots before the meeting and greeting shots—I need to move the Meeting and Greeting clip after the Coach and Wife Arrive clip. You can easily rearrange your clips on the Storyboard.

1 On the Storyboard, select the clip you want to move. I selected the Meeting and Greeting clip.

2 Hold down the mouse button and drag the clip where you want it. Watch for a vertical blue line to appear at the edge of the frame; Movie Maker will drop the clip in front of this frame.

3 Release the mouse button.

Movie Maker shifts the other clips to make room. For me, Movie Maker shifted the coach and his wife to the left.

Movie Maker moves the clip—in this case, the Meeting and Greeting clip.

assembling your clips

preview your movie

Play the movie to see how it's flowing so far.

1 Select the first clip you want to preview.

2 Use these buttons to control playback.

After Movie Maker finishes playing the clip you selected, it will automatically continue on to the next clip.

Note that you can also use the spacebar on your keyboard to start and pause playback—probably the most useful keyboard shortcut in the program.

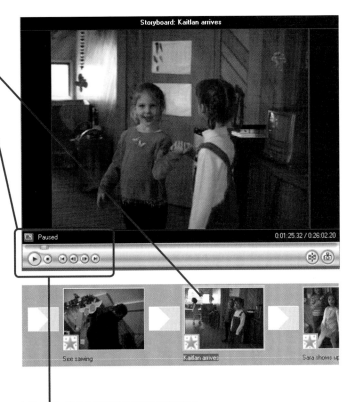

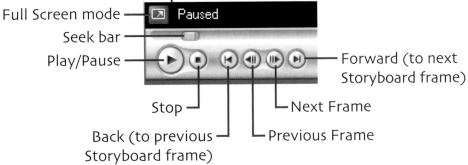

Full Screen mode ——— Paused

Seek bar ———

Play/Pause ———

——— Forward (to next Storyboard frame)

Stop ———

——— Next Frame

Back (to previous Storyboard frame) ———

——— Previous Frame

switch to timeline

After you've arranged your clips on the Storyboard, you can start trimming away unnecessary frames. To do so, you need to switch to Timeline view. Click Show Timeline.

Here's the Timeline, but with the Audio track hidden.

Click here to display the Audio track (you'll use it in Chapter 8).

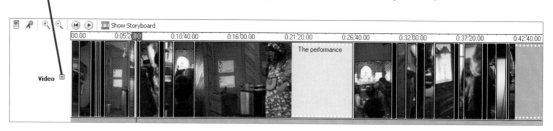

Here's the Timeline in all its glory, with the Audio track displayed. It can look intimidating, but you'll find it easy to use once you get familiar with its tools and tracks.

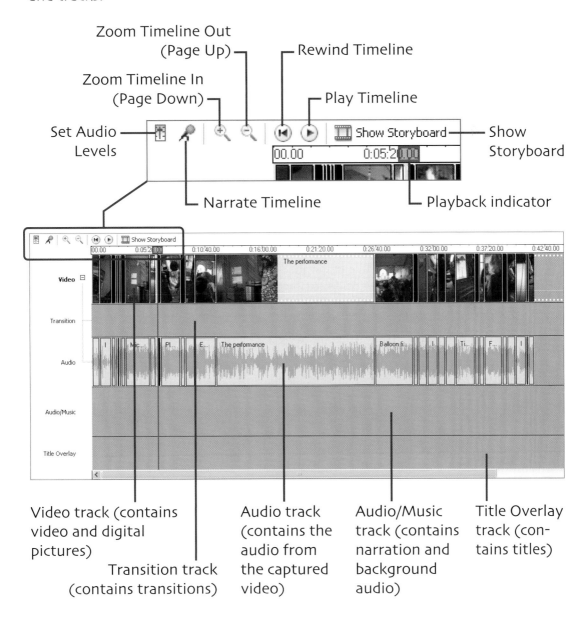

Zoom Timeline Out (Page Up)

Zoom Timeline In (Page Down)

Rewind Timeline

Play Timeline

Set Audio Levels

Show Storyboard

Narrate Timeline

Playback indicator

Video track (contains video and digital pictures)

Transition track (contains transitions)

Audio track (contains the audio from the captured video)

Audio/Music track (contains narration and background audio)

Title Overlay track (contains titles)

trim your clips

Trimming video is the process of removing unwanted frames from the beginning and end of your clips. The start trim point is the first frame that will play in your movie; the end trim point is the last frame.

You need to zoom in to trim a clip; click Zoom Timeline In until the target clip is clearly visible.

1 Click the clip.

2 Hover the mouse over the edge you want to trim until the trim cursor appears.

3 Click the mouse button.

4 If you're trimming away the beginning of a clip (as I am here), drag the left edge and watch the Monitor until the first frame you want to remain in the movie appears.

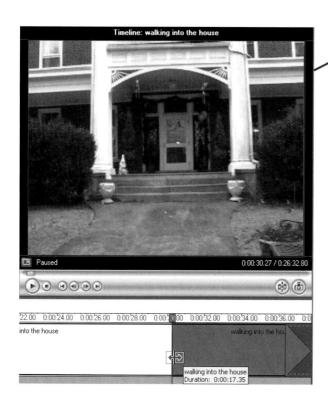

5 If you're trimming away the end of the clip, drag the right edge and watch the Monitor until the last frame you want to remain in the movie appears.

6 Release the mouse button.

Note that you can reverse the trim at any time by dragging the edge back out or by clicking the Undo button on the top toolbar.

assembling your clips

split your clips

You can also split a clip on the Timeline.

1 While watching the Monitor, drag the Playback indicator to where you want to split the clip.

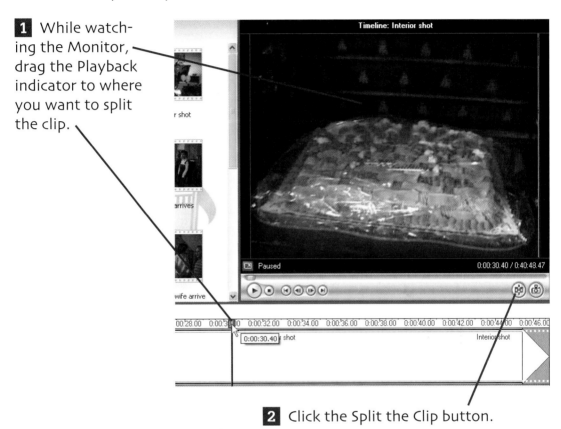

2 Click the Split the Clip button.

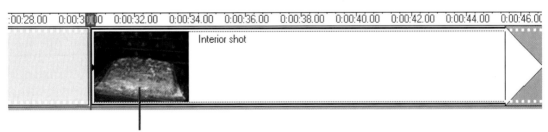

Movie Maker splits the clip, starting the new clip at the split location.

save your project

You've already put a lot of effort into your project, so it's time to save your work.

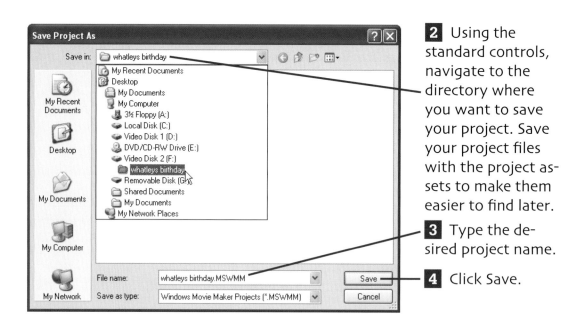

1 From Movie Maker's main menu, choose File > Save Project As.

Don't use Save Movie File. You use that menu selection to render the final movie, not to save the project.

2 Using the standard controls, navigate to the directory where you want to save your project. Save your project files with the project assets to make them easier to find later.

3 Type the desired project name.

4 Click Save.

insert pictures

Now you'll start the slide show component of the movie. Here you'll add digital pictures to the Timeline and then add background music; Movie Maker will convert this content to video when rendering the final movie. You'll be using the still pictures and a background audio file that you imported in Chapter 2. Then you'll add some transitions—visual effects that help smooth the move from one clip to the next, covered in detail in Chapter 5—between the slides. You'll start by checking the picture and transition duration settings.

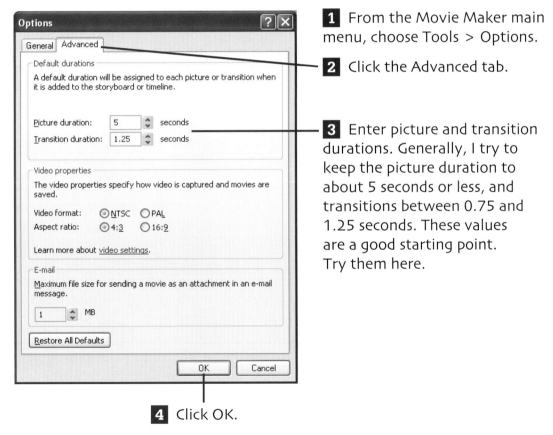

1 From the Movie Maker main menu, choose Tools > Options.

2 Click the Advanced tab.

3 Enter picture and transition durations. Generally, I try to keep the picture duration to about 5 seconds or less, and transitions between 0.75 and 1.25 seconds. These values are a good starting point. Try them here.

4 Click OK.

After applying these durations and inserting the background music clip, you'll check to see how closely the slide show and background music are synchronized.

create a slide show

Now add the pictures to the Timeline. You can insert them anywhere in the movie. For my project, I'm adding them to the end of the production, after all the trimmed video clips.

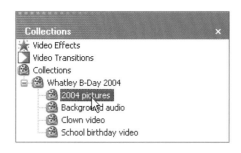

1 Click the collection that contains your pictures to open it in the Contents pane.

2 Click the Contents pane.

3 Right-click and choose Select All.

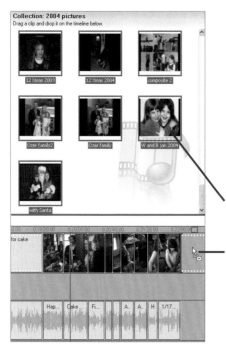

4 Click any picture in the Contents pane and hold down the mouse button.

5 Drag the picture to the Video track on the Timeline, after all of your video clips.

6 Release the mouse button.

insert music files

Your pictures are on the Video track. Now add the background audio. Select the audio collection so that the desired audio clip is showing in the Contents pane.

1 Select the audio clip in the Contents pane.

2 Hold down the mouse button and drag the audio clip to the Audio/Music track, so that the audio clip starts directly beneath the left edge of the first digital picture in the slide show.

3 Release the mouse button.

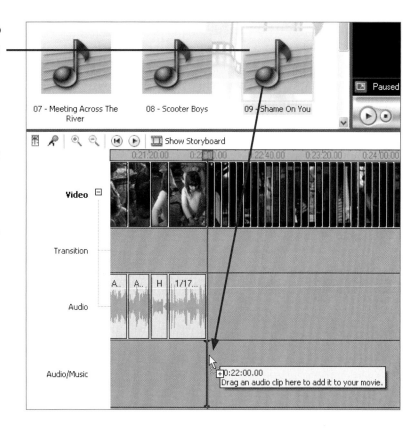

finish the slide show

Now check to see how closely the audio clip and slide show are synchronized by examining the Timeline after the audio has been inserted.

This audio clip is about 80 seconds shorter than the slide show.

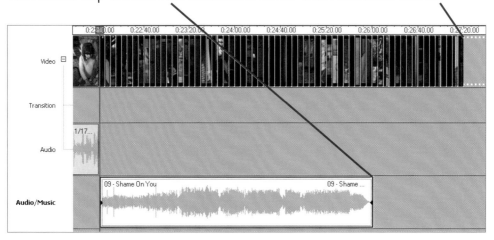

You'll need to slip in the transitions to check the final synchronization. (I'll teach you how in the next chapter. For now, just read on to see how the process works.)

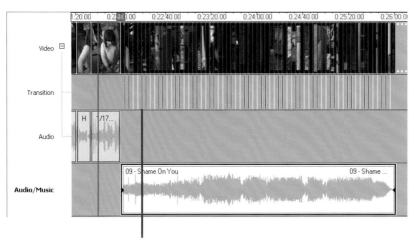

See all those little lines on the Transition track? Those are the transitions, and with them inserted, the two tracks align almost perfectly.

adjust picture duration

Zoom in to check the synchronization close up.

Not bad—the slides and audio match to within about 1 second.

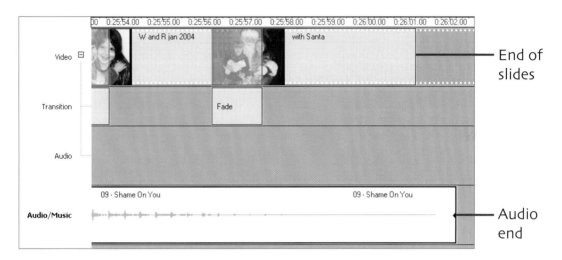

The final picture needs to be longer to make the synchronization exact.

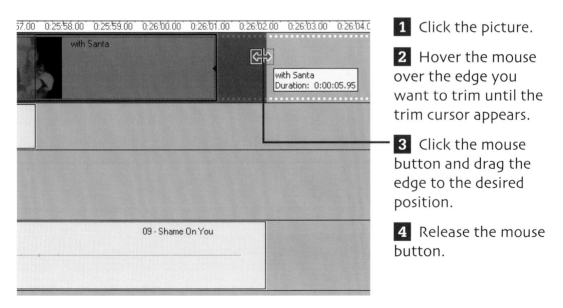

1 Click the picture.

2 Hover the mouse over the edge you want to trim until the trim cursor appears.

3 Click the mouse button and drag the edge to the desired position.

4 Release the mouse button.

extra bits

drag to storyboard p. 34

- If the video clips in the Contents pane are in the desired order, you can drag them all at once. Click the Contents pane and choose Edit > Select All from Movie Maker's main menu. Then drag the clips en masse to the Storyboard or Timeline. You can also hold down the Shift key to select contiguous clips, or Ctrl to select clips that aren't located next to each other.

- Many of the basic procedures shown in this chapter work identically in Timeline view, so if you prefer to work in Timeline view, use the same procedures.

save your project p. 42

- The project file doesn't contain the video, audio, and digital picture files that make up the project; it simply contains references to them. This keeps the project files small, but it means that you can't delete those files until after you've rendered your final movie.

- Deleting content from the Storyboard or Timeline does not delete it from your hard drive.

trim your clips p. 40

- In the next chapter, you'll learn about transitions, which are visual effects that help smooth the move from one clip to the next. If you plan to use transitions between clips, consider the transition duration when trimming your clips. For example, a 1-second fade transition creates a 1-second overlap between the two clips. When trimming, be sure that any critical action or audio in the first clip ends at least 1 second from the end of the clip, and that any critical action or audio in the second clip starts at least 1 second into that clip. Similarly, if you fade in from black (an effect discussed in Chapter 6), the first half-second of the clip will be partially obscured by the fade-in effect. When trimming, be sure that any critical action or audio starts after that half-second. Ditto at the end of a clip if you plan to fade to black at the clip's end.

5. inserting transitions

Transitions are audio and visual effects used to smooth the flow from clip to clip. For example, in movies, you may have noticed the screen fade to black at the end of one scene and then fade back in at the start of the next. You may have also noticed that the audio followed suit, growing quieter during the fade to black and then welling up as the picture faded back in. These are transitions.

Note that you don't have to insert a transition between each clip in a project. If you don't insert a transition, the second clip starts playing immediately after the first clip ends, which is commonly called a cut transition.

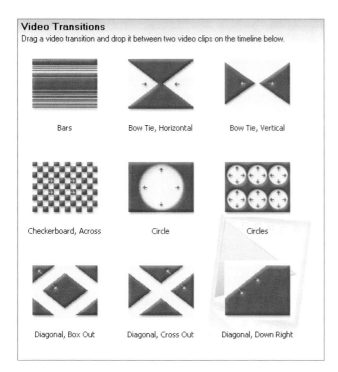

Movie Maker offers a good mix of transitions, and you can get more from Microsoft and third parties such as Pixelan.

Still, knowing which transitions to use, and when, is key to using transitions effectively.

explore transitions

1 In the Collections pane, click the Video Transitions collection to display Movie Maker's transitions in the Contents pane.

2 Double-click the transition you want to preview.

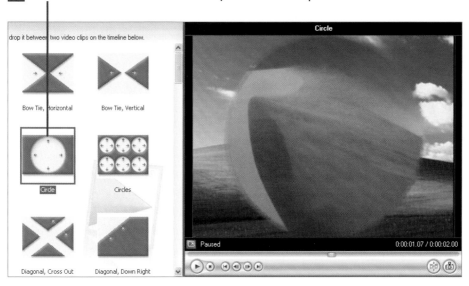

Movie Maker plays your selected transition in the Monitor.

For the Circle transition shown here, Microsoft supplies two images to help you preview the transition. The sunny hill and blue sky represent the first clip in the transition. The sand dune represents the second clip.

The Circle transition opens a widening circle in the first clip through which the second clip is visible.

Have some fun and preview any transitions that appeal to you.

insert a dissolve

I want to smooth the scene change from a view of the party room to the arrival of the first guests. This is a minor change, so I'll try a subtle dissolve transition, which blends frames from the two video clips with a touch of pixilation.

Find a similar spot in your project, where you're moving from one scene to another, making sure the change is equally minor. Working in either the Timeline or Storyboard view, have the intersection of the last clip from the first scene and the first clip from the second scene in view.

1 Display the Video Transitions collection in the Contents pane and select the Dissolve transition.

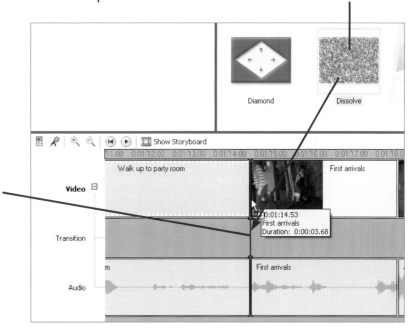

2 Hold down the mouse button and drag the transition to the intersection of the two clips.

3 Release the mouse button.

insert a dissolve (cont.)

Movie Maker inserts the transition on the Transition track.

This slightly opaque area (and the transition beneath it) represents the area of overlap between the two clips.

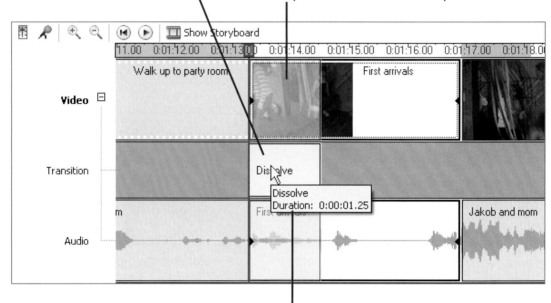

Note the information window Movie Maker displays when you hover your mouse over any content in the Timeline or Storyboard. You'll use this information in a moment to adjust the duration of the transition.

preview transitions

Now preview your transition to be sure it works like you want it to.

1 Double-click the transition in either the Timeline or Storyboard (shown).

2 Click the Play/Pause button (shown in Pause mode because the preview is playing).

When you preview your transition, Movie Maker plays it in the Monitor and then continues to play subsequent clips.

change transitions

The dissolve is pretty plain. My movie is a birthday party, so I think I should liven it up a bit. I'll try the Heart transition. See if this works for you.

1 Select the new transition. —

2 Hold down the mouse button and drag the transition to the previously inserted transition.

3 Release the mouse button.

When you replace a transition, the clip information window shows the data from the video clip above the transition, not the transition itself. Just ignore that and drop in the new transition.

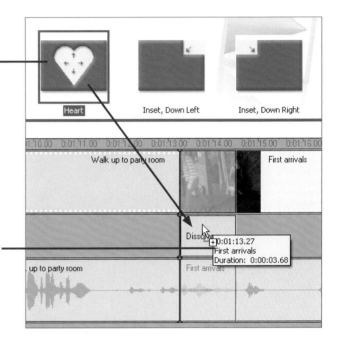

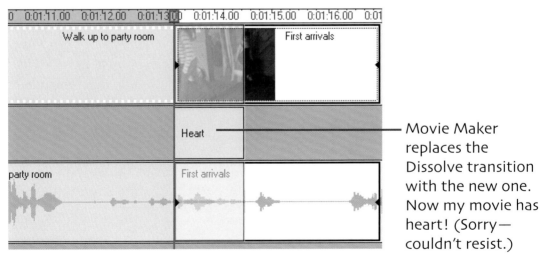

Movie Maker replaces the Dissolve transition with the new one. Now my movie has heart! (Sorry—couldn't resist.)

change duration

Preview your new transition. Mine flashes by a bit too quickly, so I'm going to make it longer. Two seconds sounds about right. Try a 2-second duration for your transition, too.

Be sure you're in Timeline view; you can't adjust the duration in Storyboard view.

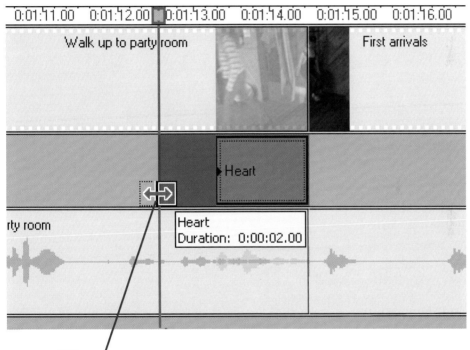

1 Hover the cursor over the left edge of the transition until the two-headed cursor appears.

2 Hold down the mouse button and drag the transition to the left, watching the information window until you've reached the target duration (2 seconds here).

3 Release the mouse.

Now preview again. With its longer duration, this transition looks a lot better.

fade audio out and in

You just inserted a video transition. Now you'll work on the audio. You'll fade out the audio on the clip before the transition—from 100% volume to 0%—and fade it back in on the clip after the transition—from 0% volume to 100%.

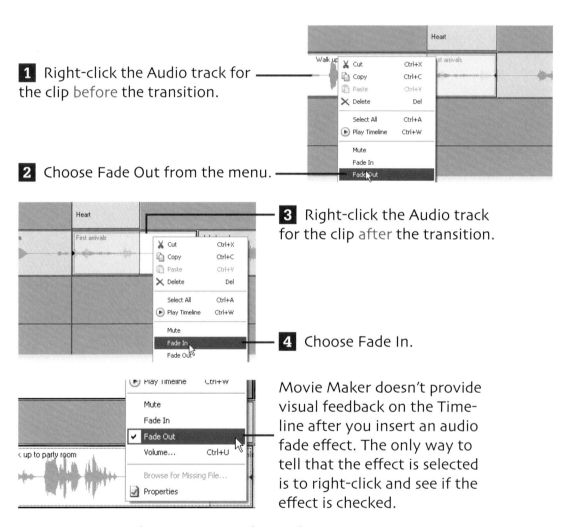

1 Right-click the Audio track for the clip before the transition.

2 Choose Fade Out from the menu.

3 Right-click the Audio track for the clip after the transition.

4 Choose Fade In.

Movie Maker doesn't provide visual feedback on the Timeline after you insert an audio fade effect. The only way to tell that the effect is selected is to right-click and see if the effect is checked.

Preview your work. You can't configure the settings, so it's take it or leave it, but if you don't like the way the fade sounds, delete it by following the same procedure: click the audio track, right-click, and choose the checked fade effect to remove the check mark.

fade video to black

Now move to the scene changes between the video portion of the project to the slide show. To let viewers know that a major change is occurring, you'll fade to black after the last video clip and then fade in from black to start the slide show.

1 Right-click the Video track of the target clip—here, the last video clip before the slide show.

2 Choose Fade Out.

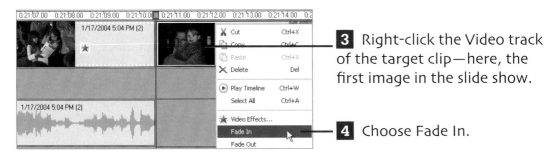

3 Right-click the Video track of the target clip—here, the first image in the slide show.

4 Choose Fade In.

To see if you've applied a fade effect, right-click the Video track and see if the option is checked.

repeat a transition

If you're building a slide show with 60 or so pictures, you'll be happy to learn that there's a way to insert the same transition between all of them at the same time. For this task, you need to work in Storyboard view.

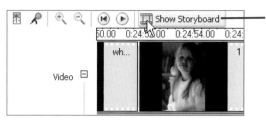 Click Show Storyboard to change to Storyboard view, if necessary.

1 Click the first picture in the slide show.

2 Hold down the Shift key on your keyboard.

3 If necessary, drag this slider bar until you can see the last slide in the slide show.

4 Click the last picture in the slide show. All of your pictures should now be selected.

inserting transitions

5 In the Contents pane, right-click the desired transition. Try the Page Curl transition.

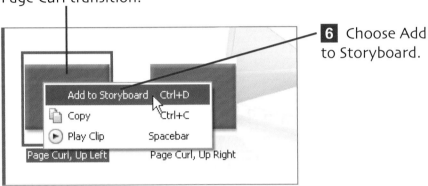

6 Choose Add to Storyboard.

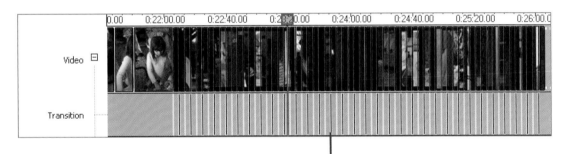

Switch to Timeline view. Each line on the Transition track is a transition that Movie Maker just inserted.

Important! Preview your work immediately to make sure that you like the transition you chose. If you don't, click Undo on the Movie Maker toolbar (at the upper left) and start over. Otherwise, if you change your mind later, you'll have to delete every single transition individually, which can be time consuming.

inserting transitions

extra bits

explore transitions p. 50

- How you use transitions is a matter of personal taste and style and should vary by the type of movie and the audience. The best way to learn how to use transitions is to pay attention to how they're used in movies and television. Serious movies and television shows usually stick to cuts, dissolves, and fades, while children's shows and comedies may use more obvious and fun transitions.

- I follow three rules when using transitions with video clips. First, I use transitions to alert the viewer to a change in scene or time, but only if I don't have video that does a better job than the transition. Second, I try to match the extent of the scene change and the transition. If it's a minor scene change, I use a modest, barely noticeable transition. If it's a major scene change, I use an obvious transition. And third, whenever I insert a video transition, I transition the audio as well, fading out the audio from the first clip and fading in the audio from the next clip.

- Slides shows are a bit of a different animal. I almost always use transitions between the slides.

- Remember that transitions overlap frames from the two affected video clips, partially obscuring the content for the duration of the transition. If you have important content at the start of the second clip or end of the first clip, make sure the transition doesn't obscure it. If it does, retrim the clip, adding the duration of the transition to the front or back of the clip, as necessary, to ensure that the transition doesn't obscure the content you want to appear.

inserting transitions

- Microsoft offers several sources of additional transitions, some free, some with a modest charge. You can download the free Windows Movie Maker 2 Winter Fun Pack 2003, which includes both a Snow Wipe and Snow Burst transition, at http://www.microsoft.com/ windowsxp/moviemaker/ downloads/winterfun.asp.

- Also consider the Microsoft Plus! Digital Media Edition, which costs $19.95 and can be found at http://www.microsoft. com/windows/plus/PlusHome. asp. The Plus! pack includes a range of useful transitions as well as other tools and effects.

- If you're serious about your transitions, surf over to http:// www.pixelan.com/mm/intro. htm. There, you'll find transitions and effects that extend Movie Maker's capabilities immensely.

change duration p. 55

- Each audio fade (in and out) lasts two-thirds of a second; you can't adjust the duration.

- All video fades (in and out) last half a second; you can't adjust the duration. There are techniques you can use to produce longer fades, but they're beyond the scope of this book. See Microsoft Windows Movie Maker 2: Visual QuickStart Guide from Peachpit Press for more details.

inserting transitions

6. applying special effects

Special effects are filters that change the appearance of video either to fix underlying problems or to enhance the video artistically. In both roles, they can help make your video much more watchable.

For example, if your video is too dark, perhaps because the lighting was inadequate during shooting, you can use effects to brighten it up before your viewers see it. In addition, you can use artistic special effects to change the pace and appearance of your video to help retain the viewer's interest.

Make no mistake, however; overusing special effects will likely have the reverse impact, like throwing too many different spices into a casserole. However, as you'll see, a dash here and a pinch there really helps make your movie more palatable to your viewers.

Use Movie Maker's Video Effects collection to cure problems with your video such as shots that are too bright or too dark.

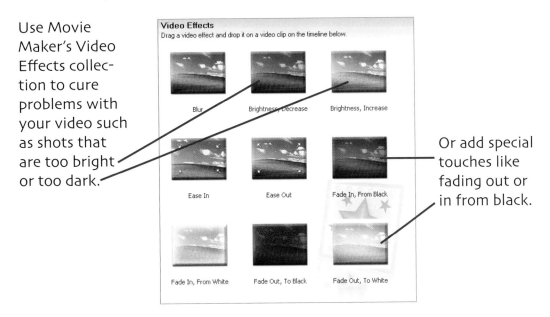

Or add special touches like fading out or in from black.

explore effects

Let's start by seeing where effects live in Movie Maker and how to preview them. You can apply effects to digital pictures as well as videos.

1 Click the Video Effects collection to display Movie Maker's effects in the Contents pane.

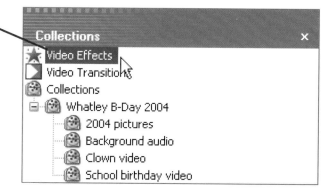

2 Double-click any effect...

...and Movie Maker previews it in the Monitor.

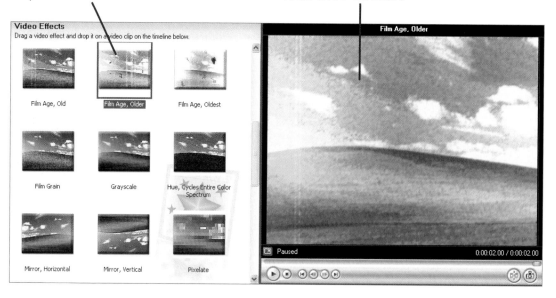

applying special effects

fade video in and out

I like to begin by fading in from black at the start of a movie. I'm working in Timeline view, but you can perform the same operations in Storyboard view.

1 Open the Video Effects collection in the Contents pane and select the Fade In, From Black effect.

2 Hold down the mouse button and drag the effect to the first clip on the Timeline.

3 Release the mouse button.

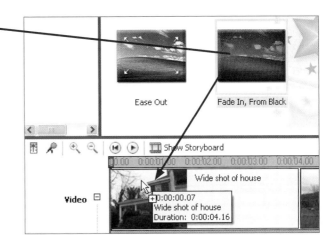

This star lets you know that you've applied an effect to the clip.

Now apply the Fade Out, To Black effect to the last clip in your project.

1 Select the Fade Out, To Black effect.

2 Hold down the mouse button and drag the effect to the last clip on the Timeline.

3 Release the mouse button.

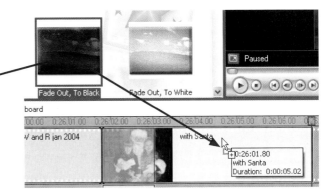

brighten a video clip

Truth be told, my daughter's birthday was a gray, dreary day, with a constant threat of snow. To create the appropriate birthday party atmosphere, I'm going to brighten my video a bit and then add some man-made snow to the mix. If you have any video that looks a bit too dark, try this effect on it. Or if you have a video that's a touch too bright, follow the same instructions but apply the Brightness, Decrease effect.

1 From the Video Effects collection, select the Brightness, Increase effect.

2 Hold down the mouse button and drag the effect to the target clip on the Timeline (in my project, I'm brightening the first two clips, the only two shot outdoors).

3 Release the mouse button. The effect is applied.

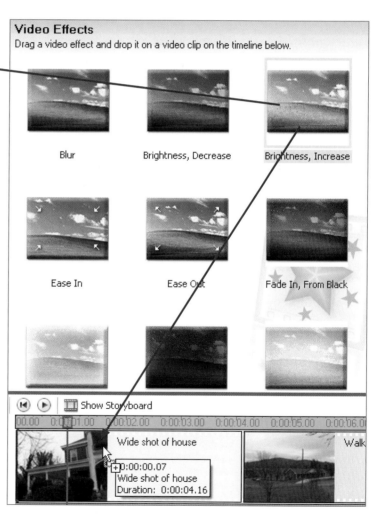

Video Effects
Drag a video effect and drop it on a video clip on the timeline below.

Blur   Brightness, Decrease   Brightness, Increase

Ease In   Ease Out   Fade In, From Black

Show Storyboard

00.00   0:00:01.00   0:00:02.00   0:00:03.00   0:00:04.00   0:00:05.00   0:00:06.00

Wide shot of house   Walk

0:00:00.07
Wide shot of house
Duration: 0:00:04.16

preview effects

Click Play on the Monitor to preview your effects to make sure they're producing the results you desire. Looks bright enough to me, but if you need to make your video even brighter, just drag the same Brightness, Increase filter down onto the clip one more time. All Movie Maker effects work this way: to increase the effect, drag it onto the clip again.

Now, if you like, try the Snowflakes effect, which comes with the free Movie Maker 2 Winter Fun Pack 2003 discussed in the "Extra Bits" sections of this chapter and Chapter 5.

1 From the Video Effects collection, select the Snowflakes effect.

2 Hold down the mouse button and drag the effect to the target clip on the Timeline.

3 Release the mouse button.

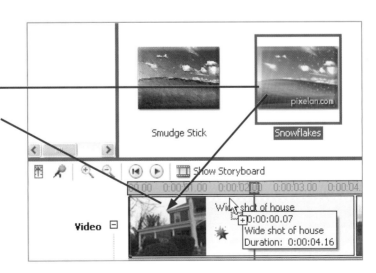

preview effects

Click Play to preview again. What do you think? Well, it probably won't fool my daughter into thinking that it snowed, but it just might make her laugh. Okay, giggle. Definitely smile. Leave it in or take it out? I'm going to leave it in (at least for now), but if I were going to remove it, here's how I would do it.

remove an effect

Okay; you applied an effect, but now you're having second thoughts. Here's how to remove the effect.

1 Right-click the Video track of the clip with the effect that you want to delete.

2 Choose Video Effects.

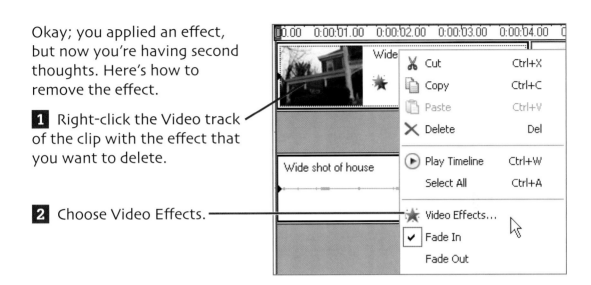

Movie Maker opens the Add or Remove Video Effects dialog box. Note that my clip has three effects applied; you can apply up to five effects to a clip.

3 In the Displayed Effects pane, select the effect that you want to delete.

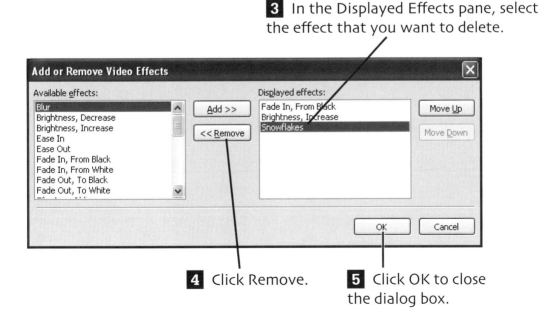

4 Click Remove.

5 Click OK to close the dialog box.

applying special effects

change playback speed

I use this effect a lot, generally to increase playback speed, but sometimes to slow it down as well. In my movie, I have a sequence of guests walking down the stairs to eat that was just begging to be speeded up, since folks walking at double speed (especially to eat cake) generally looks pretty funny. Find a sequence in your movie where there's a lot of action and try the same thing. When you preview, the audio will probably sound funny as well, as audio does when speeded up or slowed down, but you'll learn how to mute a clip in Chapter 8.

1 From the Video Effects collection, select the Speed Up, Double effect.

2 Hold down the mouse button and drag the effect to the target clip.

3 Release the mouse button.

Note that if you want to double the speed again, you just drag the effect down onto the clip again.

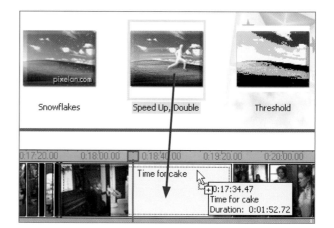

add motion to images

One of Movie Maker's strongest features is the capability that lets you add motion to still images. You have two options: the Ease In effect, which zooms into the picture, making it larger, and the Ease Out effect, which starts zoomed in and then zooms out. If you're using digital pictures in your project, such as those used for the slide show, try adding motion to them.

You can also apply both motion effects to video clips. The Ease In effect works particularly well when a clip holds steady on a single person, giving the impression that you zoomed in or out with your camcorder's zoom controls.

1 From the Video Effects collection, select the Ease In effect.

2 Hold down the mouse button and drag the effect to the target clip.

3 Release the mouse button.

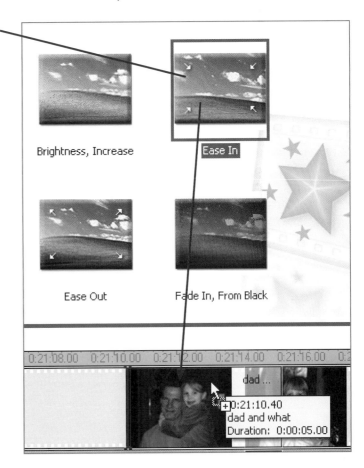

Brightness, Increase

Ease In

Ease Out

Fade In, From Black

add motion to images

With the Ease In effect applied, the video starts here...

...and slowly zooms in to here over the duration of the video clip or picture. Note that I had to apply the effect several times to achieve this level of zoom.

extra bits

explore effects p. 64

- The special effects you choose should vary by video content. For example, though I adore Movie Maker's film age effects, which make a movie look like an old black-and-white film, they're tough to use in a video documenting a six-year-old's birthday party. That said, the effects I use in this project represent a core group that seem to find their way into most movies that I create.

- You can apply up to five effects to any video or picture on the Video track.

- The Snowflakes effect used in this chapter comes in the free Windows Movie Maker 2 Winter Fun Pack 2003, which you can download from http://www.microsoft.com/windowsxp/moviemaker/downloads/winterfun.asp. When you install this package, the effects will be added to your Video Effects collection.

- Pixelan takes Movie Maker's special effects to a different level, with effects that can adjust the color of your videos as well as provide many more motion options for your still images. You can choose from a variety of effects packages, each available for less than $20, at http://www.pixelan.com/mm/intro.htm.

fade video in and out p. 65

- To paraphrase Gertrude Stein, a fade is a fade is a fade. In the preceding chapter, you used fades between video clips as transitions; in this chapter, you applied them at the beginning and end of video clips as effects. You can insert fades the same way you did in the preceding chapter, via right-click commands, or by working through the special effects collection as you did here. Either way, they're the same effects, just used in different places.

extra bits (cont.)

change playback
speed p. 70

- As you probably observed, when Movie Maker adjusts video speed, it also adjusts audio playback speed, which usually makes your audio un-usable. Generally, I mute the Audio track (turn down the volume to 0%) and add back-ground music on the Audio/ Music track that matches the speed change: slow and lugubrious for slow motion, fast and snappy for fast motion. More on this in Chapter 8.

add motion to
images p. 71

- The Ease In and Ease Out effects are great for adding motion to still pictures, but the look can get repetitive. I typically apply this effect on every third or fourth image, usually switching between the two effects.

applying special effects

7. creating titles

Titles are text-based frames that can appear full screen on the Video track or superimposed over video clips or digital pictures. I generally use titles in at least three places in my video productions.

First, I open each movie with a title so the viewer knows what he or she will be watching. I also usually insert titles at scene changes, primarily to let the viewer know what's coming and that the movie is, in fact, moving along. Finally, I close most projects with closing credits.

Movie Maker's titles have two components: text and animation scheme. Movie Maker gives you great control over font, text color, size, positioning, and transparency. In addition, Movie Maker's title animation schemes let you control how titles move on and off screen and other visual characteristics you'll learn about in this chapter.

There's nothing like a great title to begin a movie.

You can control text font and colors.

You can also choose a title animation scheme, which controls the background and the way the title appears and disappears from the screen.

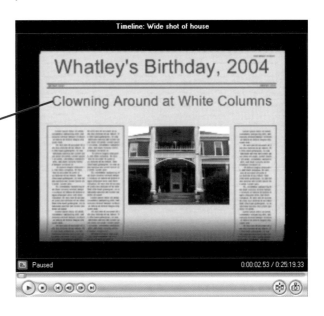

add an opening title

You'll begin by adding an opening title to your movie.

Although you can insert titles and credits in Storyboard view, I typically work almost exclusively in Timeline view by this stage in a project, so that's the view you'll use in this chapter.

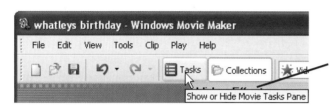

1 Since you've been working with effects, you probably have the Collections pane open. Click this button to open the Movie Tasks pane.

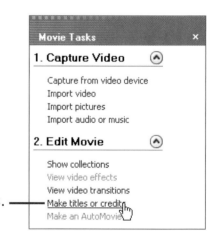

2 Click Make Titles or Credits. ————

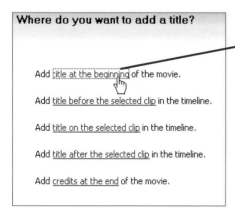

3 Click Add Title at the Beginning of the Movie.

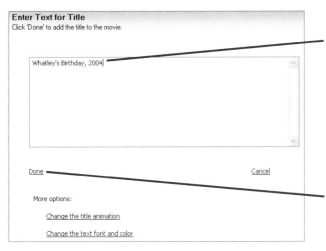

Enter Text for Title
Click 'Done' to add the title to the movie.

Whatley's Birthday, 2004|

Done

Cancel

More options:

Change the title animation

Change the text font and color

4 Type the desired text.

Note that the title I'm creating has only one text entry field, though your title may show two fields. More on this in a moment.

5 Click Done.

Movie Maker inserts the title at the start of the Video track. If you haven't yet adjusted the font, color, and animation options, Movie Maker uses the default settings; if you have, it uses the last settings that you applied. You'll learn how to change these settings in a bit.

Click the Play button to see the title in the Monitor. Kind of plain—it might work for a serious movie, but it doesn't cut it for a six-year-old's birthday party. Let's try something else.

change to title overlay

You just produced a full screen title that uses a solid blue frame as background and sits on the Video track. You'll now change to an overlay title that sits in the Title Overlay track and appears over a video or digital picture.

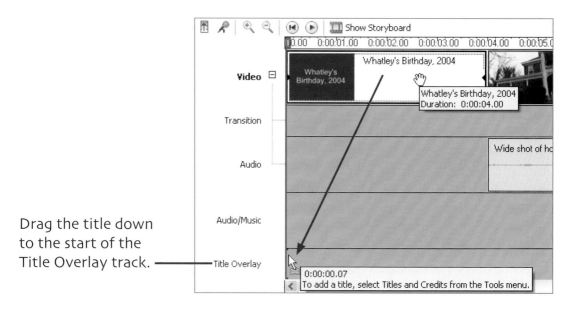

Drag the title down to the start of the Title Overlay track. ———————— Title Overlay

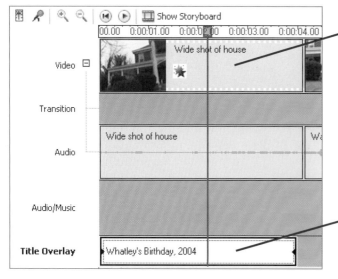

Movie Maker moves the first video clip to the left to fill the gap formerly occupied by the title.

The title is now directly below the video clip. Preview to see what that looks like.

Better, but the white text from the title is hard to see against the white background. You may not have the same problem, but I definitely need to make this text more visible. Let's take a quick look at the options.

change title animation

I could change the font color, but perhaps a different title animation would produce a better result. In Movie Maker, title animations not only animate the text, but also insert different backgrounds, banners, and special effects, which may make the text more visible.

1 Double-click the title to open Movie Maker's title controls.

2 Click Change the Title Animation.

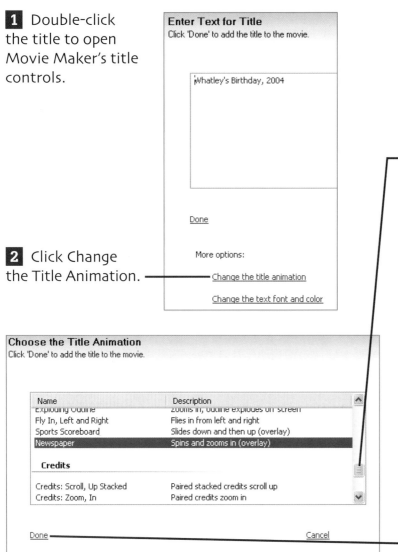

3 Select a different title animation.

Use this scrollbar to see all of your choices, which includes three groups of animations under separate headings: one-line and two-line titles and credits (which go at the end of the movie).

Click any animation scheme, and Movie Maker will display it in the Monitor. The Newspaper title animation is one of my favorites, so select that one.

4 Click Done.

creating titles

Here's the Newspaper title animation. However, it looks like there's room for another line of text. That's because this is a two-line title, and the title I created originally was a one-line title.

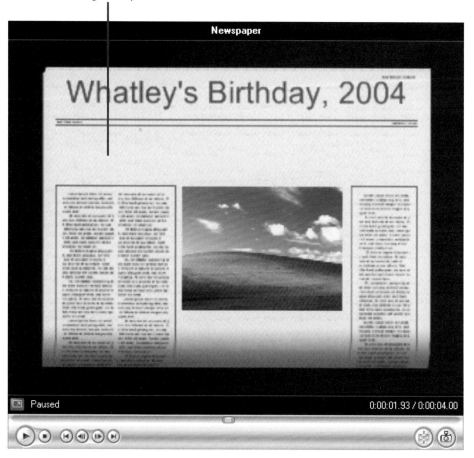

edit title text

Often, you'll have to edit the text of your title, perhaps to correct a misspelling. Or if you start with a one-line title animation and then choose a two-line title animation, as I did here, you may have room for another line of text.

1 Double-click the title to open the Enter Text for Title screen.

Now there are two lines for text where before there was only one.

2 Type the desired text.

3 Click Done.

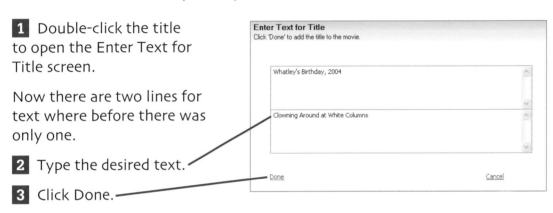

4 Preview your title.

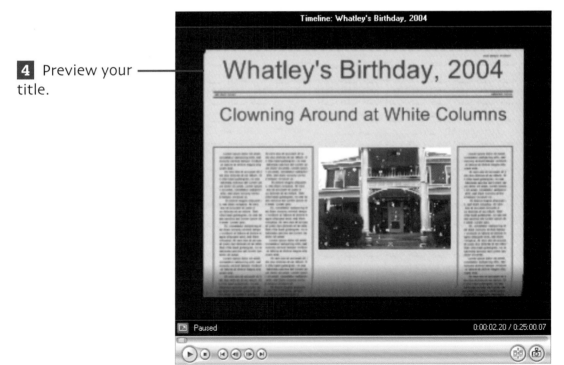

adjust title duration

So viewers have time to appreciate your title, you can make it stay on the screen longer than the 4-second default title duration.

1 Click the title.

2 Hover the mouse over the right edge until the trim cursor appears.

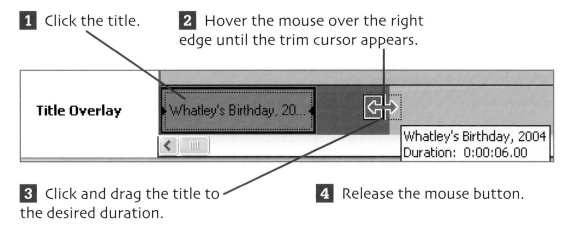

3 Click and drag the title to the desired duration.

4 Release the mouse button.

add title at new scene

The opening title is done, Now you'll add some titles at scene changes. These tell the viewers what's coming and lets them know that the movie is moving along, which helps minimize the fidgets.

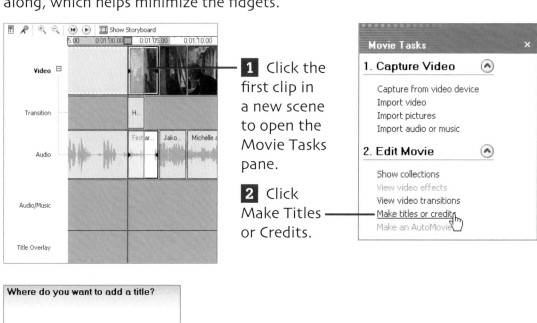

1 Click the first clip in a new scene to open the Movie Tasks pane.

2 Click Make Titles or Credits.

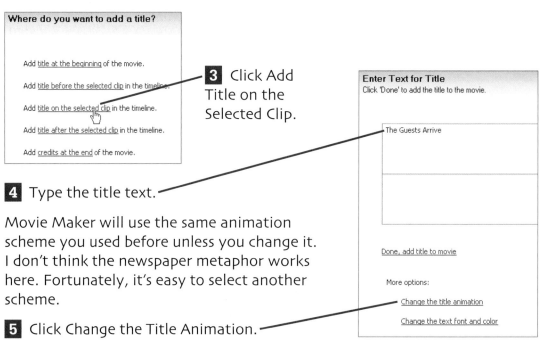

3 Click Add Title on the Selected Clip.

4 Type the title text.

Movie Maker will use the same animation scheme you used before unless you change it. I don't think the newspaper metaphor works here. Fortunately, it's easy to select another scheme.

5 Click Change the Title Animation.

creating titles

6 Choose a different animation scheme, such as this one-line News Banner title animation.

Note that titles with overlay in the name insert the text over a solid-colored back-ground, making the text more readable. I use them almost exclusively.

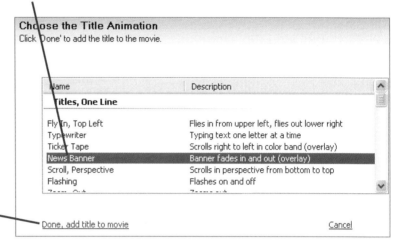

7 Click Done.

Here's the title. ——

view font controls

I like my text font to match the subject of my movies—elegant for holidays, fun for birthday parties, and so on. The title I just added doesn't quite fit the feel, so I'm going hunting for a font that screams six-year-old's birthday party.

All computers have different fonts that get loaded when you install different programs, so you may not have the font that I select. That's okay; just find another that suits the subject of your movie.

1 Double-click the title to open the Enter Text for Title screen.

2 Click Change the Text Font and Color.

The Select Title Font and Color screen opens. Most of the controls are like those in word processors.

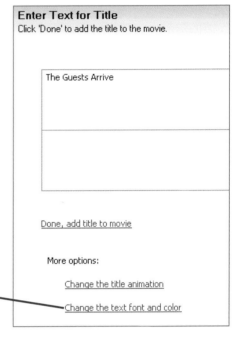

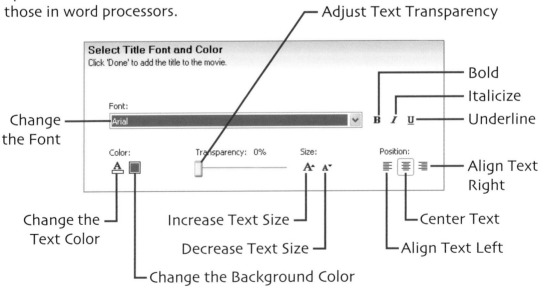

adjust fonts

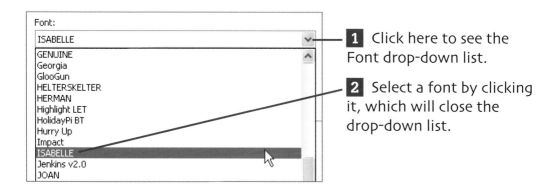

1 Click here to see the Font drop-down list.

2 Select a font by clicking it, which will close the drop-down list.

After you select the font, Movie Maker previews it in the Monitor. I'll show you ISABELLE looks after you change the background color.

3 Click the Change the Background Color icon.

adjust fonts (cont.)

4 Select the desired background color in the Color palette. Find a color that provides a good contrast with both the text and the background. Here I'm using blue.

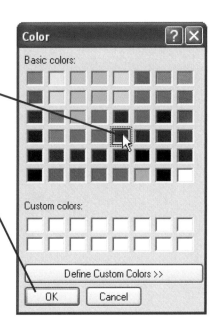

5 Click OK.

6 Movie Maker previews the title in the Monitor. After finalizing your selections, click Done (located below the font and background color buttons, at the left of the screen).

Here's the title after all adjustments. Gotta love the font, though the color may still be a touch neon. It's definitely readable, though, so I'm going to use this combination for all scene changes. Add titles for all of your scene changes. Movie Maker will continue to use the settings you apply here until you change them.

creating titles

add closing credits

Now add some closing credits.

1 In the Movie Tasks pane, click Make Titles or Credits.

2 Click Add Credits at the End of the Movie.

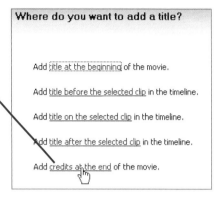

3 In the window that appears, type the desired text.

4 Click Done.

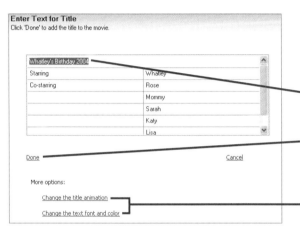

If desired, you can hunt for a different animation scheme or change the text font and colors by clicking here.

Here are my closing credits, a wonderfully suitable way to end this chapter.

extra bits

create an opening title p. 76

- Microsoft's free Creativity Fun Pack (http://www.microsoft.com/windowsxp/moviemaker/downloads/create.asp) provides three ways to enhance the visual appeal of your titles. First, it comes with 14 still images that you can use as static backgrounds for your text titles. Second, the pack includes two video backgrounds, one yellow, and one blue, which you can also use as backgrounds for your titles. Finally, the pack includes several videos designed for use at the beginning or end of your movie: for instance, the Countdown video counts down from five to zero and then flashes the word START.

change to title overlay p. 78

- You can apply transitions and effects to full-screen titles located on the Video track: for example, fading into the opening title of a movie or fading out of the closing credits. However, you can't apply either transitions or effects to titles on the Title Overlay track.

8. using audio

Audio is an incredibly powerful medium. The right background music can set the proper mood for a movie or slide show and amuse and entertain in its own right, and narration can provide additional information and context to help the viewer appreciate the visual aspect of the presentation.

In this chapter, you'll add both background music and narration to your movie, and you'll learn how to integrate it smoothly with the audio you captured with your camcorder. Note that you can perform these activities only on the Timeline, not on the Storyboard.

Movie Maker has two audio tracks. The Audio track contains only audio captured with the video file.

The Audio/Music track contains all other audio, including narration and background music.

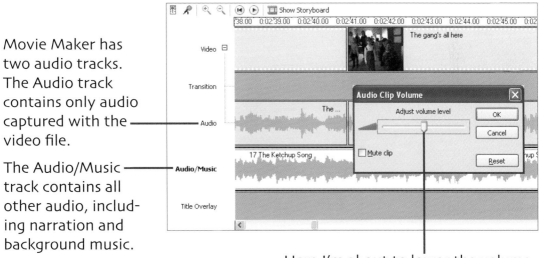

Here I'm about to lower the volume of the background music track so I can hear the conversation in the video more clearly.

91

add background music

Let's start by inserting some background music into the project. Find some music appropriate for your project and import it into a collection as described in Chapter 2.

1 In the Collections pane, click the collection that contains the audio file.

Movie Maker displays the collection in the Contents pane.

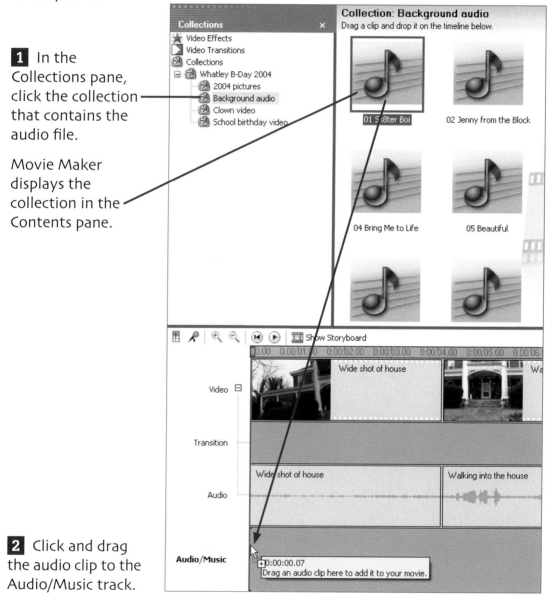

2 Click and drag the audio clip to the Audio/Music track.

Here's the inserted audio track.

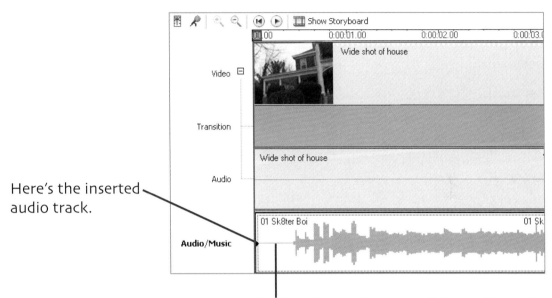

The flat line at the start of the audio track indicates that it's silent there. The silence is less than a second long, but to make the music start right away, the silence needs to be trimmed off.

trim audio clips

You trim audio clips like any other content: you simply grab an edge and drag it to the desired length.

1 Click the clip on the Timeline to select it.

2 Hover the mouse over the edge until the trim cursor appears.

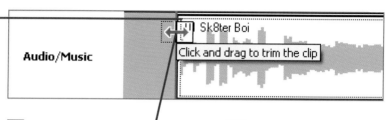

3 Click the mouse button and drag to the right (or left if you're trimming the end of the clip).

4 Release the mouse when the clip starts where you want it to.

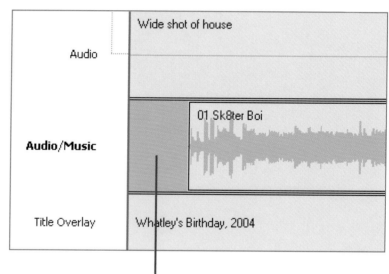

Movie Maker left a gap on the Audio/Music track when the clip was shortened. Unless the gap is removed, the audio won't start playing immediately.

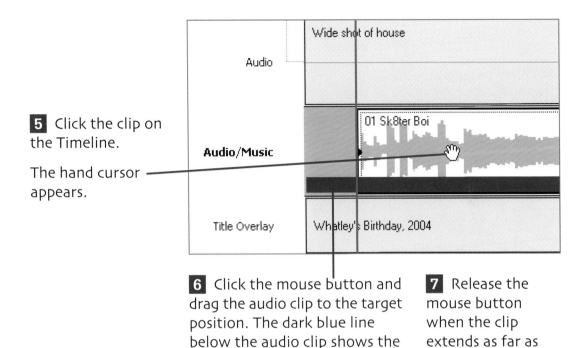

5 Click the clip on the Timeline.

The hand cursor appears.

6 Click the mouse button and drag the audio clip to the target position. The dark blue line below the audio clip shows the clip's new position as you drag.

7 Release the mouse button when the clip extends as far as you want it to.

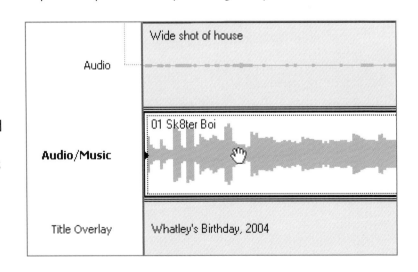

The gap is filled, and the audio will start at the same time as the video.

the big picture

Here's a big-picture view of how I want the background music to integrate with the audio from the camcorder.

Each track displays a waveform, which is a graphical representation of the audio file.

A small waveform indicates low volume.

A larger waveform indicates higher volume.

A mix of high and low volumes often indicates someone talking.

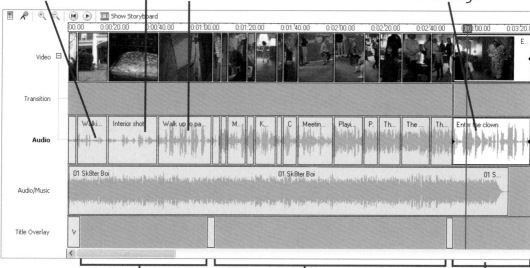

These are my outdoor and indoor establishing shots, which give the viewer the lay of the land. Here I want to turn off the audio on the Audio track (captured with the video) and solely use the background music track.

Here guests are arriving. Now I want primarily to hear the conversation, with the music track much lower in the background.

Now the clown starts performing, so I want to disable background audio completely so the audience can hear the show.

Your project will likely have scenes with similar characteristics: some where you want just the background music, some where you want just the audio that is part of your video, and some where you want a mix of both. Follow along to see how to make this happen.

mute the audio

Find a scene in your project that you want to mute (turn down the audio to 0%). I'm muting the Audio track for the opening scene of my movie.

1 Click the clips that you want to mute (hold down the Shift key to select multiple clips).

2 Right-click.

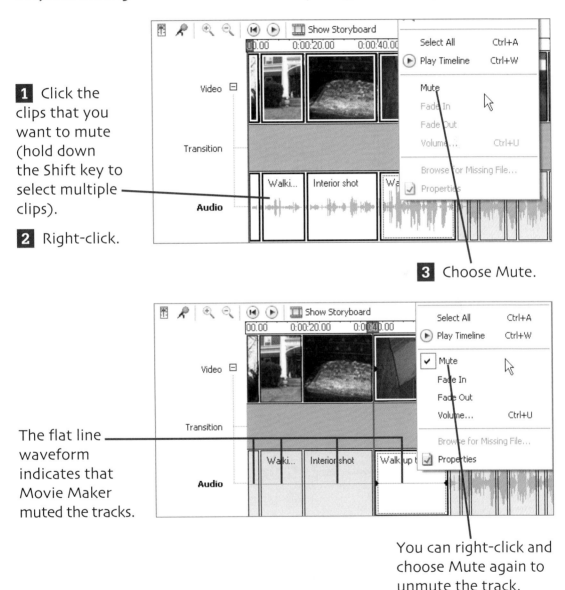

3 Choose Mute.

The flat line waveform indicates that Movie Maker muted the tracks.

You can right-click and choose Mute again to unmute the track.

turn down music

Now find a scene where you want to turn down the background audio so you can hear the sound you recorded with your video. I want to turn down the background music in the second scene of my movie, so the conversations I recorded with the video can be heard. Since Movie Maker doesn't let you adjust the volume of just a portion of an audio clip, you first have to split the audio clip at the scene change. Then you can reduce the volume of the second part of the audio clip.

1 Click the audio clip to select it.

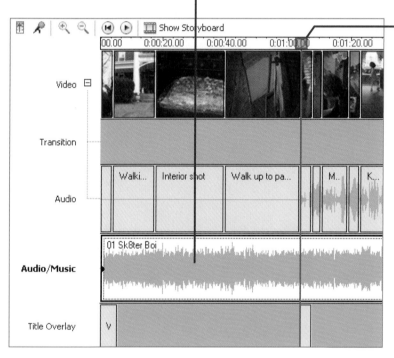

2 Move the Playback indicator to the start of the new scene.

3 From Movie Maker's main menu, choose Clip > Split.

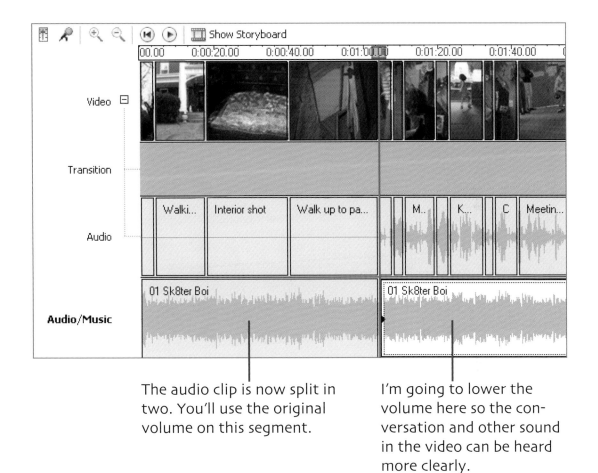

The audio clip is now split in two. You'll use the original volume on this segment.

I'm going to lower the volume here so the conversation and other sound in the video can be heard more clearly.

adjust the volume

Now let's adjust the volume of the background music. Find a scene in your project where you've inserted background music, but also want your viewers to be able to hear the audio shot with the video.

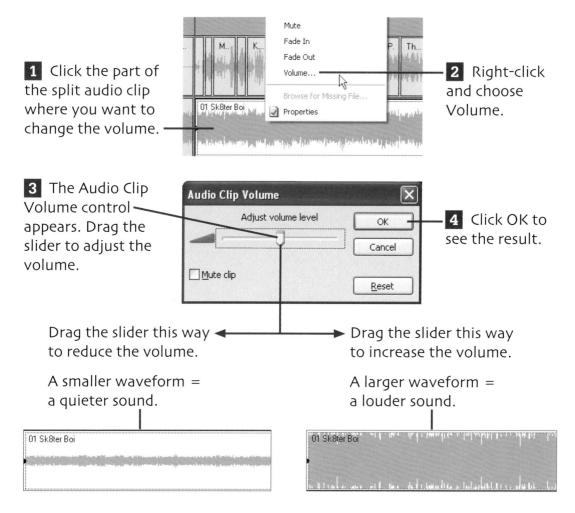

1 Click the part of the split audio clip where you want to change the volume.

2 Right-click and choose Volume.

3 The Audio Clip Volume control appears. Drag the slider to adjust the volume.

4 Click OK to see the result.

Drag the slider this way to reduce the volume.

Drag the slider this way to increase the volume.

A smaller waveform = a quieter sound.

A larger waveform = a louder sound.

These waveforms are useful, but you'll really have to preview to hear the new levels. Keep adjusting the background music until you achieve the desired volume mix between the two tracks.

trim and fade audio

If you inserted background music into your movie, there may be a place where you want the music to stop playing, so that your audience hears only the audio you recorded with your video. In my movie, when the clown performs, I want the background music to stop, so the viewers can focus on the performance. Here's what to do.

Here's where the clown starts performing. This is where I want the background music to stop.

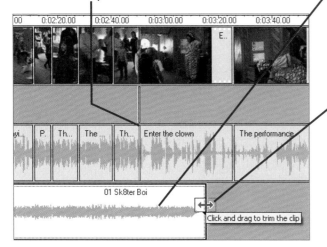

1 On the Audio/Music track, click the audio clip to select it.

2 Hover the mouse over the clip's edge until the trim cursor appears.

3 Click the mouse button and drag to the left to shorten the clip.

4 Release the mouse button when you reach the place where you want the background audio to end.

Now fade out the background audio so the ending isn't abrupt.

5 Click the background audio clip.

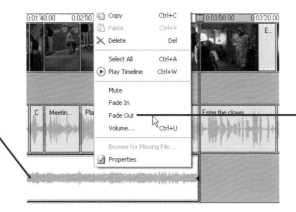

6 Right-click and choose Fade Out.

set up for narration

In Chapter 4, I built a slide show with digital pictures and music. Now I'm thinking it would be better to have my daughter narrate the slide show, putting the year's worth of pictures in her own words. I often add narrations to digital pictures and videos if the descriptions will enhance the viewing experience. Find a part of your own project that could use narration and give it a try.

To create your narration, you'll need a microphone. Here are two types of microphone you can use.

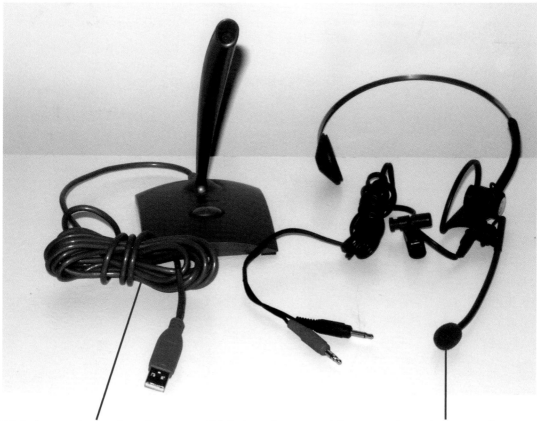

This is a universal serial bus (USB) microphone that connects to the computer's USB port.

This headset combines a microphone and headphones. The red plug always goes into the microphone connector, and the black plug goes into the speaker or headphone connector.

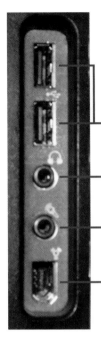

Connect the microphones to your computer. Here are the connections on my HP xw41000 computer.

Plug a USB microphone into one of the USB ports.

This is the headphone connector for a headset microphone; plug in the black connector here.

This is the microphone connector for a headset microphone; plug in the red plug here.

This is the FireWire port where you connect your camcorder for video capture.

create narration

1 On the Timeline, move the Playback indicator to the place where you want the narration to begin.

2 Click the Narrate Timeline button.

The Narrate Timeline window appears. Here's where you adjust the volume and start and stop recording.

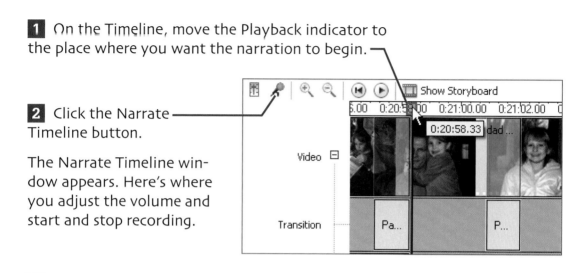

3 Speak into the microphone normally. Adjust the volume control...

...until the volume line stays consistently between 50 and 75%.

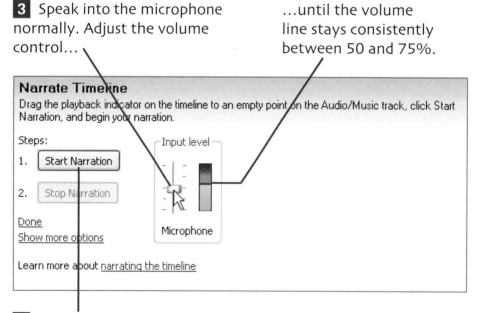

4 Click Start Narration to begin the narration. Movie Maker will start playing the video from the narration starting point so you can watch it in the Monitor as you record.

5 Start talking into the microphone.

Watch the volume meter so you stay within the 50 to 75% volume range.

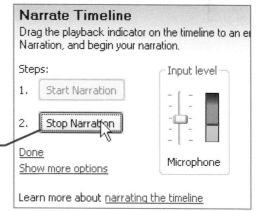

Narrate Timeline

Drag the playback indicator on the timeline to an e
Narration, and begin your narration.

Steps:

Input level

1.   Start Narration

2.   Stop Narration

Done

Show more options

Microphone

Learn more about narrating the timeline

6 Click Stop Narration when you're done. The Save Windows Media File dialog box appears.

create narration (cont.)

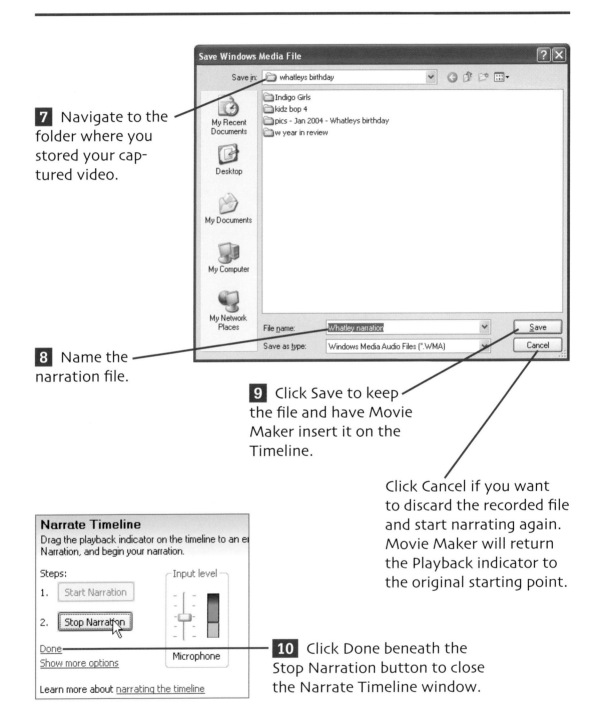

7 Navigate to the folder where you stored your captured video.

8 Name the narration file.

9 Click Save to keep the file and have Movie Maker insert it on the Timeline.

Click Cancel if you want to discard the recorded file and start narrating again. Movie Maker will return the Playback indicator to the original starting point.

10 Click Done beneath the Stop Narration button to close the Narrate Timeline window.

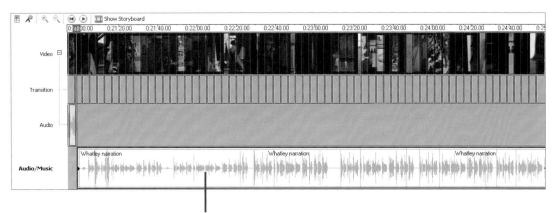

The completed narration
underneath the slide show.

extra bits

add background music p. 92

- I use Windows Media Player to copy audio tracks from a CD-ROM so I can include them in a movie. It's very simple to use, but if you want step-by-step guidance, see Microsoft Windows Movie Maker 2: Visual QuickStart Guide from Peachpit Press for details.

- You can also add sound effects to your videos on the Audio/Music track. Although Movie Maker doesn't come with any sound effects or background music, Microsoft offers two free sources of both. The Creativity Fun Pack (http://www.microsoft.com/windowsxp/moviemaker/downloads/create.asp) comes with 53 sound effects in five categories: animal, fun random, graduation, party and sports, and background music. Microsoft's Windows Movie Maker 2 Winter Fun Pack 2003 (http://www.microsoft.com/windowsxp/moviemaker/downloads/winterfun.asp), also free, includes 92 sound effects and 7 music tracks.

set up for narration p. 102

- There's a big difference between the microphone port and the line-in port available on some computers. The line-in port is used for the output from stereo systems and other independently powered devices and requires a significantly stronger signal than you get with the typical computer microphone. Line-in ports won't work with a microphone, so be sure you connect your microphone to the microphone port.

9. creating automovies

Music videos have been a powerful component of movies since the "Raindrops Keep Falling on My Head" bicycling scene in Butch Cassidy and the Sundance Kid (boy am I dating myself). Movie Maker makes it simple to build such a scene with the AutoMovie feature.

AutoMovie takes your video, trims away all but the most interesting short clips, and synchronizes the clips with a song that you select. It's almost like having an MTV music video producer inside your computer. It's fast, it's fun, and the results can be surprisingly compelling.

Here's the AutoMovie I'll build in this chapter. Note the short video clips as trimmed by Movie Maker and the inserted transitions and titles on their respective tracks.

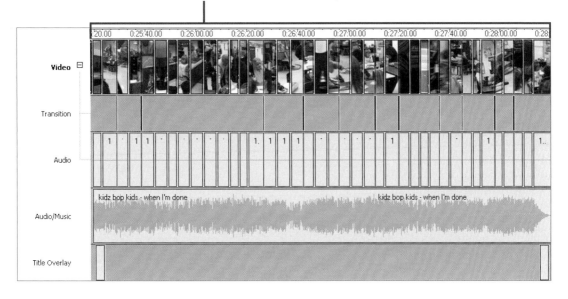

build an automovie

Yikes! Whatley looked over the movie while creating the narration in the last chapter and asked, "Where's the footage from the party at school?" Ruh-roh, daddy forgot, and I'm running out of editing time. Rather than manually edit that party, I'll create an AutoMovie and add it to the project. Grab a stretch of your own video footage and a favorite tune and join in.

Note that Movie Maker places any AutoMovies you create at the end of the project.

1 In the Contents pane, choose the video clips you want to include in the AutoMovie. Press the Shift key to choose multiple consecutive clips, and the Ctrl key to choose multiple noncontiguous clips.

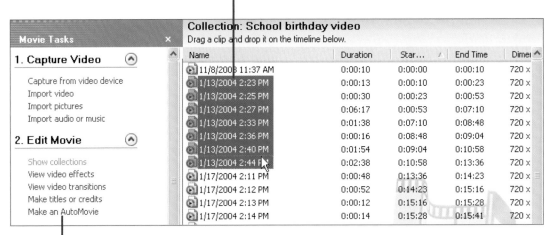

2 In the Movie Tasks pane, click Make an AutoMovie.

3 In the Select an AutoMovie Editing Style window that opens, click the desired editing style. The editing style controls the nature of the effects and transitions Movie Maker applies and the pace of the video. I've always liked the Music Video style, so try that one.

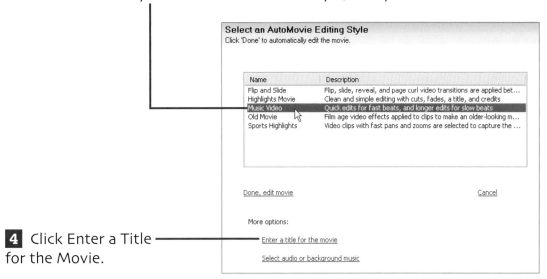

4 Click Enter a Title for the Movie.

5 In the Enter Text for Title window that opens, type the title text.

Note that each style has specific font and color options that you can't modify.

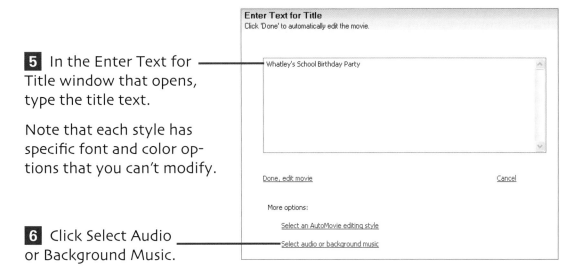

6 Click Select Audio or Background Music.

build an automovie (cont.)

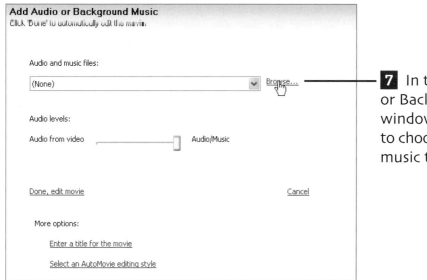

7 In the Add Audio or Background Music window, click Browse to choose a background music track.

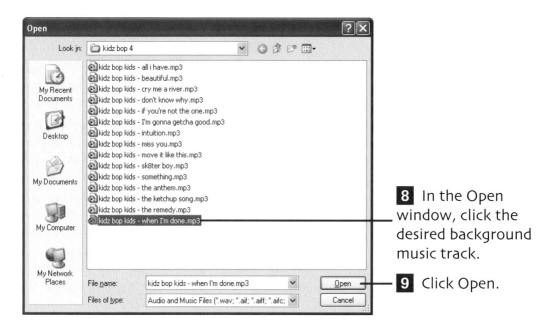

8 In the Open window, click the desired background music track.

9 Click Open.

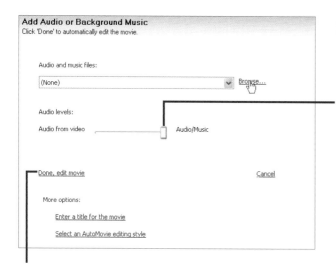

10 In the Add Audio or Background Music window, drag the Audio Levels slider all the way to the right, to 100% Audio/Music.

AutoMovie doesn't work well if you want to hear what people are saying, because it tends to randomly cut people off in mid-sentence. I never use this feature when I want to hear the audio shot with the video.

11 Click Done, Edit Movie. Movie Maker builds the AutoMovie and inserts it at the end of the Timeline.

Here's the finished AutoMovie. All video segments are very short.

Movie Maker muted the audio on the Audio track.

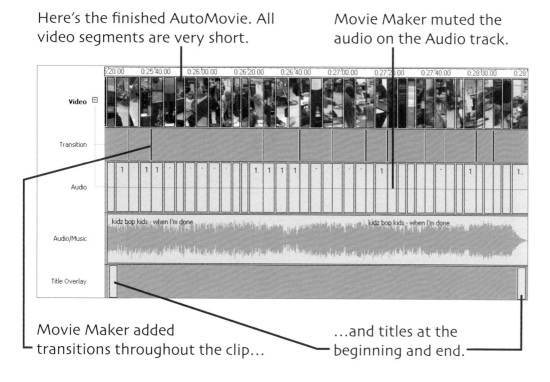

Movie Maker added transitions throughout the clip...

...and titles at the beginning and end.

extra bits

build an automovic p. 110

- Play yor AutoMovie right away after you create it, and if you don't like it, simply click Undo to make it go away and then start over. Otherwise, you'll have to delete all the parts manually, which can take a while.

- After Movie Maker produces the AutoMovie, you can edit any component as desired.

- If your footage contains any clips or portions of clips that you absolutely don't want included in the AutoMovie, delete them in the Contents pane before producing the AutoMovie. See Chapter 3 for details.

10. that's a wrap

You've finished your project, and now it's time to show it off to the world. The challenge, of course, is that the world is a big place, so you may need to deliver the video in different formats over different media.

Fortunately, Movie Maker offers a range of output formats. Figure out which ones work for you and then follow along.

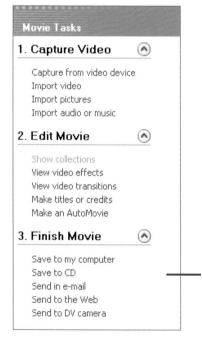

No matter how you intend to send your movie to your target audience, it all starts here in the Movie Tasks pane.

save on computer

I keep a copy of most movies I produce on my editing station, if only to amuse my daughters when they're spending time in my office. If you plan on playing the finished movie on the computer that produced it, this is the best option.

1 In the Movie Tasks pane, click Save to My Computer.

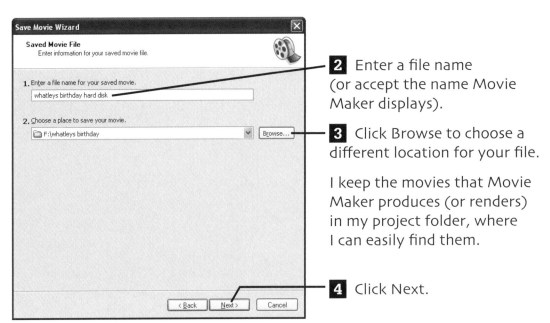

2 Enter a file name (or accept the name Movie Maker displays).

3 Click Browse to choose a different location for your file.

I keep the movies that Movie Maker produces (or renders) in my project folder, where I can easily find them.

4 Click Next.

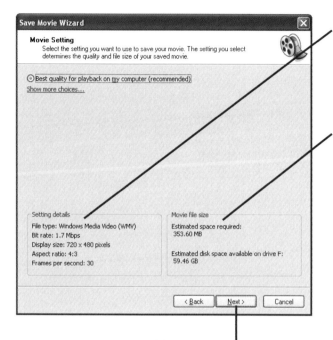

The Setting Details area shows the default output parameters Movie Maker uses to produce videos for playback on your computer.

The Movie File Size area reports the size of the rendered file and remaining hard disk space. If disk space is insufficient, Movie Maker will tell you and won't let you continue.

5 Click Next to start encoding— the process during which Movie Maker produces the digital file.

save on computer (cont.)

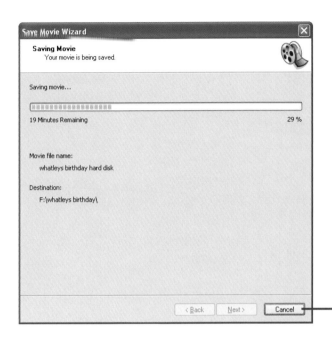

My project is about 28 minutes long and took about 33 minutes to produce on a 3.2 GHz Pentium 4 HP xw4100 workstation. Your mileage will definitely vary by processor speed, with slower machines taking much longer.

Click Cancel if you want to stop the encoding.

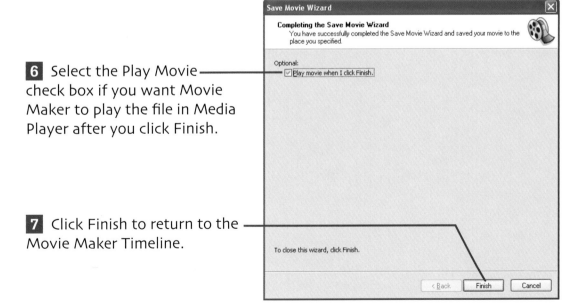

6 Select the Play Movie check box if you want Movie Maker to play the file in Media Player after you click Finish.

7 Click Finish to return to the Movie Maker Timeline.

that's a wrap

save on cd

You may also want to burn your movie file to a CD to archive it or to send it to a friend or relative.

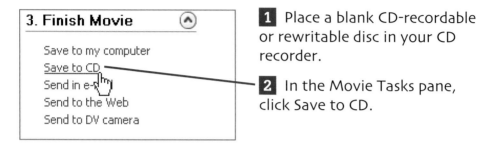

1 Place a blank CD-recordable or rewritable disc in your CD recorder.

2 In the Movie Tasks pane, click Save to CD.

3 Enter a file name for the movie (or accept the name Movie Maker displays).

4 Enter a name for the CD (or accept the name Movie Maker displays).

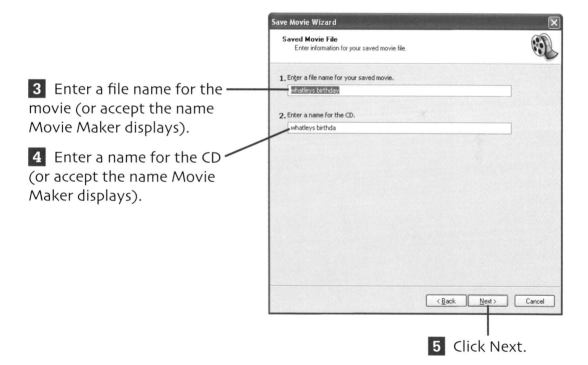

5 Click Next.

save on cd (cont.)

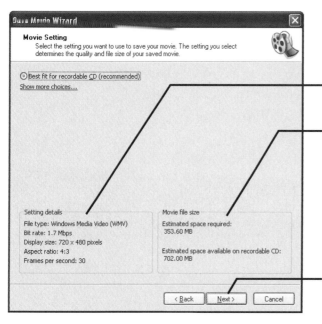

The Setting Details area shows the default output parameters Movie Maker uses to produce videos for burning to CD-ROM.

The Movie File Size area tells you the size of the file and the capacity of the CD-recordable disc. If the space is insufficient for your project, Movie Maker will tell you and won't let you continue.

6 Click Next to continue.

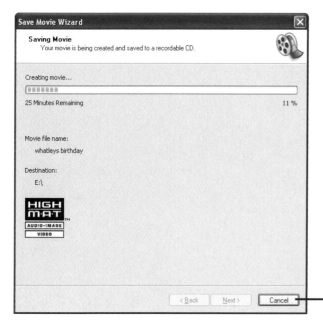

Movie Maker is encoding the file. When encoding is done, Movie Maker will burn the file to the CD-R. The CD-R should play on virtually all current Windows and Macintosh computers and on any HighMAT-compatible consumer electronics device.

Click Cancel if you want to stop the process.

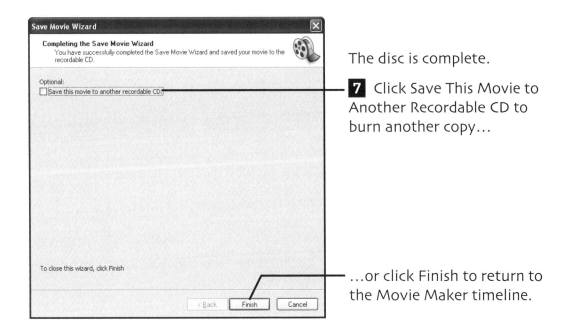

The disc is complete.

7 Click Save This Movie to Another Recordable CD to burn another copy...

...or click Finish to return to the Movie Maker timeline.

send in e-mail

My project is fairly long; if yours is similarly long, sending via e-mail won't be an option (as you'll see in a moment). However, for shorter projects, say around 3 minutes or less, e-mail is a great way to send movies to friends and family.

1 In the Movie Tasks pane, click Send in E-mail. —————

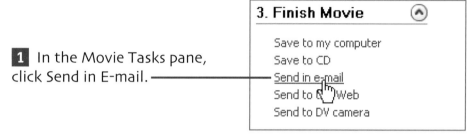

This is what you'll see if your project is too long.

Either increase the file size limit here (but only if you are absolutely certain that your Internet service provider and your recipient's accept the higher limit)...

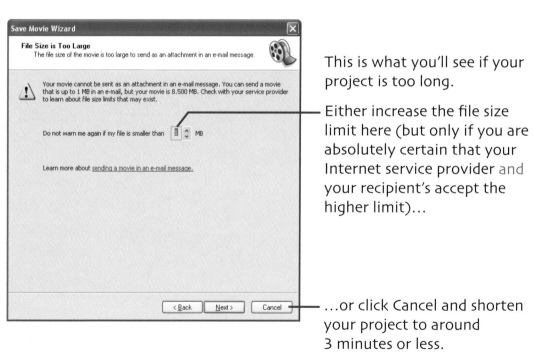

...or click Cancel and shorten your project to around 3 minutes or less.

that's a wrap

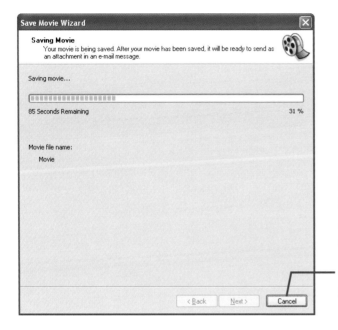

If your project is short enough to send via e-mail, Movie Maker will immediately start encoding.

Click Cancel if you want to stop the process.

Rendering is complete.

Click here if you want to play the movie.

Click here if you want to save the movie to your hard disk.

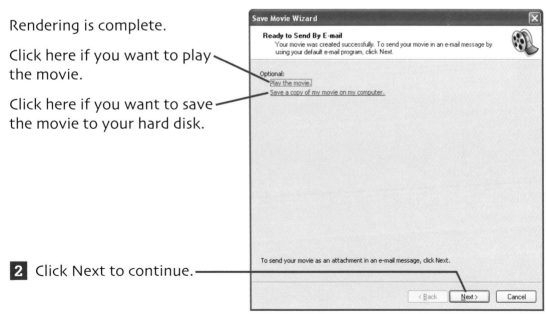

2 Click Next to continue.

send in e-mail (cont.)

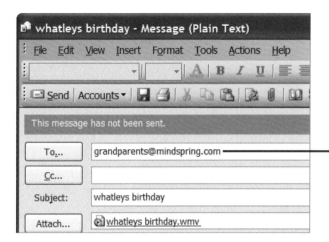

Movie Maker opens your e-mail program, opens a new message, and inserts the rendered file as an attachment.

3 Enter an e-mail recipient and message as desired and send the e-mail as you normally would.

that's a wrap

upload to the web

Use this option to send video files to www.neptune.com or other Web hosting services supported by Movie Maker (as I write, Neptune is the only supported service). Once you've uploaded your project (and joined Neptune), you can invite others to view your video from the pages that Neptune supplies. Neptune offers a free three-day trial account and a one-year membership for $59. You'll need an Internet connection and a trial membership with Neptune to complete the process described here. (To set up a trial account, go to www.neptune.com.)

1 In the Movie Tasks pane, click Send to the Web.

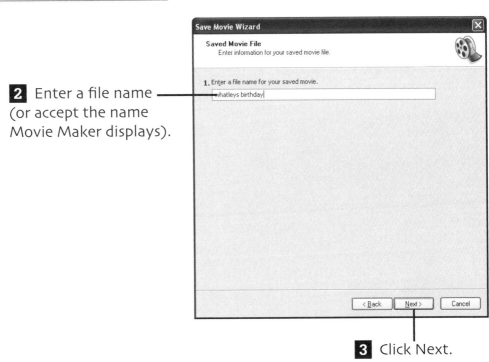

2 Enter a file name (or accept the name Movie Maker displays).

3 Click Next.

upload to the web (cont.)

4 Select the connection speed used by the person who will watch the video over the Internet. If you're not sure, select Dial Up Modem.

The files uploaded to the Neptune Web site are much smaller than those produced for viewing from your hard disk or CD-ROM (160x120 as opposed to 720x480), which means they won't look quite as good. This reduction in display size is necessary to ensure that the video plays smoothly over the connection speed used by your viewers.

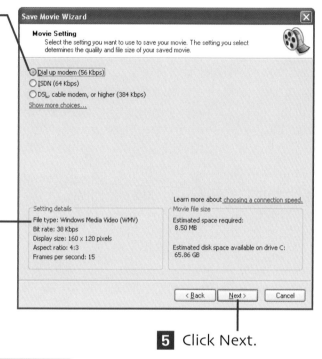

5 Click Next.

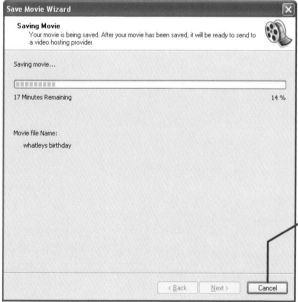

Movie Maker starts encoding your file.

Click Cancel if you want to stop encoding. After it finishes encoding, Movie Maker automatically advances to the next screen in the wizard.

that's a wrap

6 Select a provider and enter a user name and password.

If desired, click the Remember My Password check box to avoid having to log in during future sessions.

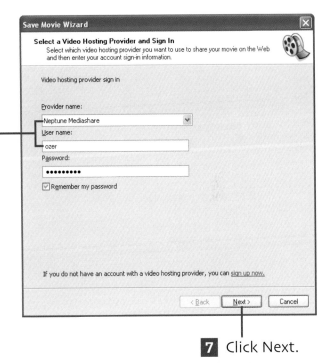

7 Click Next.

Movie Maker starts uploading the file to Neptune.

Click Cancel if you want to stop uploading. After it finishes uploading, Movie Maker automatically advances to the next screen in the wizard.

that's a wrap

upload to the web (cont.)

8 Click the Watch My Movie on the Web After I Click Finish check box to view your file on the Web after you click Finish.

9 Click Finish.

Movie Maker opens your browser to your Neptune home page.

that's a wrap

save on tape

I write all my Movie Maker projects back to tape, usually for archival purposes, but sometimes to copy (or dub) the movie to VHS tape for viewers who don't have computers. This is probably a good idea for you as well. Start by going back to Set Up for DV Capture in Chapter 2 and getting your DV camera connected and ready. Then proceed as decsribed here.

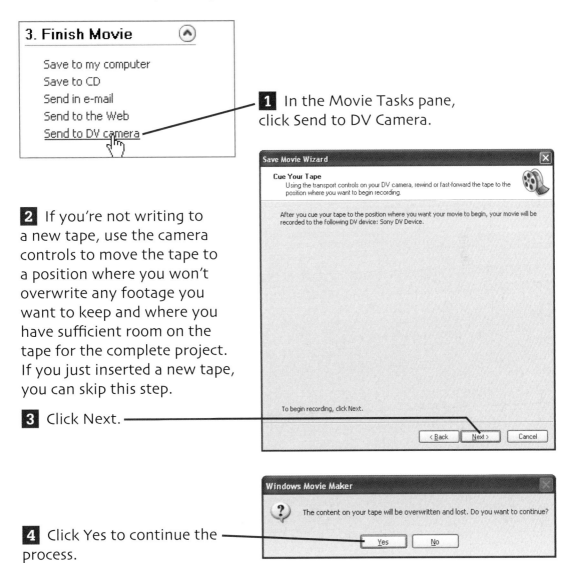

1 In the Movie Tasks pane, click Send to DV Camera.

2 If you're not writing to a new tape, use the camera controls to move the tape to a position where you won't overwrite any footage you want to keep and where you have sufficient room on the tape for the complete project. If you just inserted a new tape, you can skip this step.

3 Click Next.

4 Click Yes to continue the process.

save on tape (cont.)

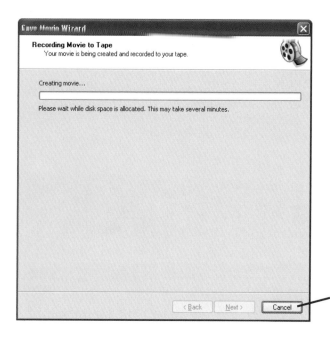

Movie Maker starts rendering your project and then writing the video back to tape.

Click Cancel if you want to cancel the process.

5 Click Finish to return to the Movie Maker Timeline.

that's a wrap

save to create dvd

After producing my movies in Movie Maker, I sometimes create DVDs of the movies, usually with Sonic Solutions MyDVD, an inexpensive yet highly functional program. When producing a DVD, I want to start with the best possible file, so I render back to DV video, the highest-quality format Movie Maker can output. If you're producing a file to include on a DVD, render the file as described here.

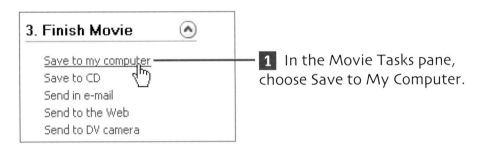

1 In the Movie Tasks pane, choose Save to My Computer.

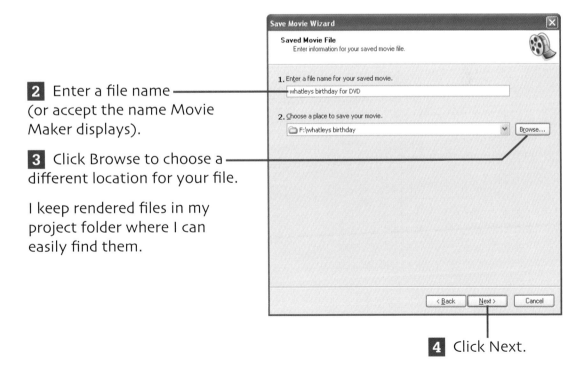

2 Enter a file name (or accept the name Movie Maker displays).

3 Click Browse to choose a different location for your file.

I keep rendered files in my project folder where I can easily find them.

4 Click Next.

save to create dvd (cont.)

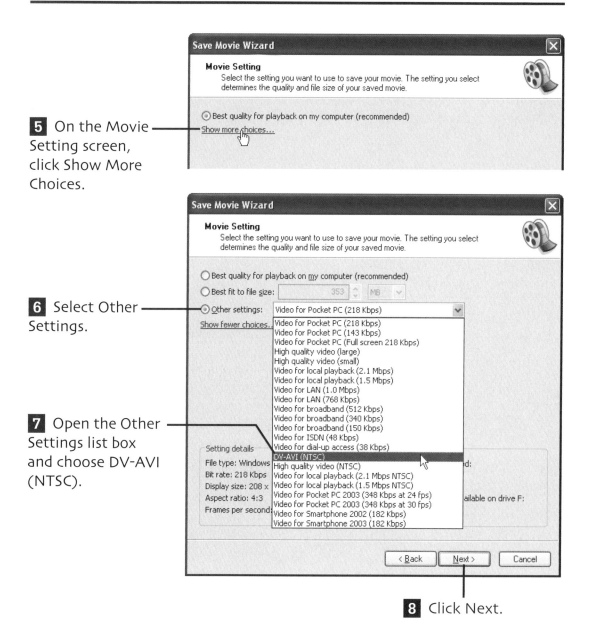

5 On the Movie Setting screen, click Show More Choices.

6 Select Other Settings.

7 Open the Other Settings list box and choose DV-AVI (NTSC).

8 Click Next.

that's a wrap

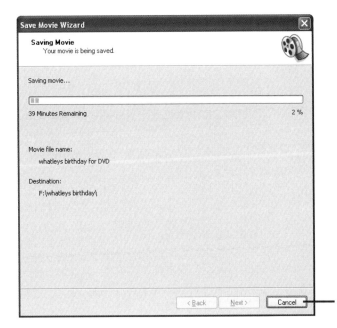

Movie Maker starts encoding.

Click Cancel if you want to stop the encoding.

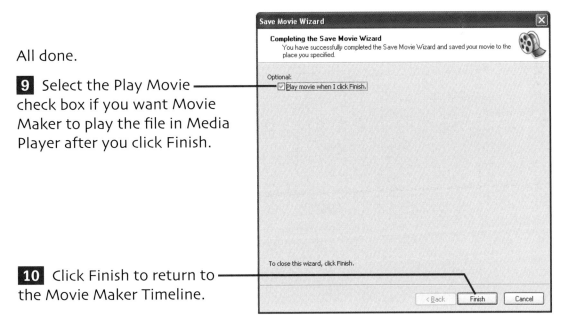

All done.

9 Select the Play Movie check box if you want Movie Maker to play the file in Media Player after you click Finish.

10 Click Finish to return to the Movie Maker Timeline.

extra bits

save on cd p. 119

- Most DVD recorders can also write to CD-recordable media. Movie Maker can write to a DVD recorder with CD-recordable media loaded, but it can't write to a DVD recorder with DVD-recordable media loaded.

- Movie Maker can store about one hour of video on a CD using the techniques described in this chapter.

- HighMAT is a Microsoft-sponsored format designed to allow one CD-recordable disc to play on consumer electronics devices and computers. At the time of this writing, only a few consumer electronics devices support this format, and I don't own one. Thus, I use Movie Maker's Save to CD function solely to produce discs for playback on computers.

send in e mail p. 122

- I do most of my e-mailing from my Dell laptop rather than my encoding station, so I use the Save a Copy of My Movie on My Computer option to save an e-mail-sized file, which I transfer to the Dell over my network and then e-mail from there.

save on tape p. 129

- If you're interested in learning more about how to dub your movies from DV to VHS tape, check out Microsoft Windows Movie Maker 2: Visual QuickStart Guide, also published by Peachpit Press, where this process is described in detail.

that's a wrap

index

index

index

Visual QuickProject

Managing
Your Personal Finances
with Quicken

TOM NEGRINO

managing your
personal finances
with quicken

Visual QuickProject Guide

by Tom Negrino

Peachpit Press

Visual QuickProject Guide
Managing Your Personal Finances with Quicken
Tom Negrino

Peachpit Press
1249 Eighth Street
Berkeley, CA 94710
510/524-2178
800/283-9444
510/524-2221 (fax)

Find us on the World Wide Web at: www.peachpit.com
To report errors, please send a note to errata@peachpit.com
Peachpit Press is a division of Pearson Education

Editor: Nancy Davis
Production Editor: Connie Jeung-Mills
Compositor: Owen Wolfson
Indexer: Rebecca Plunkett
Cover design: The Visual Group with Aren Howell
Interior design: Elizabeth Castro
Cover photo credit: Photodisc

ISBN 0-321-29365-7

Printed and bound in the United States of America

To my father, Joe Negrino, who has led his accounting clients through the thorny underbrush of the tax system for half a century.

Special Thanks to...

My superb editor, Nancy Davis.

The book's production editor,
Connie Jeung-Mills.

Aruna Harder and Chris Repetto of
Intuit, for their help with questions
about Quicken 2005 for Windows
and Macintosh.

contents

contents

introduction

The Visual QuickProject Guide that you hold in your hands offers a unique way to learn about new technologies. Instead of drowning you in theoretical possibilities and lengthy explanations, this Visual QuickProject Guide uses big, color illustrations coupled with clear, concise step-by-step instructions to show you how to complete one specific project in a matter of hours.

Our project in this book is to gain control of your personal finances using the latest version of the best-selling personal finance program, Quicken. You can use either Quicken 2005 for Windows or Quicken 2005 for Macintosh. These are the latest versions, but if you haven't upgraded yet, don't fret; because Quicken doesn't change too much from year to year, things will look pretty familiar if you have earlier versions.

I'll show you how to use Quicken to handle your paycheck; manage your checkbook; bank and pay bills online; balance your accounts to the penny every month; manage your credit cards; and handle your investments.

what you'll create

Create a data file in Quicken to contain all of your financial information.

Create accounts in Quicken that correspond to your checking, savings, credit card, and investment accounts in the real world, and see at a glance your account balances.

Set up your paycheck and schedule it so that Quicken automatically enters the paycheck information every time you get paid.

You'll learn how to write checks in Quicken, and, if you like, print checks from the program on pre-printed check forms.

Never forget a bill again—just put regular bills into Quicken and tell it to memorize the bill. Quicken reminds you to pay the bill every month, banishing late fees forever!

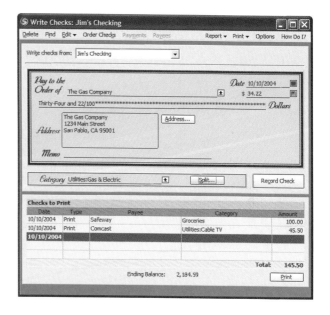

Tired of writing checks? You can pay your bills from within Quicken with online banking and online bill payment. This saves you time and effort, and as a bonus, it takes literally seconds each month to reconcile your checkbook.

Credit cards are great, but they can be cruel masters if you let your spending get out of hand. You'll learn to use Quicken to keep on top of credit card debt and prevent it from spiraling out of control.

Quicken's reports and graphs are great tools to let you know where your finances stand. You'll see how to use them for a quick financial checkup.

Looking forward to retirement? Smart investing now will pay off in the years ahead. You'll see how to set up your investment accounts, and how you can keep on top of your portfolio as it grows in value.

introduction

how this book works

The title of each section explains what is covered on that page.

Important terms and Web site addresses are shown in orange.

Captions explain what you're doing and why. They also point to items of interest.

Numbered steps explain actions to perform in a specific order.

add transactions (Win)

1 Choose Buy – Shares Bought from the investment transactions pop-up menu.

2 Enter the Transaction date.

3 Choose the security you want to purchase from the Security name pop-up menu. This menu lists all the securities you have previously bought. If you are buying a security that is new to your portfolio, click the Add New Security button at the bottom of the pop-up menu, and Quicken will walk you through a quick Wizard to add the new security.

Pixar
Janus Global Technology
Janus Mercury
Janus Worldwide
JDS UNIPHASE CORP
Lucent
Pixar
S&P Mid Cap Spdr
TIME WARNER INC

Add New Security

Add New Security

4 Enter the number of shares you have bought in the Number of shares field.

5 Enter the price you paid per share in the Price paid field.

6 If you paid a broker commission, enter its dollar amount in the Commission field. Quicken calculates the cost of the transaction (number of shares times price per share plus commission) and places the result in the Total cost field.

7 If you want to add a memo, type it in the Memo field.

8 The money to pay for your purchase can either come from the cash balance in your portfolio account or from another Quicken account, such as your checking account. If it comes from the portfolio cash balance, in the Use cash for this transaction section, click From this account's cash balance. If the money comes from another account, click From, and then choose the account from the pop-up menu next to it.

9 If you want to save the current transaction and immediately enter another, click Enter/New. If you are done entering transactions, click Enter/Done. The investment transaction is saved, and it appears in the Transactions tab of the investment account.

manage investments

135

x

introduction

The extra bits section at the end of each chapter contains additional tips and tricks that you might like to know—but that aren't absolutely necessary for creating the presentation.

The heading for each group of tips matches the section title.

extra bits

add transactions (Win) p. 134

- You'll find explanations of the more exotic investment actions found in the Enter transaction pop-up menu, such as short selling, in the Quicken User Guide.
- The column at the right edge of a single mutual fund account register and a portfolio account register differs. In a portfolio account, the column shows the running Cash Balance in the account. Mutual fund accounts don't have cash balances, so the column is called Share Balance, and shows a running total of [...]s in the [...]

- The number of investment transactions available in a mutual fund account is smaller than the transactions available in a portfolio account, because a portfolio account provides a wider array of investment options. For example, you can short sell a security in a portfolio account, but you can't short sell a mutual fund.

deal with dividends p. 138

- Unlike online banking, online investment transactions through Quicken are a one-way trip; you can enter transactions in Quicken by downloading them, but you can't use Quicken to create new transactions, such as buying or selling securities. For that, you'll need to use your online broker's Web site, or even talk to your broker on the telephone.
- You enable an investment account for online transactions in the same way that you online enable any other account. If you need help, see Chapter 5.

manage investments

deal with dividends

There are many transactions that can occur in your investment accounts that are not the result of buying or selling shares of securities with cash. The most common are dividends in a portfolio account and capital gains distributions and reinvestments in single mutual fund accounts.

To enter these transactions manually, you will use the investment action forms again. On Windows, select the investment account in the Account Bar, click the Transactions tab, then click Enter Transactions. In the investment actions dialog, choose the kind of transaction you need to enter, then fill out the dialog.

On the Mac, choose Activities > Investment Actions. The Investment Actions window appears. Double-click the investment action you want, and the associated action form appears. Fill out the form, and click Record.

If your financial institution supports it, downloading investment transactions gives you many of the same benefits as online banking, namely less manual entry, better accuracy, and a significant time savings.

To download investment transactions on Windows, click the One Step Update button in the toolbar, then choose the accounts that you want to update in the One Step Update dialog, then click Update Now. Quicken will go online, connect to your financial institutions, and download any transactions that are available.

Accounts that have downloaded investment transactions that need to be reviewed will be flagged in the Account Bar.

Flag —⚑ Ameritrade IRA   9,638.55

The page number next to the heading makes it easy to refer back to the main content.

138   **manage investments**

useful tools

Quicken is pretty self-contained in terms of managing your finances, but there are lots of useful sites on the Web that can help you manage your money.

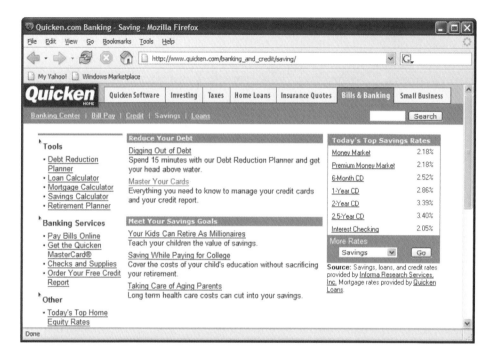

To view these sites, you'll need an Internet connection (a broadband connection is best) and a Web browser. On Windows, you'll probably use Internet Explorer, and on the Mac, Apple's Safari. If you're a Windows user, I suggest using Mozilla Firefox as your Web browser (shown); it's much less susceptible to viruses and other bad software than is Internet Explorer for Windows. When you're talking about your money, the more security, the better. You can obtain Firefox at http://www.mozilla.org.

1. explore quicken

Before you start working with Quicken, you need to see the tools that Quicken gives you. In this chapter, you'll explore the user interface from two versions of Quicken: Quicken 2005 for Windows and Quicken 2005 for Macintosh. Though the two programs look different, both deliver all of the financial savvy you need to manage your money.

On Windows, there are four versions of Quicken 2005, with increasing amounts of features and capabilities: Basic, Deluxe, Premier, and Premier Home & Business. On the Macintosh, there's just one version, called Quicken 2005 for Mac.

Start up Quicken. On Windows, point at the Start menu, choose Programs, then choose Quicken, and then choose Quicken 2005.

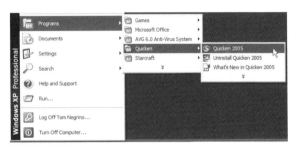

On the Mac, open the Applications folder, then open the Quicken 2005 folder, and double-click on the Quicken 2005 icon.

create data file (Win)

When you start up Quicken for the first time on Windows, it launches the Get Started Assistant.

Choose I am new to Quicken and click Next. In the next screen, Quicken asks you what you want to call your data file. By default, the name is QDATA and will end up in your My Documents folder. That's a fine location, but the name isn't very helpful, so select I want to choose a different file name and location and click Next.

In the resulting Create Quicken File dialog, give the file a descriptive name (I suggest your last name) and click OK. In this book, we'll be following the financial adventures of the fictional Carroll family, so I named the file Carroll Family.

When the file is created, Quicken Guided Setup starts up automatically. This is another assistant in which you enter a bunch of information, and it tries to set up your accounts for you. I think it's overkill, so we'll enter data on just one of the Guided Setup screens, then strike out on our own. The first screen is just informational, so read it and click Next Step.

On the About You screen, enter all the information requested, including your name and birthdate (Quicken uses your birthdate for retirement calculations); if you're married, enter your spouse's information. Then click Exit Setup. Quicken saves what you entered.

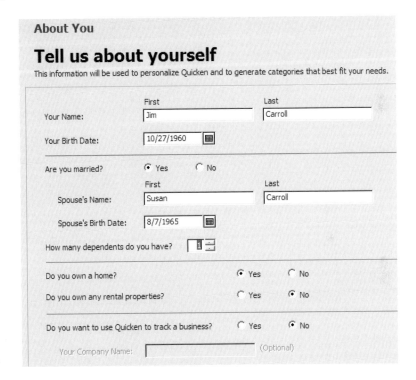

create data file (Mac)

On the Mac, Quicken displays an Open dialog, asking for the location of your data file (it assumes that you are upgrading from a previous version). Click Cancel, then choose File > New File. In the resulting Save dialog, give the data file a descriptive name (something more interesting than Quicken Data, such as Carroll Family), and choose where you want to save it. Quicken comes with a set of categories that will help you organize your finances. You'll learn more about categories in Chapter 2; for now, if you'll be using Quicken for your home finances, just select the Home check box, and if you also plan to manage a small business, also select the Business check box (most people will only need the Home categories). Click Save.

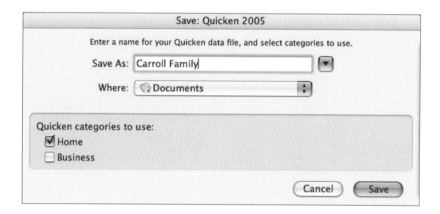

Quicken for Mac will then show you the New Account Assistant. You'll set up accounts in Chapter 2, so for now just click Cancel.

explore quicken

quicken for windows

The Quicken Home screen appeared when you finished with the Quicken Guided Setup. It's pretty blank now (because you haven't entered any of your accounts yet), but here's what it looks like when there's a bit more information in Quicken.

The menu bar contains the commands you use to accomplish tasks with Quicken.

The toolbar gives you an easier way to get to Quicken's features.

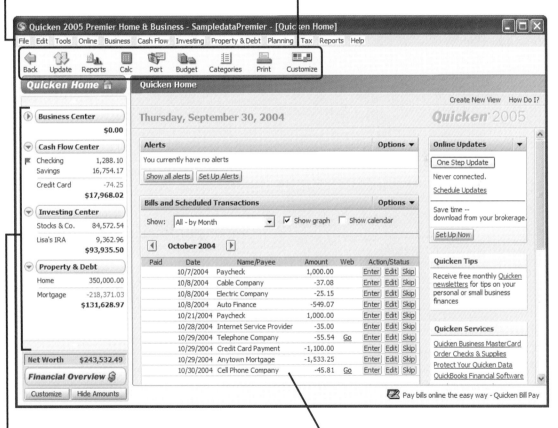

The Account Bar shows all your accounts, with their current values. You'll learn more about the Account Bar in Chapter 2.

The Bills and Scheduled Transactions list shows you upcoming financial events.

explore quicken 5

quicken for windows

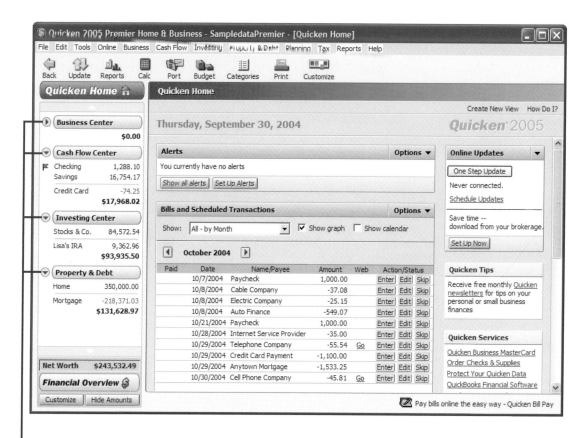

Quicken has several activity centers for different kinds of financial transactions; click on these buttons to display them.

Depending on the version of Quicken you're using (Basic, Deluxe, Premier, or Premier Home & Business), what you see may differ a bit from what is shown here (I'm using the Premier Home & Business version).

When you click on one of the accounts in the Account Bar, you see the register for the account. It looks much like your paper checkbook register, except that it's neater, and Quicken does all the math for you, giving you a running balance.

Checking		Register	Overview					
Delete Find Transfer Reconcile Write Checks Update Now					View ▼ Report ▼ Options ▼ How Do I?				

Date△	Num	Payee Category	Memo	Payment Exp	Clr	Deposit	Balance
6/29/2004		Telephone Company Utilities:Telephone		67 00			1,997 17
6/29/2004		Mortgage Mortgage Interest		1,200 00			797 17
6/30/2004		Safeway Groceries		45 00			752 17
7/1/2004	DEP	Paycheck Net Salary				1,000 00	1,752 17
7/1/2004		Deposit				1,000 00	2,752 17
7/8/2004	Sched	Auto Finance Auto:Loan	sports car	549 07			2,203 10
7/15/2004	DEP	Paycheck Net Salary				1,000 00	3,203 10
7/21/2004 ▶	117	Dr. Siegler Medical:Doctor		240 00			2,963 10
7/30/2004 ▦	Num	Payee Category	Memo	Payment Exp		Deposit	Enter Edit Split

Online Balance: 750.40 **Ending Balance:** 2,963.10

quicken for windows

Let's take a closer look at one of the transactions in the check register. Each transaction line contains all of the information about that transaction.

The Date field records when the transaction occurred.

Enter the check number or transaction type here.

The check's payee (or if it's a deposit, the source of the money) goes here.

For checks and other payments, this is the payment amount.

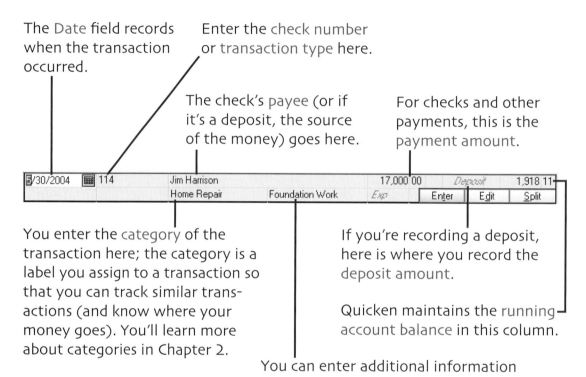

You enter the category of the transaction here; the category is a label you assign to a transaction so that you can track similar transactions (and know where your money goes). You'll learn more about categories in Chapter 2.

If you're recording a deposit, here is where you record the deposit amount.

Quicken maintains the running account balance in this column.

You can enter additional information about the transaction in the Memo field.

explore quicken

quicken for mac

Quicken for Mac has a similar user interface to its Windows counterpart, but there are some differences.

The menu bar contains the commands you use to accomplish tasks with Quicken.

You switch between Quicken's different financial areas with the activity area tabs.

The toolbar gives you an easier way to get to Quicken's features.

You can add custom account buttons to the toolbar.

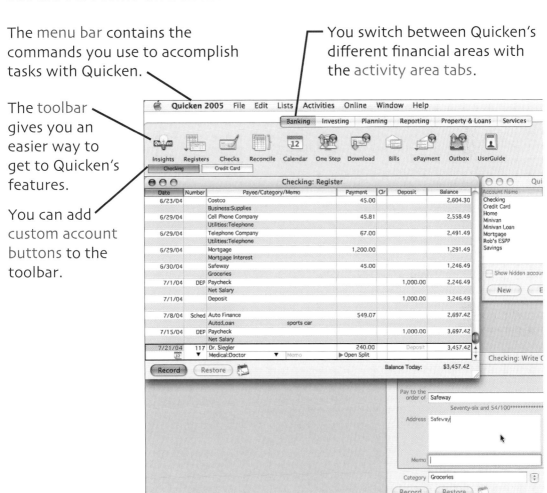

quicken for mac (cont.)

The Account List shows all your accounts, with their current values. You'll learn more about the Account List in Chapter 2.

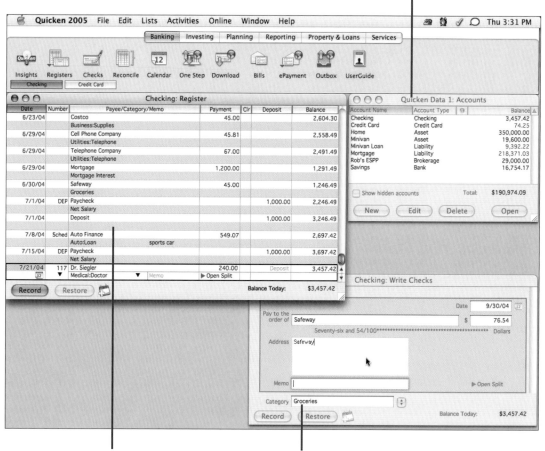

I've double-clicked the Checking account in the Account List, which opens its account register.

You can add transactions directly in the register, but sometimes the Write Checks window is more convenient.

explore quicken

Some transactions are assigned to more than one category; this is called a split transaction. You can spot these because they have split in the Category field of the register.

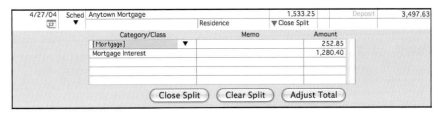

4/27/04	Sched	Anytown Mortgage		1,533.25	Deposit	3,497.63
📅	▼	split	Residence	▶ Open Split		

Clicking the Open Split button in the register shows the multiple categories. You'll learn more about split transactions in Chapter 4.

4/27/04	Sched	Anytown Mortgage		1,533.25	Deposit	3,497.63
📅	▼		Residence	▼ Close Split		

Category/Class		Memo	Amount
[Mortgage]	▼		252.85
Mortgage Interest			1,280.40

(Close Split)   (Clear Split)   (Adjust Total)

The Mac equivalent of the Windows' Quicken Home page is Quicken Insights, which gives you a good overview of your finances.

Account List

Expense graph

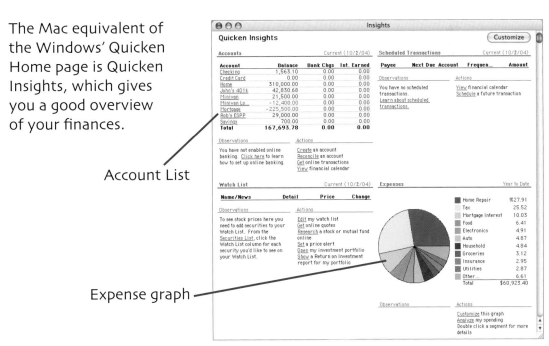

explore toolbars

On Windows, the default toolbar has a set of buttons that Intuit thinks will be the most useful for you.

Back to the last screen you were viewing.

One Step Update, which gets all of the online financial information that you have set up to download.

Open the Reports window.

Customize the toolbar.

Open an on-screen Calculator.

| Back | Update | Reports | Calc | Port | Budget | Categories | Print | Customize |

Open the Investing Center, so you can view your portfolio.

Open the Budget window.

View the Categories window.

Print the current window or register.

Clicking the Customize button brings up the Customize Toolbar dialog. You can use the Add and Remove buttons to change the buttons on the tool-bar, and the Move Up and Move Down buttons to modify button order.

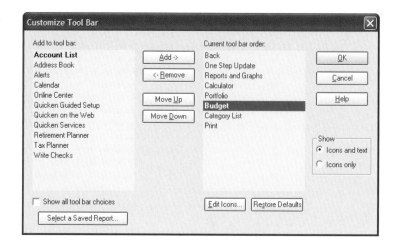

The toolbars on the Mac work differently; they are linked to their activity areas, and each area has a different set of buttons. For example, the Banking area has these buttons:

Activity area tabs

And the Planning area has these buttons:

In all of the activity areas, buttons with a badge of the world, such as the TurboTax icon above, indicate online features that require an Internet connection.

explore toolbars (cont.)

You can also customize the toolbars on the Mac. Click the button for the activity whose toolbar you want to change, then choose Quicken > Configure Toolbar. The Configure Toolbar dialog opens.

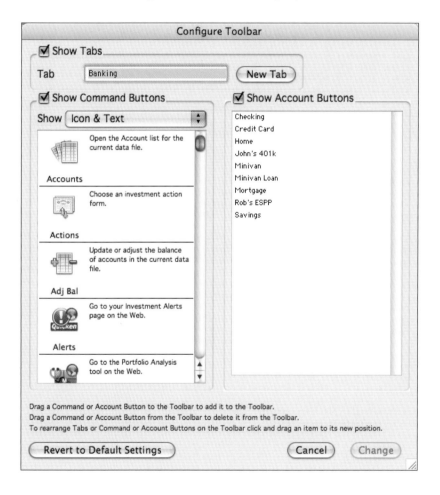

Follow the directions at the bottom of the dialog to modify the buttons, and then click Change.

extra bits

create data file (win) p. 2

- Here's a hard fact of life: Computers crash. Although they don't crash that often, it happens. Or your computer could become infected by a virus that trashes your files (especially on Windows). Besides computer problems, there are plenty of other things that can go wrong, including fires, mudslides, earthquakes, hurricanes—well, you get the idea. That's why you need to be thinking right now about backing up your data files.

  A backup is a recent copy (or better yet, multiple copies) of your documents. If your computer has a CD-RW drive, you can burn backup copies onto rewritable CDs. Another good solution is to buy an external hard drive, hooking it up via FireWire or USB2.

  No matter how you backup, you should get into the habit of backing up regularly. Establish a schedule. Get into the habit of backing up your files before you shut down your computer, for example. If you never shut your computer down, do your backup first thing in the morning when you're fresh; doing backups at the end of the day when you want to get away from the computer doesn't work as well.

  Having multiple backup copies is the extra safe way to go. Keep one of your backups off the premises in a safe place, such as a safe deposit box. Bring in that backup and update it periodically—once a month, for example. Then take the backup off-site again. Having multiple backups does you no good if all of your backup disks are destroyed along with your computer.

extra bits

explore toolbars p. 12

- On the Mac, you can use the Configure Toolbar dialog to add custom buttons to the toolbars for your accounts, which makes it easier to open the individual accounts, instead of opening the Account List, then double-clicking the account name.

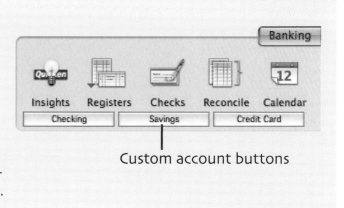

Custom account buttons

2. set up your finances

As you saw in the last chapter, Quicken stores all of your financial information in a single data file. Inside that data file, you'll create a number of accounts. An account represents an asset (something that you own, such as the money in your checking account or some property) or a liability (a debt that you owe, such as the balance on your credit cards or the mortgage on your home).

Quicken allows you to have as many or as few accounts as you wish. Some people prefer to use Quicken to track only their main checking account, and other people create many accounts to track every aspect of their financial life.

In this chapter, you'll set up the different accounts that you will initially use; learn about the different account types in Quicken; and learn about categories, the most important tool you'll use in Quicken to manage your finances.

decide what to manage

Before you dive into Quicken, it's useful to spend a few minutes deciding what parts of your financial life you'll manage with the program. Though Quicken can handle every aspect of your finances, I suggest that you start with just a few areas, like your checking and savings accounts and the credit card you use the most. The reason is simple: You're making a transition from paper systems to a computerized one, and there's a bit of a learning curve and some information to enter into Quicken. I'll help you with that learning process, and you can help yourself by not trying to enter in every last bit of your financial information at one time. As you become more comfortable using Quicken, and as you discover its benefits, you can add more accounts and manage more of your financial life in the program.

This is a great time to sit down for a moment with a pen and paper and jot down two short lists. At the top of the first list, write "This is what I want to do with Quicken." Then give yourself some clear, short goals, things like "Manage my checkbook" and "Pay my bills." As we work through this book, you'll make these goals happen.

In the second list, write down the names of the accounts you have chosen to set up now in Quicken. If you have only one checking account, it's OK to use the name "Checking" in Quicken. But if you want to manage more than one checking account, it's a good idea to give each a descriptive name, such as "Jim's Checking" and "Susan's Checking."

This is what I want to do with Quicken:

1. Balance my checkbooks
2. Pay the bills
3. Manage my credit cards
4. Keep track of my IRA

Account List:
1. Jim's checking
2. Susan's checking
3. Joint checking
4. Citibank Visa

set up accounts (Win)

Let's set up your accounts in Quicken for Windows, including your main checking account, savings account (if you have one), and a credit card account (ditto). If you have them, get the last paper statements from each of these accounts. If you don't have them, that's OK; you can make changes later.

On Windows, you saw the Quicken Home screen when you finished with the Quicken Guided Setup in Chapter 1. In the Account Bar, click the Cash Flow Center button. The window changes to display the Cash Flow Center.

Let's add your main checking account. In the Spending & Savings Accounts section, click Add Account. The Quicken Account Setup window appears, asking you to enter the financial institution for the account (in other words, the bank where you have your checking account).

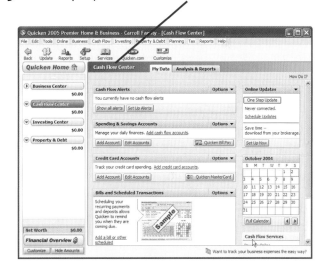

As you type the name, a pop-up list appears with choices. Keep typing until you find your bank. If your bank isn't in the list (unlikely, but possible), just type in the bank name.

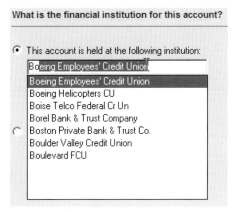

set up accounts (Win)

When your bank is selected, click Next. Quicken asks if you want to set up your account online or manually. Click Manual, and then click Next. (We'll cover setting up accounts for online access in Chapter 5.)

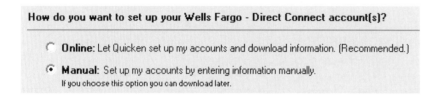

We're setting up a checking account, so click Checking on the next screen, then click Next. Give the account a name. If it's going to be the only checking account, then the default name of Checking is fine. Otherwise, give it a more descriptive name, so you can tell the different checking accounts apart. Click Next. On the next screen, enter the ending date from the last paper statement for the checking account and the ending balance, then click Done.

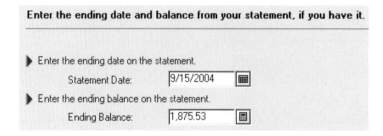

Quicken displays the register for your new account, with the opening balance filled in.

Repeat this process for the rest of the checking and savings accounts you want to set up.

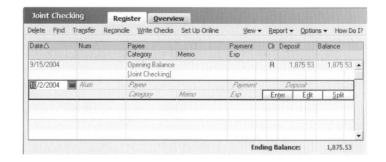

To set up the credit card account, click the Add Account button in the Credit Card Accounts section of the Cash Flow Center. Follow the prompts to add the account information; it's much like adding the checking account.

As you finish setting up each account, it appears in the Account Bar and the Cash Flow Center. You also get handy totals of the amounts in your accounts, and for the credit cards, the amount of credit you have available.

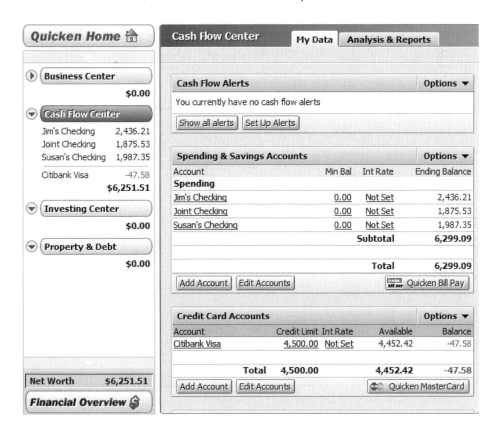

set up accounts (Mac)

Let's set up your accounts in Quicken for Mac, including your main checking account, savings account, and a credit card account. If you have them, get the last paper statements from each of these accounts. If you don't have the statements, don't worry; you can make changes later.

If the Account List isn't open, display it by choosing Lists > Accounts, or by pressing Cmd-A. Then click the New button in the Account List. The New Account Assistant opens.

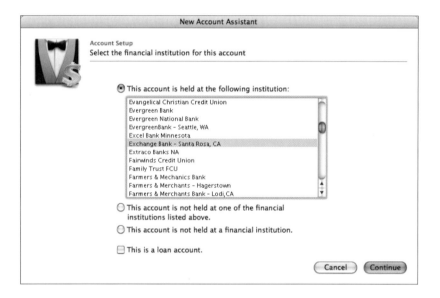

Let's add your main checking account. Type the first few letters of your bank's name to scroll the list of financial institutions, and then select your bank. If your bank isn't in the list, click This account is not held at one of the financial institutions listed above. Then click Continue. Quicken next asks if you want to set up your account online or manually. Click Manual, and then click Continue. (We'll cover setting up accounts for online access in Chapter 5.)

This screen shows the different kinds of accounts you can set up. Click Checking, and then click Continue. On the next screen, give the account a name. If it's going to be the only checking account, then the default name of Checking is fine. Otherwise, give it a more descriptive name, so you can tell the different checking accounts apart. Click Continue.

On the next screen, enter the ending date from the last paper statement for the checking account and the ending balance, and then click Continue. Quicken displays the register for your new account, with the opening balance filled in.

Repeat this process for the rest of the checking, savings, and credit card accounts you want to set up.

As you finish setting up each account, it appears in the Account List, with the balance for all your accounts.

about categories

The whole point of using Quicken is to gain better control over your finances. To achieve that control, you'll need to know where your money comes from and where your money goes. You use Quicken's categories to track the flow of money. For example, when you buy food at the grocery store and record the transaction in a Quicken register, you can record it under the Groceries category. Later, when you're curious about how much money you spend on groceries, you can create a report that adds up all of your grocery transactions. You can—and should—assign a category to each transaction that you enter into Quicken.

By categorizing all of your transactions in Quicken, you can generate reports and graphs about the details of your income and expenses; save time and money while preparing your tax returns; and get a clearer view of your financial picture.

Because categories are used to track the flow of money, you need to be concerned about whether the money is flowing in or out. Money that is flowing in, such as your paycheck, is tracked using income categories. Money that you spend on your mortgage, utilities, groceries, and other bills is tracked using expense categories. A third type of category, the transfer category is used just to keep track of money that you move from one Quicken account into another.

You'll often want to track several types of income or expenses that are related to a single category. Quicken lets you use subcategories to handle these relations. For example, under the Medical category, you might have several subcategories for Doctors, Dentists, Prescriptions, and Insurance. Later, when you run an expense report, you'll be able to see just how much money you spent on each of the medical subcategories.

Quicken comes with a preset category list, but most people end up customizing their categories to better reflect their particular financial situation. For example, I write books for a living, and I want to know how much money each book brings in. So in my Quicken file, I set up a Writing category, and then I use the name of each book as a subcategory. At the end of the year, my income report shows me how much money each book brought in, and also shows the total for everything that is part of the Writing category.

set up categories (Win)

It's easy to add a new category or subcategory. The Carroll family lives in California, so they need to set up a subcategory for earthquake insurance. On Windows, choose Tools > Category List. The Category List opens.

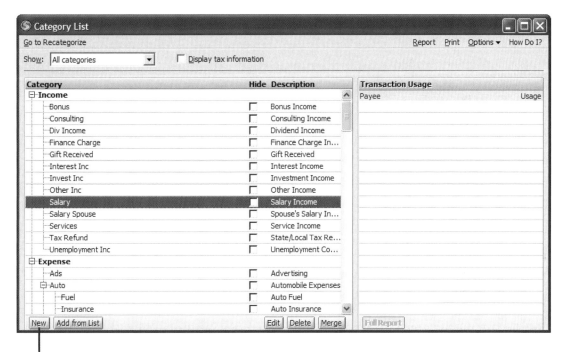

Click the New button at the bottom of the list.
The Set Up Category dialog appears.

set up categories (Win)

Give the new category or subcategory a name, then press the Tab key to get to the next field. Enter a short description. You can skip the Group field.

Next, click Income, Expense, or Subcategory of. If the latter, choose the parent category for the subcategory in the pop-up list.

If the category or subcategory is tax-related (meaning that you want to use it to track tax-related income or expenses), click the Tax-related check box, and choose the tax form line item from the pop-up menu that matches the category or subcategory.

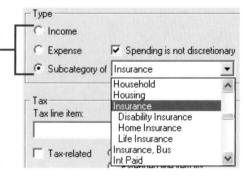

Quicken shows you a brief description of the tax form line item. For example, here is the Tax section of the IRA Contributions category. When you're done, click OK to save your new category or subcategory.

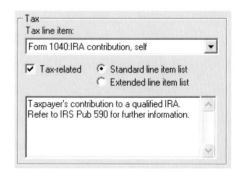

set up your finances

set up categories (Mac)

On the Mac, choose Lists > Categories & Transfers > List, or press Cmd-L. The Categories & Transfers List opens.

To add a category, click New. To add a subcategory, first select the parent category in the list, and then click Add Subcategory. In either case, the Set Up Category dialog appears.

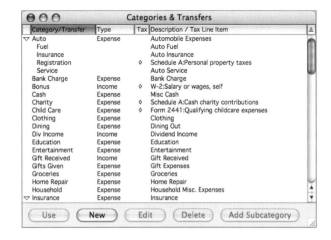

Enter the name and description for the category or subcategory. If you are adding a new category, choose the Category Type by clicking Income or Expense (if you're adding a subcategory, these buttons will be inactive, because a subcategory must always be of the same type as its parent category). If necessary, click the Tax-related check box. Then you can click Assign tax link and select the line item tax form for that category or subcategory. Click Create when you are done.

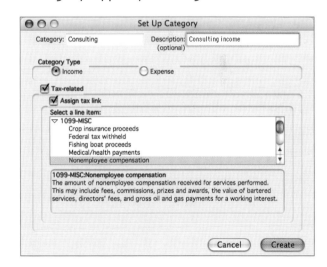

extra bits

decide what to manage p. 18

- The number one contributor to marital strife is disagreements over handling money. So it's a good idea to set up your finances to help minimize stress. Here's one proven way to manage a couple's finances: instead of having one joint checking account, use three checking accounts. Each person has his or her own account (to which their paychecks are deposited, which they can use for their own expenses), and each contributes an agreed amount every month to a joint checking account, which is used for shared expenses. This allows each person a certain amount of financial freedom, and both contribute to pay the common bills. Some couples contribute equal amounts every month; others contribute in proportion to the salary that each earns. Either way, it's a good way to handle a family's finances.

set up accounts (Win & Mac) p. 19

- Quicken allows you to have a Cash account, which is unlike the rest of the accounts because no corresponding account exists at a financial institution. You use a Cash account to track out-of-pocket expenses, or simply to record that spending money has come out of your checking account. For example, let's say that you withdraw $100 from an ATM. In Quicken, that amount comes out of your checking account and goes into the Cash account (because it is money flowing out of the checking account, it has to go somewhere). As you spend the money, you can make notations in the Cash account to track how that cash has been spent. This can be a useful exercise if you are having trouble figuring out how you spend your cash; keep really detailed records for a week or so, and you'll get a better look at your spending habits.

However, this may be more detail than you're willing to deal with; most people aren't going to keep receipts for small expenses like stopping at Starbucks in the morning. For my finances, I compromise; spending money comes out of my checking account and goes into the Cash account, but I don't bother to enter expenses in the Cash account. Naturally, Quicken thinks that the Cash account keeps growing (because there are credits and never any debits). This will eventually affect your net worth statement, because Quicken thinks that you're carrying thousands of dollars in cash in your pocket. I deal with this by occasionally entering a balance adjustment in the Cash account register, returning it to zero.

about categories p. 24

- It's important to use the same category names consistently throughout your Quicken accounts. For example, if you go to the doctor and pay with a check, you would enter that check under the Medical category in your checking account register. If on a subsequent visit you pay with a credit card, you would enter the transaction in your credit card account register using that same Medical category. This consistent categorization leads to accurate reports, and correct reports give you a better picture of your finances.

- If needed, you can create multiple levels of subcategories.

- If you delete a category, the transactions in your data file that were assigned to that category end up with no category at all. As a result, those transactions won't show up where you expect them in reports that are sorted by category and could be hard to find. It's better to try to avoid deleting categories altogether, but if you need to you should first reassign categories for the affected transactions using the Find/Replace feature in Quicken for Mac or the Recategorize feature in Quicken for Windows.

3. set up your paycheck

Now that you've set up your accounts and added categories, it's time to tell Quicken how to handle one of your most important financial transactions: your paycheck. Your paycheck isn't just a simple deposit; it's the amount you are paid (your gross pay) minus all of those deductions for taxes and other things like 401(k) contributions. You are left with your net pay, which is what gets deposited to your checking account.

Your paycheck is an example of a split transaction, which is a transaction that has amounts assigned to more than one category. Your gross pay is a positive number, say $1,000. Each kind of tax (Federal, state, Social Security, etc.) or other payroll deduction is a negative number. The remainder after deductions is your net pay.

On Windows, Quicken provides a handy wizard to help with your paycheck setup. On the Mac, you'll enter the different amounts into the register. On both platforms, you can memorize the paycheck and have Quicken automatically enter it for you the next time, so you only have to do the paycheck setup once.

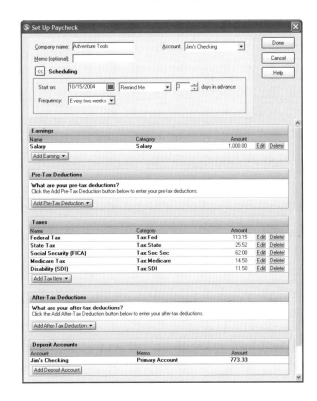

paycheck setup (Win)

To set up your paycheck so Quicken can use it, you'll need your latest paycheck stub. In Quicken, choose Cash Flow > Banking Activities > Set Up Paycheck. The first screen of the Paycheck Setup assistant appears. It's just informational, so click Next.

On the next screen, tell Quicken if this is your paycheck or your spouse's, then enter the name of your employer. Click Next.

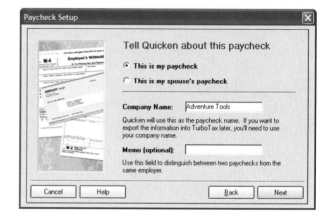

This next screen allows you to enter details of the transaction or just the net pay. Choose to track all earnings, taxes, and deductions, then click Next.

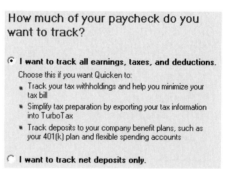

The main Set Up Paycheck dialog appears. It's a big dialog, so I'll show it in pieces as we work through it. At the top of the dialog, the Account pop-up menu shows the account to which the paycheck will be deposited. If the account is correct, move on; otherwise choose the proper account.

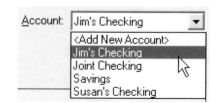

The Scheduling area is next. This allows Quicken to automatically enter your paycheck every pay period. Begin here by entering the date of your paycheck next to where it says Start on. You can type in the date, or you can click the calendar icon to get a pop-up calendar. Click a day in the pop-up calendar to enter it in the Date field. Next, choose Remind Me or Automatically Enter from the pop-up menu, and choose how many days in advance you want to be reminded to enter the paycheck. Depending on your choice, Quicken will give you a reminder that the deposit will be made, or will just enter it automatically in the register. If your paycheck is regular and the amount doesn't change from check to check, I recommend that you choose Automatically Enter here. If your paycheck amount varies, choose Remind Me; that way, when the paycheck arrives, you can change the split amounts in the transaction based on the amounts in your paycheck stub. Finally, choose how often you get paid from the Frequency pop-up menu.

Calendar icon

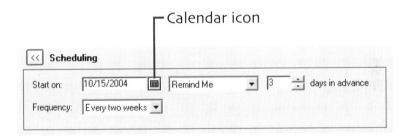

In the Earnings section, enter the gross amount of your salary, before any deductions. If you have other earnings that are included in the paycheck, such as a bonus, vacation pay, profit-sharing, and so on, choose the type of earning from the Add Earning pop-up menu. In the resulting Add Earning dialog, enter the amount, and then click OK.

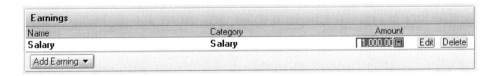

set up your paycheck

paycheck setup (Win)

Many people have deductions that are taken out before taxes, such as contributions to a 401(k) or other retirement account, or deductions for medical or dental insurance. If you have such pre-tax deductions, click the Add Pre-Tax Deduction button to get a pop-up menu with the possible choices.

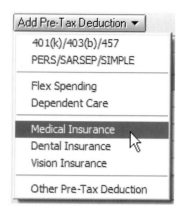

If you choose any of the first four choices, the Quicken Account Setup assistant starts up to help you create a Quicken account for the retirement or benefits plan you selected. Work through the assistant to create the account; you will return to the Set Up Paycheck

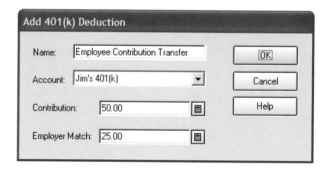

dialog and will be presented with a dialog that allows you to enter the contribution amounts. For example, if you set up a 401(k), the Add 401(k) Deduction dialog appears. Fill out the dialog, then click OK.

If you have other pre-tax deductions, add them now. Otherwise move on to the Taxes section, which is filled out for you with a standard set of taxes.

Taxes				
Name	Category	Amount		
Federal Tax	Tax:Fed	113.15	Edit	Delete
State Tax	Tax:State	25.52	Edit	Delete
Social Security (FICA)	Tax:Soc Sec	62.00	Edit	Delete
Medicare Tax	Tax:Medicare	14.50	Edit	Delete
Disability (SDI)	Tax:SDI	11.50	Edit	Delete
Add Tax Item ▼				

Click the Edit button next
to each line item, and in the
resulting Edit Tax Item dialog,
enter the amount of that tax
from your paycheck stub,
then click OK. If you don't
have some of the listed taxes
(if, for instance, you live in

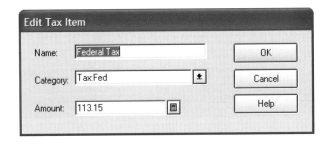

a state with no state income tax), click the Delete button next to that line
item. Continue through the line items until you are done.

Some people have payroll deductions that are
taken after taxes. For example, if you participate
in an Employee Stock Purchase Plan (ESPP), you
can purchase your company's stock with every
paycheck. If you have such ESPP deductions,
click the Add After-Tax Deduction button to get
a pop-up menu with the possible choices, then
work through the resulting dialog.

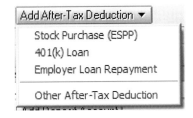

The bottom of the Set Up Paycheck dialog shows you the account to which
the paycheck will be deposited, your net pay, and the W-2 Gross pay (the
W-2 Gross is less than the Salary because of the 401(k) contribution, which
comes off the top). You're done setting up your paycheck; at the top of the
Set Up Paycheck dialog, click Done.

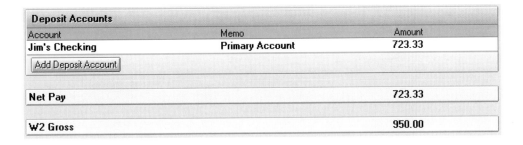

paycheck setup (Mac)

To set up your paycheck so Quicken can use it, you'll need your latest paycheck stub. You'll enter your paycheck information as a scheduled transaction, which is just a future transaction that you set up in advance, and that Quicken remembers so you don't have to enter all of the details each time. When the transaction comes due, Quicken either enters it automatically into your check register, or asks you if it's okay to add.

If you have pre-tax deductions from your paycheck, such as a 401(k) or other retirement plan, you must create that account before you begin setting up your paycheck. The same goes for post-tax deductions, such as Employee Stock Purchase Plans. See Chapter 2 for more information on setting up accounts.

Begin by choosing Lists > Scheduled Transactions. The Upcoming Bills and Scheduled Transactions window opens. Click the Scheduled Transactions tab.

Click New. The Enter Transaction dialog appears.

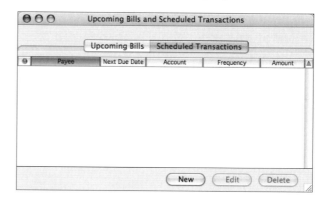

Account pop-up menu   Open Split button

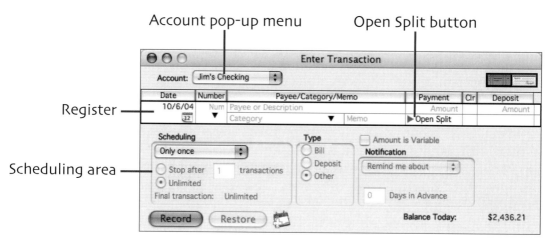

Register

Scheduling area

Check to make sure that the account shown in the Account pop-up menu is the one to which you want the paycheck deposited. In the Date field, enter the paycheck date from the pay stub. You can type in the date, or you can click the calendar icon to get a pop-up calendar. Click a day in the pop-up calendar to enter it in the Date field.

In the Number field, type d. Quicken will fill the field in with DEP, which means deposit. Press the Tab key to move to the Payee field, then type a description of the paycheck (I used Jim's Paycheck).

Now you'll begin entering the split transaction. Click the Open Split button to show the multiple lines for the split.

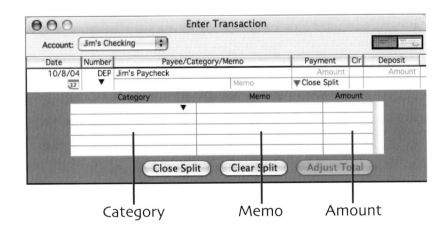

The first line is for your gross pay. In the first Category field, type Salary, then press the Tab key until you are in the Amount column for that line. Enter the amount of your gross pay. Pressing the Tab key brings you to the next line. Note that you don't have to finish typing Salary; Quicken's QuickFill feature finishes the word as soon as you type a few letters. Quicken tries to make data entry easier for you whenever it can; for instance, if you enter a figure without a decimal point, Quicken puts the cents (.00) in for you.

set up your paycheck   **37**

paycheck setup (Mac)

The next several lines are for your paycheck deductions, such as 401(k) contributions and taxes. If you have a retirement account deduction, you need to show that money is going into the retirement account. You'll use a transfer category for this, which is a special category that Quicken uses to denote money flowing between two of its own accounts. Transfer categories always have square brackets [] around their names. Press the left square bracket, then begin typing the name of the retirement account. When Quicken finishes entering the name, press the Tab key until you are in the Amount field. Because this is a deduction, enter it as a negative number, so that it will be subtracted from your gross pay. For example, if the 401(k) contribution is $50, type -50.

Category	Memo	Amount
Salary		1,000.00
[Jim's 401k] ▼		-50.00

Continue entering deductions on each line as negative numbers until you are done. Quicken scrolls the list of line items if needed.

Category	Memo	Amount
Salary		1,000.00
[Jim's 401k]		-50.00
Payroll Taxes, Self:Federal		-113.15
Payroll Taxes, Self:State		-25.52
Payroll Taxes, Self:Soc Sec ▼		-62.00

Some people have payroll deductions that are taken after taxes. For example, if you participate in an Employee Stock Purchase Plan (ESPP), you can purchase your company's stock with every paycheck. As you recall from Chapter 2, a transfer category is used to keep track of money that you move from one Quicken account into another. Use the transfer category Quicken automatically created when you set up the ESPP account to denote the transfer of funds to the ESPP stock account and then enter the deduction as a negative number.

Finally, you'll set up the schedule for this transaction, so Quicken remembers it for you. In the Scheduling section, choose the frequency of the transaction from the pop-up menu, depending on how often you get paid. Click Deposit in the Type section. Under Notification, choose Remind me about or Automatically enter from the pop-up menu, and choose how many days in advance you want to be reminded. Depending on which you choose, Quicken will give you a reminder that the deposit will be made, or will just enter it automatically in the register. If your paycheck is regular and the amount doesn't change from check to check, I recommend that you choose Automatically enter.

Notification pop-up menu

Frequency pop-up menu

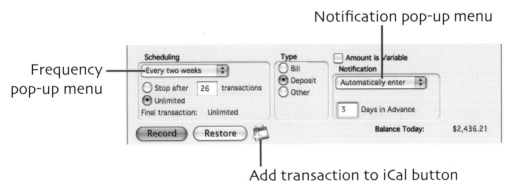

Add transaction to iCal button

If you use Apple's iCal calendar program, you can add a reminder of the transaction to your calendar by clicking the iCal button. When you are done with the transaction, click Record. Quicken asks if you want to record the current transaction and future

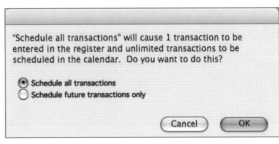

transactions, or if you are just creating a scheduled transaction for future transactions. If you choose Schedule future transactions only, Quicken will think that you are just creating a future scheduled transaction, and will not enter the instance of the paycheck that you hold in your hand. You need to enter the paycheck for which you have the pay stub, so select Schedule all transactions and click OK.

extra bits

paycheck setup (Win) p. 32

- It's possible to enter just your net pay into Quicken, but I don't recommend it. The reason is that there are real benefits to knowing the total amount of deductions from your paycheck, especially at tax time. You (or your accountant) can look at a report of all of the paycheck deductions and get the information you need to complete your tax returns more quickly.

- If your paycheck varies each pay period, you should still set up your paycheck as a scheduled transaction. You'll be able to enter the varying amounts in each split line without having to recreate them each time.

paycheck setup (Mac) p. 36

- The QuickFill feature is very useful to enter categories, but sometimes you need a quick list of all the categories to figure out which category you want to apply to the transaction. The triangle in the Category field of a register brings up a pop-up menu with all of the categories. Click the triangle, then choose from the pop-up menu.

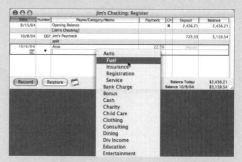

- Subcategories appear in the Category field separated by a colon. For instance, the Fire subcategory of the Insurance category would appear in the Category field as Insurance:Fire. When typing in the Category field, you can enter subcategories by typing the colon, then the first few letters of the subcategory.

set up your paycheck

4. write and print checks

On a day-to-day basis, you'll primarily use Quicken to handle the transactions in your various checking, savings, and credit card accounts. A transaction can be anything that changes the balance of an account. For a checking account, it could be writing a check, making a deposit, or withdrawing cash from the ATM.

Every account in Quicken has an account register in which you enter transactions. Quicken's registers look and act much like paper checkbook registers, which makes them familiar and easy to use. However, a Quicken register does the math for you and keeps a running balance automatically.

In this chapter, you'll learn how to enter transactions in the account registers, write checks, enter deposits, transfer money between Quicken accounts, and print checks from Quicken, rather than writing them by hand.

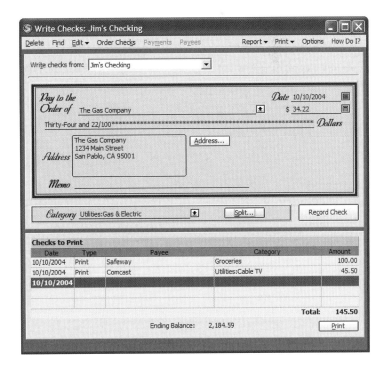

explore registers

Checks, deposits, and funds transfers from one account to another are all transactions that need to be entered in your account register. An account register uses boxes, called fields, to record all the information you need about the transaction, including the date, check number, payee, payment or deposit amount, category, and memo field. There's also a status box to indicate whether the transaction has cleared your bank or been reconciled with a bank statement. There is always a blank transaction at the bottom of the register, with labels to help you remember what information to enter. On Windows, there are also three buttons in the line item: Enter, which saves the transaction; Edit, which is a pop-up menu that offers you a variety of options; and Split, which opens the Split Transaction window (you'll learn more about splitting transactions later in this chapter). Account registers look slightly different, depending on the kind of account you are viewing. For instance, a credit card register uses Charge and Payment instead of Payment and Deposit.

Cleared/reconciled status box   Running balance

10/8/2004	Num	Payee		Payment	Deposit		
		Category	Memo	Exp	Enter	Edit	Split

On the Mac, the register looks much the same, except that there is an Open Split button, and the button you click to save the transaction is called Record and is at the bottom of the register window.

10/7/04	▼	Payee or Description			Payment	Deposit	
12	▼	Category	▼	Memo	▶ Open Split		
Record	Restore				Balance Today:	$2,436.21	
					Balance 10/8/04:	$3,159.54	

enter transactions

To enter a check or deposit, first open the account by clicking it in the Account Bar (Windows). On the Mac, click the Banking tab and choose the account you want from the Registers pop-up menu in the toolbar.

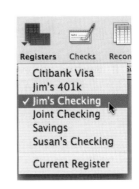

The account register opens with the Date field highlighted and the current date filled in. If you want to change the date, type in a new date or click the calendar icon in the date field to get a pop-up calendar. Click to select a date in the pop-up calendar. You can also use keyboard shortcuts to enter dates. Press the Tab key to get to the Number field.

Press d (for deposit), and Quicken will fill in the field with DEP. You can use other keyboard shortcuts to enter transaction types in the Number field, or you can use the pop-up menu in the Number field.

Tab and enter the payee (for a check) or a description (for a deposit or transfer). Next, tab across to the Payment or Deposit field and enter the transaction amount.

Press Tab to get to the Category field, then assign a category to the transaction by typing it into the field. The QuickFill feature fills in a category name from your list after you enter the first few letters. You can also use the pop-up menu in the Category field to select a category.

Optionally, in the Memo field, enter a memo about the transaction.

Press Enter (Return) to save the transaction and add it to the register.

| 10/9/2004 | 1452 | Safeway | | 83 62 | | 2,352 59 |
| | | Groceries | | | | |

enter transactions (cont.)

date field keyboard shortcuts

shortcut	what it does
+	next day
-	previous day
t	today
m	beginning of the current month
h	end of the current month
y	beginning of the current year
r	end of the current year
[	same date last month
]	same date next month

number field keyboard shortcuts

shortcut	what it does
+	enters the next check number
-	subtracts a check number
a	ATM, an ATM transaction
d	DEP, a deposit
e	EFT, Electronic Funds Transfer
p	PRINT, a check to be printed
s	SEND, an electronic payment to be sent
t	TRANS, a transfer to another Quicken account

write and print checks

split transactions

Many transactions need to be divided among multiple categories. This is called splitting the transaction. For example, let's say that you write a check for both groceries and a prescription at a grocery store that has a pharmacy. You will want the grocery portion of the check recorded in the Groceries category, and the prescription portion recorded in the Medical category (of course, you can also split a deposit).

Let's enter a split transaction now. In the register, enter the date, check number, payee, and the payment or deposit amount. Click the Split button (Open Split button). On Windows, the Split Transaction window appears.

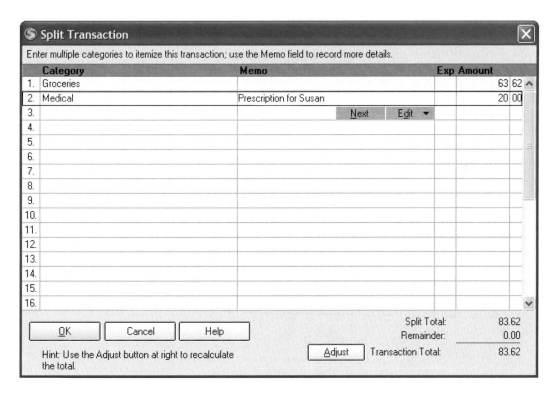

Enter the category in the first Category field in the split, either by typing it in or by choosing it from the pop-up menu.

Press the Tab key and (optionally) type a memo in the first Memo field.

split transactions (cont.)

Type the amount that you want to allocate to the first category in the first Amount field. Quicken subtracts that amount from the total and puts the remainder in the next Amount field. Enter the next category and amount on the next line. Repeat this until you have allocated the entire payment or deposit amount. Click OK to dismiss the Split Transaction window, then click Enter in the register to save the transaction.

On the Mac, clicking the Open Split button opens split lines in the register, rather than in a new window.

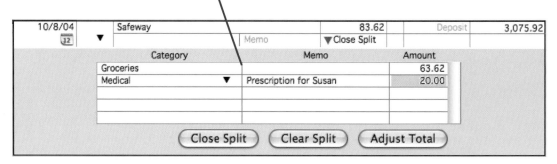

Follow the instructions above to allocate the amounts among the different categories in the split. When you have allocated the entire payment or deposit amount, click the Record button.

edit transactions

Unlike some other financial programs, Quicken allows you to make changes to transactions at any time, if you make a mistake in data entry. You can edit, delete, or void transactions whenever necessary.

To edit a transaction, open the account register that contains the transaction. Click the transaction in the register to select it, then in any field of the transaction select the incorrect information and type over it to replace it. Click Enter (Record) to save the changed transaction.

To delete a transaction, click on the transaction to select it, then choose Edit > Transaction > Delete (Edit > Delete Transaction). Quicken will ask you to confirm the deletion. Click Yes to delete the transaction.

To void a transaction, click anywhere in the transaction to select it, then choose Edit > Transaction > Void Transaction (Edit > Void Transaction). Quicken places the word VOID at the beginning of the Payee field. Click Enter (Record) to save the transaction. Quicken removes the amount in the Payment or Deposit field and recalculates the account balance.

| 10/9/2004 | 🔳 | 1453 | **VOID**Arco | | *Payment* | c | *Deposit* | 2,330 | 09 |
| | | | Auto:Fuel | *Memo* | *Exp* | | Enter | Edit | Split |

schedule transactions

One of the best ways to save time in Quicken is to set up scheduled transactions for recurring transactions that need to be paid on a regular schedule. Scheduled transactions can be entered automatically, saving you the drudgery of data entry. They are especially good for automatic deductions from your checking account, such as monthly service fees; because you don't initiate those kinds of transactions, it's easy to forget to enter them in your register. I also like to use them for bills that are the same from month to month, such as my cable TV bill.

Any transaction in your register can be turned into a scheduled transaction. You'll do the job a little differently on Windows and the Mac, but the idea is the same. On either platform, open the account register and click to select the transaction that you want to schedule.

On Windows, choose Edit > Transaction > Schedule Transaction. The Create Scheduled Transaction dialog appears.

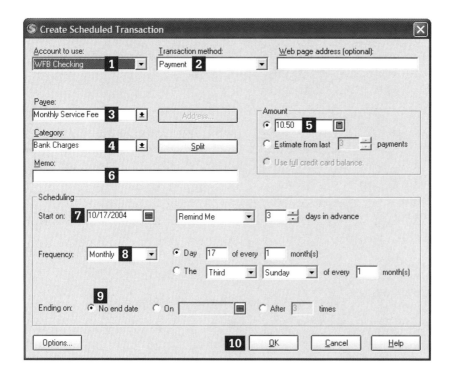

write and print checks

1 Pick the account from the Account to use pop-up menu.

2 The Transaction method can be Payment, Online Payment from Quicken, Printed Check, Deposit, or Transfer. Pick the one you want from the pop-up menu.

3 Type the payee in the Payee field, or choose it from the pop-up menu.

4 Type the category in the Category field, or choose it from the pop-up menu.

5 In the Amount area, if the transaction will be a fixed amount every time, click the first button and enter the amount. If the transaction amount is variable (i.e., it changes from month to month), you can have Quicken estimate an amount, so you

have a rough entry in your register of the amount of the transaction. When you get the bill with the exact amount, you can edit the transaction to put in the actual payment. Click Estimate from last payments and choose how many payments you want Quicken to use for the estimate. If you are making a credit card payment, and want to pay the card balance off, choose Use full credit card balance.

6 If you want, enter a Memo for the scheduled transaction.

7 In the Scheduling area, enter the date you want the scheduled transaction to start in the Start on field, then decide if you want Quicken to give you a reminder of the scheduled transactions that you can enter yourself, or if you want Quicken to enter the transaction automatically in the register. You should also tell Quicken how many days in advance you want to be reminded of the transaction to be entered.

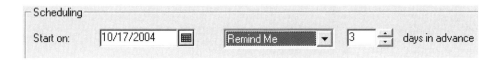

write and print checks 49

schedule transactions

8 Choose the Frequency of the scheduled transaction. This section changes depending on what you choose from the first pop-up menu.

9 In the Ending on section, choose when Quicken will stop adding the scheduled transaction. You can choose No end date, to end on a particular date, or to end after a certain number of times (this last choice is good for loans).

Ending on: ⦿ No end date   ○ On [   ] 🔲   ○ After [3]   times

10 Click OK to save the scheduled transaction.

On the Mac, choose Edit > Schedule Transaction. The Schedule Future Transaction window opens.

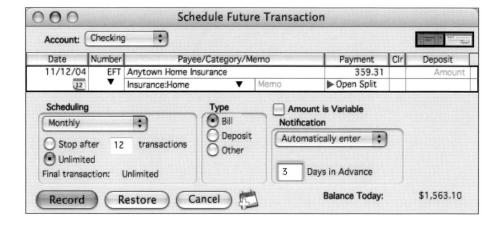

1 Enter the date you want the scheduled transaction to start in the Date field.

2 In the Scheduling area, choose the frequency of the scheduled transaction.

3 In the Type area, click Bill, Deposit, or Other.

4 Under Notification, choose Remind me about or Automatically enter from the pop-up menu, and choose how many days in advance you want to be reminded of the transaction to be entered.

5 If the transaction amount varies by a few cents from one time to the next, click Amount is Variable, and Quicken will show you and confirm the transaction each time before it is recorded in the register. If you check this box, the Notification pop-up menu will become inactive, because you will always be reminded, rather than having the transaction automatically entered.

6 Click Record to save the scheduled transaction.

transfer money

You often need to transfer money between accounts. For example, when you write a check to make a payment to your credit card account, money flows out of the checking account and into the credit card account, decreasing the credit card's balance. Quicken makes it easy to update both accounts with one transaction so you don't have to enter the same transaction in both registers. To accomplish this, Quicken uses a special kind of category called transfer categories, which refer to other Quicken accounts. Quicken creates transfer categories automatically when you create an account. You can view the transfer categories in your data file by choosing Tools > Category List (Lists > Category & Transfers > List) and scrolling to the bottom of the resulting window. The transfer categories are the ones enclosed in the square brackets [ ].

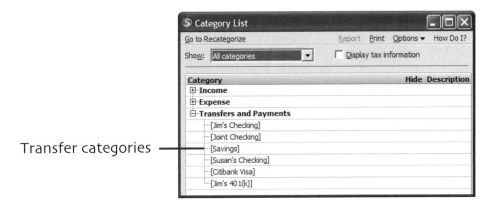

Transfer categories

On Windows, you'll find a Transfer button at the top of every account register.

Transfer button

write and print checks

Click the Transfer button. The Transfer dialog appears.

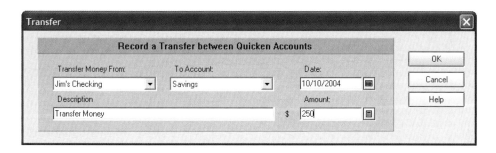

Using the Transfer Money From pop-up menu, choose the source account for the transfer, then choose the destination account for the transfer from the To Account pop-up menu. Quicken fills in the Date and Description fields for you, but you can change them if you like. Finally, enter the Amount of the transfer, then click OK.

On the Mac, choose Activities > Transfer Money > Between Registers. From the resulting dialog, enter the Amount and choose the From and To accounts. Quicken fills in the Date and Payee fields for you, but you can change them if you want. Click Transfer to record the transaction.

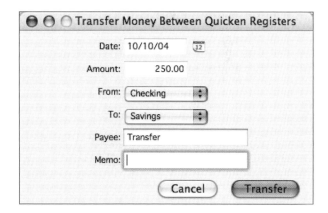

write checks

One minor drawback to using Quicken is that if you handwrite checks in your paper checkbook, you must reenter the check information into Quicken. There are two ways that you can avoid this double work. The most convenient is to use online banking and bill paying (see Chapter 5). You can also enter checks in Quicken, then print them onto preprinted check forms using your inkjet or laser printer. You'll need to order computer checks from your bank or a check printing company.

To set up a check to print, you can enter PRINT in the Number field when entering a check in the account register, or you can use the Write Checks window. On Windows, you'll find the Write Checks button at the top of the account register.

On the Mac, click the Checks button on the toolbar under the Banking tab.

Write Checks button

Checks

write and print checks

The Write Checks window looks like a real paper check, and you fill it out in much the same way. Enter the Date, Payee, and Amount. Quicken then turns the amount you enter into its text form on the next line. If you'll be using windowed envelopes to mail your checks, enter the name and address of the payee in the Address field. Otherwise, don't bother. Add a Memo if you like, then fill in the Category. Click Record Check (Record) to save the transaction and add it to the Checks to Print list (which only appears on Windows). When you're done entering checks, close the Write Checks window.

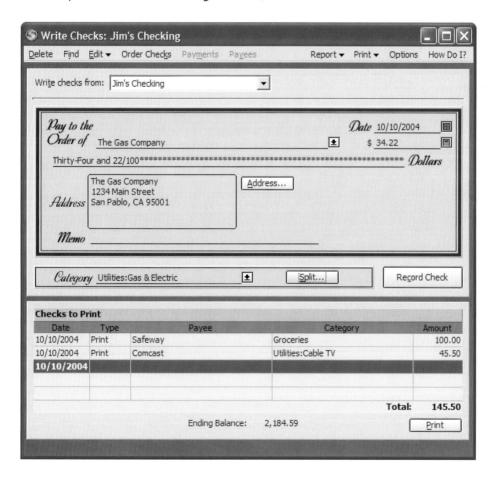

print checks

To print checks, make sure the checks are in your printer tray and positioned correctly for printing. You might want to run a test on some plain paper before you print on real checks for the first time. Verify that the printer is turned on and that it is online.

Choose File > Print Checks. The Select Checks to Print (Print Checks) window appears, telling you how many checks are ready to print.

The starting check number should match the first number of the checks that you put in the printer. If it doesn't match, change it. Click OK (Print) to print your checks.

After the checks have been printed, Quicken will ask you whether all the checks printed correctly. If they did, click OK. If not, type the number of the first check which printed incorrectly, click OK and you will reprint checks from that number.

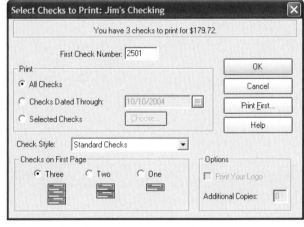

Select Checks to Print window (Windows)

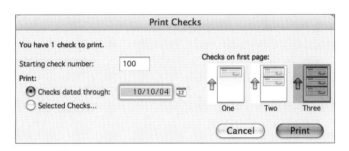

Print Checks window (Mac)

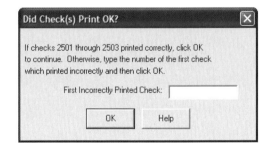

extra bits

enter transactions p. 43

- If you need to write a postdated check, simply enter a future date in the Date field. At the bottom of the register, Quicken will display the Balance Today and a future balance showing the balance as of the date of the post-dated check.

- To quickly enter a date in the current month, type the day in the Date field and press the Tab key. Quicken automatically enters the current month and year.

- In any field in which QuickFill works, you can use the up-and-down arrow keys to scroll alphabetically through the possible matches. For example, if you type Hom in the Description field, QuickFill might guess Home Depot. Pressing the down arrow key would tell QuickFill to try the next possibility in the QuickFill list, Home Savings. Pressing the up arrow key scrolls up alphabetically through the list.

- Most of the time you'll want to keep your account registers sorted by date, but sometimes (like when you're trying to track down a particular check) you'll want to sort by the check number. Click the Date column header to sort by date; click the Number column header to sort by number. On Windows, you can also click the other column headers to sort by those fields.

- Sometimes it's useful to do a quick calculation while entering a transaction. For example, you might need to add up several checks when making a deposit. Quicken's QuickMath feature gives you a calculator right in the account register. QuickMath works a bit differently on Windows and the Mac.

On Windows, most fields where you can enter numbers have a small calculator icon. Click the icon to pop up a calculator, then type numbers and click the arithmetic operator buttons to complete the calculation. The calculation's result appears in the number field when you're done.

You can also access the calculator by pressing any of the arithmetic operator keys (+, -, *, /, or =).

continues on next page

extra bits

On the Mac, in any field where you can enter an amount, press any of the arithmetic operator keys (+, -, *, /, or =) to pop up a "paper tape." Enter the numbers you wish to calculate, and press an operator key between each number. When you have entered all your numbers, click the Total button at the bottom of the paper tape or press Enter. Quicken places the calculation's result in the number field.

Bank Charge				
Jim's Paycheck			+	12.25
split			+	14.65
Checks from eBay Auctions		Payment	+	119.85
Category ▼	Memo	▶ Open Split		62.50
				total

split transactions p. 45

- If you decide that you don't want to split the transaction after all, on Windows, click the Cancel button in the Split Transaction window. On the Mac, click the Clear Split button, which deletes all the information in the split lines.

- You can add as many lines of categories as you need to a split transaction.

write and print checks

schedule transactions p. 48

- On both Windows and Mac, you can view your scheduled transactions in a list. On Windows, choose Tools > Scheduled Transactions List. On the Mac, choose Lists > Scheduled Transactions.

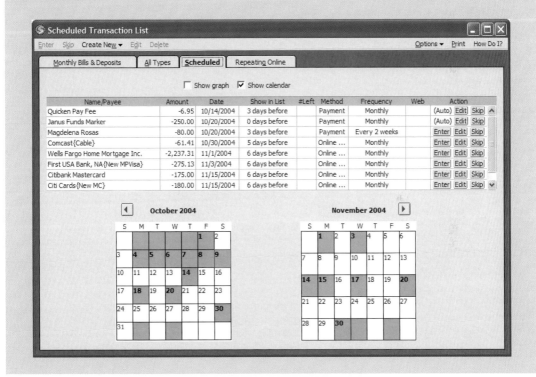

extra bits

write checks p. 54

- When you're away from home, you can write checks from the checkbook that your bank provided when you opened your account, or you can use your preprinted computer checks and fill them out by hand. I prefer to use my regular bank checkbook and enter the information into Quicken when I return home. I differentiate between the checks that Quicken prints and ones I handwrite by using two widely different sets of check numbers for each kind of check. For example, I started my computer checks at 1000 and my hand written checks start in the 4000 range. Quicken has no problem dealing with different sets of check numbers.

print checks p. 56

- You can buy preprinted computer checks from Intuit, but they're more expensive than other sources such as ASAP Checks (www.asapchecks.com) and Checks for Less (www.checksforless.com).

5. bank and pay bills online

The major portion of dealing with your finances is keeping your checkbook up to date and paying your bills. These tasks are probably not your idea of fun; they certainly aren't mine. So I'm ready to sign up for anything that makes these chores easier. Online banking and bill payment through Quicken doesn't make the job fun—heck, it's not a miracle cure—but it will make dealing with the bulk of your finances easier. You can save a lot of time and a bit of money.

Banking online saves you time because you don't need to record your checks, ATM withdrawals, or credit card transactions by hand. Instead, you download them from your bank, review the transactions to catch any possible errors and make sure they are properly categorized, then add them to your account registers with the click of a button. You can balance your checkbook in minutes every time you download your statement. Best of all, there's never any waiting in line when you're online.

Online bill payment lets you transfer money from your checking account directly to your creditors. You don't have to write or print checks, stuff envelopes, find stamps, or go to the post office. You simply enter a payment instruction in an account register and have Quicken send it over the Internet to your bank, which then transfers the money to your payees.

In this chapter, you'll learn how to enable your accounts for online banking and bill payment, download and compare transactions to your account registers, and pay bills and transfer money online using Quicken.

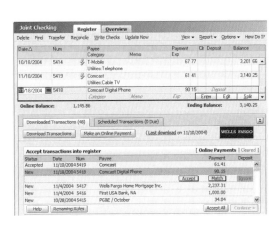

set up online accounts

To use online banking, you must first have access to the Internet, because Quicken uses the Internet to transmit and receive financial information from your bank. You must contact your bank or other financial institution (for example, a credit union or credit card company) to get online access for checking, savings, and credit card accounts. Not all financial institutions support online banking, and some support it only for certain account types, such as checking, but not credit card accounts. If you have accounts at more than one financial institution that you want to enable for online access, you'll need to apply to each one separately.

After you have signed up for online banking, your financial institution will mail you a kit with information to help you set up your Quicken accounts for online banking. For security purposes, this kit will usually be sent by U.S. Postal Service. You'll also receive an initial personal identification number (PIN), which you should change in your first online banking session. After you have received this kit, it's time to online-enable your accounts; that is, you'll set them up for online access.

To enable an existing account for online use on Windows, begin by selecting the account in the Account Bar. Choose Online > Online Account Services Setup. The Online Account Setup dialog appears. Click Edit Existing Quicken Account.

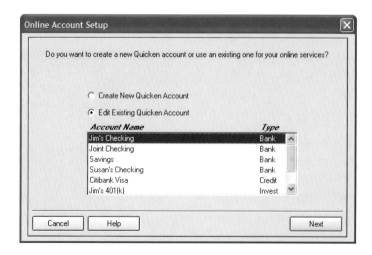

bank and pay bills online

Select the account that you wish to online-enable in the scrolling list, and click Next. The login screen for your financial institution appears (you told Quicken the financial institution for the account when you created the account; see Chapter 2 for more details). Enter the information requested in the login screen, then click

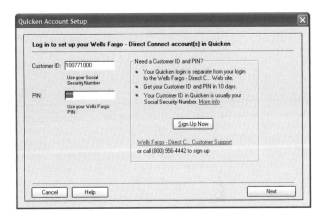

Next. In this example, Wells Fargo Bank uses the Direct Connect method, which requires my Social Security number (as the account name) and the PIN that the bank sent to me. Your financial institution may require different information.

Quicken connects to your financial institution, and confirms that your account name and PIN are correct. Many financial institutions require that you change the PIN at this time, and will display a screen where you put in a new PIN. Enter and confirm the new PIN, and then click Next.

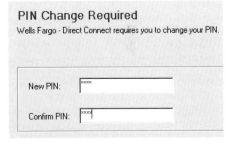

If you have multiple accounts at the financial institution, Quicken will detect them and ask which of the accounts you want to use. Choose the account from the pop-up menu, and then click Next.

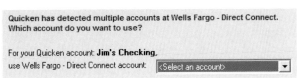

set up online accounts

If there are additional accounts and your financial institution uses Direct Connect, Quicken may ask you to match the financial institution accounts with your Quicken accounts. If you don't want to do that, choose Do not use this account in Quicken from the pop-up menu. Otherwise, choose an account from the pop-up menu next to each account Quicken found, then click Next.

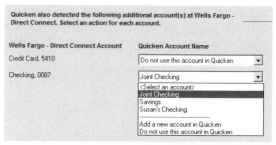

Quicken shows you a summary screen with a list of the accounts that you have online-enabled. Click Done. Quicken automatically connects to your financial institution and downloads all transactions from the last 60–90 days, then displays the Online Update Summary dialog.

See the compare transactions section later in this chapter to learn how to deal with the downloaded transactions.

To online-enable an existing account for the Mac, click the Banking tab on the Toolbar, then choose Lists > Accounts. The Accounts list appears.

Select the account you wish to online-enable, then click Edit. The account's setup dialog appears.

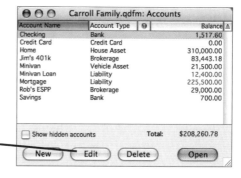

From the Financial institution pop-up menu, choose Select financial institution. Quicken will connect to the Internet and update the list of financial institutions, then will display the Financial Institutions window.

Scroll through the list to find your financial institution, click to select it in the list, then click Use. Quicken will ask for your Customer ID and PIN.

Many financial institutions require that you change the PIN at this time, and will display a screen where you put in a new PIN. Enter and confirm the new PIN, and then click OK.

If you have multiple accounts at the financial institution, Quicken will detect them and display the Review Accounts dialog, asking which of the accounts you want to use.

If you don't want to online-enable an account, uncheck it in the list. For accounts you want to online-enable, choose the Quicken account you want to associate it with using the pop-up menus in the Store in the Quicken Account column. When you're done, click OK.

Quicken connects to your financial institution and downloads the recent (60–90 days, depending on your institution) transactions for the selected accounts. The Download Transactions screen appears; see the compare transactions section later in this chapter to learn how to deal with the downloaded transactions.

use Web Connect

If your financial institution supports the Direct Connect connection method to download transactions, you should always use that, as it is more convenient than Web Connect. But some institutions only support Web Connect, which uses a Web browser to connect to the financial institution's Web site, where you can then download a file containing your transactions. You then import the downloaded file into Quicken. On Windows, Quicken uses an embedded version of Internet Explorer to connect to the financial institution's Web site. On the Mac, you can use Safari or Internet Explorer. To use Web Connect for the first time, you will need to obtain a welcome kit from your financial institution, which will include a user ID and PIN.

To download transactions using Web Connect on Windows, click to select the account in the Account Bar, then click the Download Transactions button on the account register.

A new browser window will open to the login page of your financial institution's Web site. Enter your account name and password, and log in.

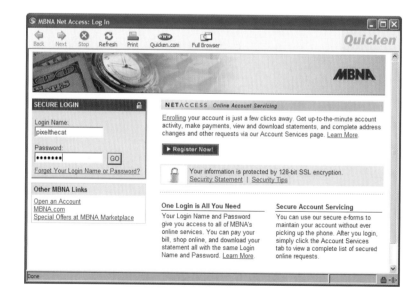

Use the Web site to navigate to where you can download your account statement. Each financial institution's Web site differs, and they may call the option "Download statement," "Download account activity," or something similar. Follow the on-screen instructions to download the file.

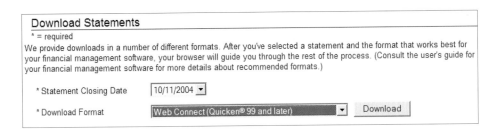

Quicken automatically imports the file, and the Online Update Summary window appears. Click the Go to Register button for the account you just downloaded.

The register appears, with the downloaded transactions in the bottom pane of the register. See the compare transactions section later in this chapter to learn how to deal with the downloaded transactions.

On the Mac, use your Web browser to log in to your financial institution's Web site. Navigate to where you can download your account statement, then follow the on-screen instructions to download the file. After the file has downloaded, Quicken will automatically launch and import the file (if you are using Safari or Internet Explorer). When Quicken is done with the downloaded transactions, the Online Transmission Summary appears. Click OK, and Quicken displays the Download Transactions window. See the compare transactions section to learn how to deal with the downloaded transactions.

compare transactions

After downloading banking transactions, Quicken compares those transactions to ones already in your account registers. Some downloaded transactions will match items that exist in the register, and Quicken labels these as Matched. Other transactions that aren't already in the register will be labeled as New. In either case, you may need to properly categorize the transaction, and then you accept the transaction into Quicken. Quicken will then mark all of the accepted transactions as cleared in your account register.

To compare, match, and accept downloaded transactions on Windows, begin by looking for the flagged accounts in the Account Bar. The flag signifies that you have downloaded transactions that need to be dealt with (a flag can also denote an account with scheduled transactions that are due).

Flags —————

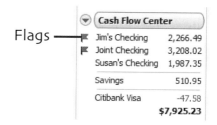

Click one of the flagged accounts in the Account Bar. The Transactions tab of the account will appear, split in two. The top pane is the account register, and the bottom pane contains the downloaded transactions.

Account register ———

Downloaded ——— transactions

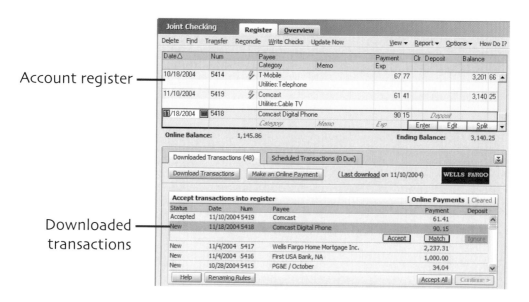

In the Accept transactions into register section, transactions that already exist in your account register will be labeled as Match in the Status column. Transactions not in your register will be labeled New.

Status column

Transaction date   Payee   Charge or Payment

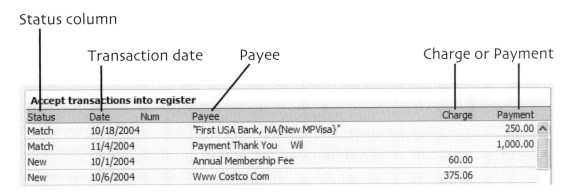

Click the first downloaded transaction. Two buttons, labeled Accept and Edit, will appear below the transaction.

Status	Date	Num	Payee	Charge	Payment
Match	10/18/2004		"First USA Bank, NA{New MPVisa}"		250.00
				Accept	Edit ▾

compare transactions

If it is a matched transaction, Quicken will highlight the transaction in the register in the top half of the window. Click Accept. The status for the transaction will change to Accepted.

If the transaction is labeled New, you may have to enter the payee or category of the transaction (Quicken will remember this category for subsequent similar transactions). Click to select the new transaction, and it will appear in the account register.

New transaction in register

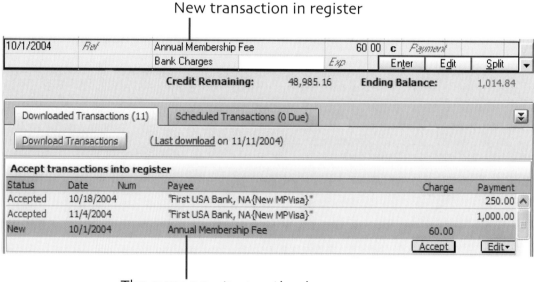

The same new transaction in
the downloaded transaction list

If necessary, categorize the transaction in the account register, then click Enter in the account register. The downloaded transaction will change to Accepted. Repeat matching and accepting transactions until all of them have been accepted, then click Done at the bottom of the Accept transactions into register section.

On the Mac, after you have completed downloading transactions, the Download Transactions window appears. Because you could have download-ed transactions from multiple financial institutions, choose the one that you want from the Financial Institution pop-up menu. You may also have multi-ple accounts at the same financial institution, so choose the account that you want from the Account pop-up menu.

Account pop-up menu   Financial Institution pop-up menu

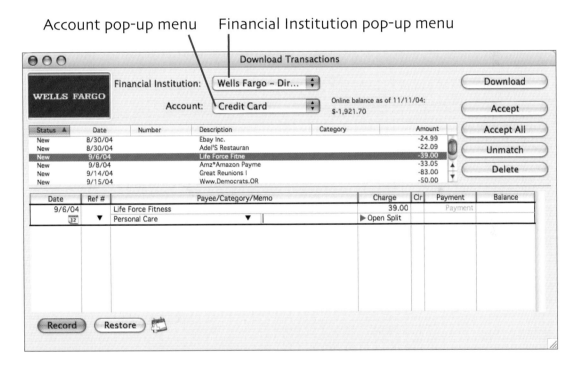

Quicken displays the downloaded transactions for the selected financial institution and account in the top half of the Download Transactions win-dow. Quicken compares the downloaded transactions with transactions that are already in your account register. If the transactions correspond, the word Matched appears in the Status column, otherwise the word New appears. You will first convert all of the New transactions to Matched transactions, then you can accept them into your account register.

compare transactions

Click to select the top New downloaded transaction. It will appear in the register in the bottom half of the window. If necessary, enter the payee or category of the transaction, then click the Record button at the bottom of the window. The transaction will change to Matched. Repeat this process for all of the New transactions.

New transaction in downloaded transaction list

New	9/15/04	Www.Democrats.OR	-50.00
New	9/18/04	Merch Interest	-21.94
New	9/17/04	Applebee'S Hop39	-51.53

Date	Ref #	Payee/Category/Memo		Charge	Clr	Pay
8/7/04		Adel'S Restaurant		36.18		
		Dining				
9/6/04		Life Force Fitness		39.00	C	
		Personal Care				
9/15/04		Www.Democrats.org		50.00		
12 ▼		Political Contribution ▼	Memo	▶ Open Split		

New transaction in register after category added

After you have matched all the transactions, select each transaction and click the Accept button, or click Accept All. Quicken removes the accepted items from the transaction list in the Download Transactions window. Close the Download Transactions window by clicking its close box.

organize your pins (Win)

All of the online financial accounts that you use will require a PIN in order to access them. It's not a good idea to use the same PIN for all of your accounts, because you don't want a situation where someone learns the PIN for one of your accounts, and then has access to all of them. But it can be difficult to remember different PINs for many accounts. Quicken's PIN Vault consolidates all of the PINs for the online accounts you access through Quicken, allowing you to unlock all of the accounts by entering just one password.

To set up your PIN Vault on Windows, choose Online > PIN Vault > Set Up. The PIN Vault Setup dialog appears, set to the Welcome tab, which explains what the PIN Vault does. Click the Summary tab.

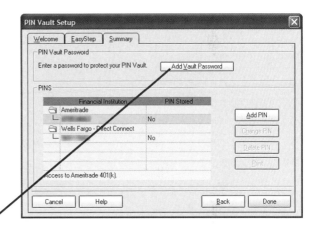

The first thing you need to do is to add the password that you will use to unlock the PIN Vault. Click Add Vault Password. In the resulting dialog, enter the password, then enter it again, and then click Add.

Next, you'll add the PINs for each account to the Vault. You'll only have to do this once. Click to select the account number of the first account, then click Add PIN. In the resulting dialog, enter the PIN twice, then click Add. Under the PIN Stored column of the PIN Vault Setup dialog, the status will change to Yes.

Continue adding PINs for each of the remaining accounts, then click Done.

organize your pins (Mac)

To set up your PIN Vault on the Mac, choose Online > PIN Vault. The Online Account Updates window appears, set to the PIN Vault tab. Click Create PIN Vault.

In the resulting dialog, enter the password you want to use, then enter it again, and then click OK.

To add the PINs for your accounts, click on the first account, and click Edit. The Enter PIN dialog appears. Enter the PIN as requested, then click OK.

Continue adding PINs for each of your remaining accounts, then close the Online Account Updates window by clicking its close box.

use one step update

Quicken allows you to have many different online-enabled accounts, at different financial institutions. For example, you could have different checking accounts at different banks, plus one or more online brokerage accounts from which you can download your investment transactions. It wouldn't be convenient for you to have to check each one of these accounts separately, so Quicken's One Step Update feature allows you check all of your online accounts at once. Almost anything that you want to do online in Quicken, you can do with One Step Update, including download transactions from your banking, credit card, and investment accounts; update investment prices; pay bills; and upload financial information to Quicken.com so that you can view it wherever you are.

One Step Update uses the PIN Vault to store the different PINs for each account. The PIN Vault feeds your personal identification numbers to One Step Update as needed.

If your financial institution uses the Web Connect method to download transactions, you can't include that institution in your One Step Update. Instead, you must download transactions through the financial institution's Web site.

To start up a One Step Update on Windows, click the Update button on the Toolbar, or choose Online > One Step Update.

Update

The One Step Update dialog appears. Click to select which items you want to include in the update, then click Update Now.

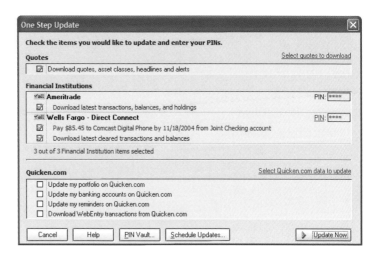

use one step update (cont.)

Quicken will connect to your financial institutions, and will keep you apprised of its progress with the One Step Update Status dialog.

After the download is complete, the Online Update Summary window appears. If there are transactions that need to be reviewed, you can click the Go to Register button to go directly to that account's register. Otherwise, click Continue to close the window.

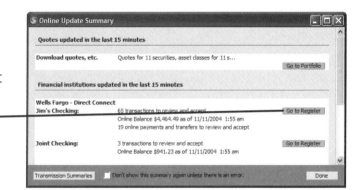

To start up a One Step Update on the Mac, click the One Step button on the Toolbar, or choose Online > One Step Update.

One Step

In the Online Account Updates window, choose the items that you wish to update, then click Update Now.

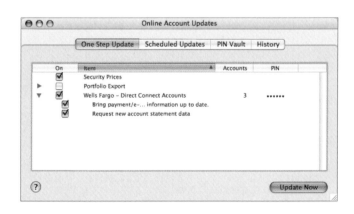

Quicken will connect to your financial institution. After the download is complete, the Online Transmission Summary Window will appear. Click OK. If transactions were downloaded from your financial institutions, the Download Transaction window will appear, allowing you to review and accept the transactions.

bank and pay bills online

create online payees

Making online payments with Quicken makes paying your bills extremely quick and convenient. You'll begin by setting up the payment recipients in the Online Payees list.

To create an online payee, choose Online > Online Payees List (Online > Payments > Online Payees). The Online Payees List opens. Click New.

Online Payees List for Windows

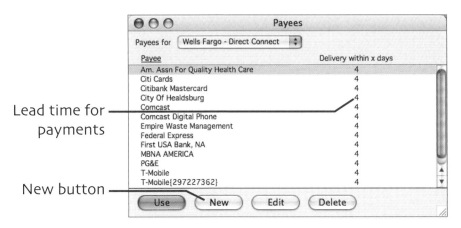

Online Payees List for Mac

create online payees

The Set Up Online Payee dialog appears. Enter the name of the online payee, the billing address, your account number with the payee, and the contact number of the payee. You can usually find all of this information on your billing statement. When you're done entering the information, click OK. A confirmation dialog will appear allowing you to check your work. Check it carefully, as you want to make sure that any payments you make are correctly credited to your account. Click Accept.

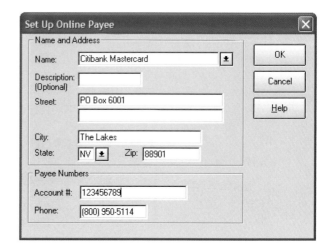

pay bills online

Paying bills online is a lot like entering any other payment in your checking account register, except that you don't have to actually write a paper check. Just enter the payment in Quicken and send it off.

Begin by opening the account register that you want to use to make the payment. Click in the blank transaction at the bottom of the register. Enter the date that you want the online payment to occur. This date can't be today's date; because it takes a few days to process the online payment, you must pick a future date. Different payees take different amounts of time to be paid, and your bank knows how long it takes for most payees. If you want to know how many days it takes for a payment to post, open the Online Payees List, and look at the Lead Time column. Press Tab.

In the Num field of the register, type S, which will bring up the pop-up menu set to Send Online Payment (on the Mac, it's just Send). Press the Tab key to get to the Payee field.

In the Payee field, begin typing the name of one of your online payees. Quicken's QuickFill feature will complete the name after a few letters. If you type a name that is not in the Online Payees List, it will walk you through the process of adding a new online payee. Enter the payment amount, category, and (optionally) a memo, then click Enter (Record). Repeat as needed to enter more payments.

| 11/18/2004 | Send | Comcast Digital Phone | 85 45 | | 5,692 54 |
| | | Utilities:Telephone | | | |

To send your payments, do a One Step Update.

transfer money online

If you have more than one online-enabled account at a particular financial institution, and if that institution allows you to transfer money online between those accounts, you can transfer the funds electronically through Quicken.

On Windows, click the Online Center button in the Toolbar or choose Online > Online Center..

Online

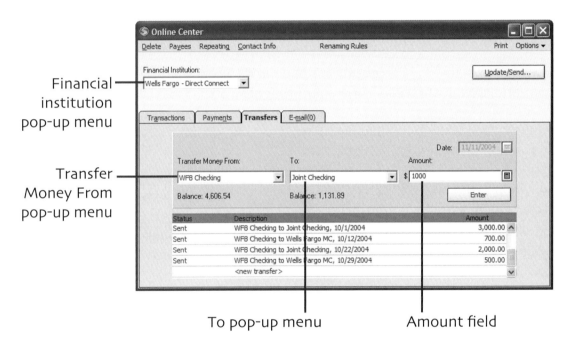

Financial institution pop-up menu

Transfer Money From pop-up menu

To pop-up menu

Amount field

Choose the financial institution you want from the Financial Institution pop-up menu. Choose the source of the funds from the Transfer Money From pop-up menu, and the destination of the funds from the To pop-up menu. Quicken shows you the balance of each account underneath the source and destination. Enter the transfer amount in the Amount field, then click the Enter button. To send the payment, click the Update/Send button.

The Online Center window appears. Click the Transfers tab.

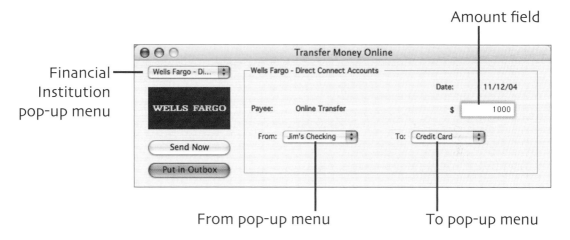

Amount field

Financial
Institution
pop-up menu

From pop-up menu

To pop-up menu

On the Mac, choose Online > Transfer Money Online.

In the resulting dialog, choose the financial institution you want from the Financial Institution pop-up menu. Enter the transfer amount in the Amount field. Choose the source of the funds from the From pop-up menu, and the destination of the funds from the To pop-up menu. To send the payment, click the Send Now button.

extra bits

set up online accounts p. 62

- Even if your financial institution doesn't support online banking, you can still use online bill payment through Intuit, which allows you to pay anyone, regardless of whether they can accept online payments (if necessary, Intuit writes and mails a paper check for you).

- Each financial institution sets its own fees for online banking, and the amount varies from bank to bank, so it's a good idea to shop around for the best deal.

- There are approximately 2,000 financial institutions that support online access for Quicken for Windows, and about 1,300 that support online access for Quicken for Mac. You can get an up-to-date list of the financial institutions by choosing Online > Participating Financial Institutions on Windows or by choosing Online > Financial Institutions on the Mac, then clicking the Update List button.

- Depending on your financial institution, you'll connect and download transactions in one of two fashions. The first, Direct Connect, is the easiest and best way to connect. It allows Quicken to connect directly with your bank's computers to download transactions, exchange payment instructions, transfer funds between accounts, and exchange e-mail about your accounts. Financial institutions that don't support Direct Connect instead offer Web Connect, which uses the bank's Web site in conjunction with your Web browser to do some of the work of displaying and downloading your financial information. Financial institutions that use Web Connect require you to go to the bank's Web site and log in before you can download your account transactions. Web Connect downloads a file with the transactions to your computer; Quicken then reads the file and imports the transactions.

- Worried about the security of online banking? Don't be. Besides the security provided by your PINs, Quicken encrypts all of the information that is transferred back and forth. Encryption is a technique that scrambles data before it is sent using a mathematical algorithm. At the other end, your bank unscrambles the data. Quicken uses 128-bit DES (Data Encryption Standard) encryption along with SSL (Secure Sockets Layer) transfer protocols. This makes online banking through Quicken even more secure than, for example, purchasing goods and services from online merchants.

compare transactions p. 68

- Your financial institution may label ATM transactions and service charges as EFT, which stands for Electronic Funds Transfer.

- If you turn on Auto-Reconcile, Quicken will automatically begin the reconciliation process after you complete comparing transactions. See the Quicken User Guide for information about turning on Auto-Reconcile.

organize your pins p. 73

- Make the password that you use to lock up the PIN Vault different from any of the PINs that are stored in the Vault. That way if the password for the Vault is compromised, you

haven't given away the keys for any of the individual accounts.

- When you pick a PIN, don't use easy to figure out numbers such as the numeric portion of your street address, or your birthday, or the last four digits of your telephone number. The whole point of a PIN is security. Instead, use combinations of numbers that you don't have trouble remembering but that other people wouldn't know or couldn't easily find out, like the number of your college dorm room.

- Once your PINs are in the PIN Vault, you cannot view them within Quicken, because they appear as asterisks in the program. But on Quicken for Windows, you can print a listing of them, revealing each PIN. Choose Online > PIN Vault > Edit. You'll be asked for your PIN Vault password. Enter the password, then in the PIN Vault dialog, click the Print button.

extra bits

pay bills online p. 79

- If your payee is set up to receive electronic funds transfers, payment is transferred directly from your account to your payee's account. This takes between two and four business days. If the payee doesn't accept EFTs, your financial institution prints a paper check and sends it to the payee by U.S. mail. It's important that you allow sufficient time for the payment to get to the payee to avoid a late charge, so make sure that you schedule payments at least three or four days before a payment due date.

- Don't forget that a payee will often need a day or two after receiving a check to process the payment and credit your account.

transfer money online p. 80

- Money transferred between online accounts will usually be transferred between those accounts on the next business day.

- Transfers and credit card accounts are dealt with as payments, and transfers from credit card accounts to checking or savings accounts are usually considered to be cash advances. You should check with your bank for their detailed policy on such transfers, since fees may apply.

6. balance your accounts

Balancing your checkbook by hand is a pain, especially if you have slacked off for a few months and need to catch up. It's even worse if you've never been in the habit of balancing your checkbook. I know this, because I used to be one of those people. For me, one of the biggest benefits of using Quicken to balance my checkbook was that a chore that often took an hour to do by hand became easy to do in just a few minutes. If you use online banking and turn on Quicken's Auto-Reconcile feature, it can even do the account balancing for you.

Quicken isn't limited to just reconciling your checkbook, however. You can also balance your savings and credit card accounts. In this chapter, you'll learn how to reconcile accounts and resolve any differences between the bank's records and your own.

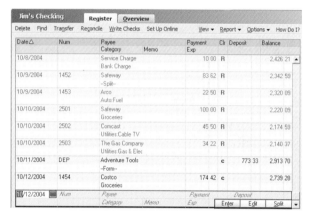

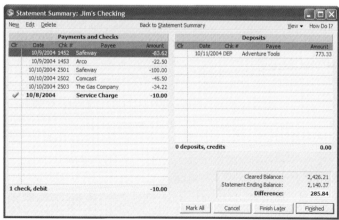

85

balance accounts

You'll use the same procedure to balance a checking, savings, money market, or credit card account. You'll need your bank or credit card statement. First, you enter your statement closing balance, and then you match transactions on your statement with transactions in your Quicken account register.

Before you begin, you should make sure that you have entered into Quicken all transactions that occurred between the date of your last statement and the date of your current statement. If you need to reconcile for more than one month, you first need to reconcile your account with the bank statements for each of the prior months before you try to reconcile the current month's statement.

To get started, open the register for the account you want to balance, then choose Cash Flow > Reconcile (Activities > Reconcile). The Statement Summary (on the Mac it's called Reconcile Startup) dialog appears. The Opening Balance field will be filled in (with the ending balance from the last time that you reconciled; if you have never reconciled before, you may have to go back and reconcile a prior month).

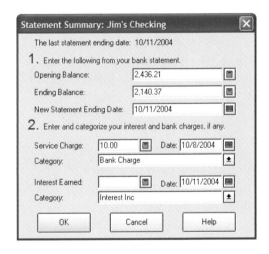

In the Ending Balance field, enter the ending balance from your bank statement, and enter your statement closing date in the New Statement Ending Date field. If the account has a service charge associated with it, enter it in the Service Charge field, and enter the date the charge was applied to your account (often it's the same date as the statement closing date). If necessary, choose the Category for the service charge. If the account earns interest, enter the amount, date, and category of the interest payment. Click OK. The Reconcile dialog opens.

Any service charges or interest payments will show up in the Payments and Checks section already cleared. Compare your bank statement with the transactions shown, and click on each transaction that matches. As you clear each transaction, a check mark appears next to it in the Clr column.

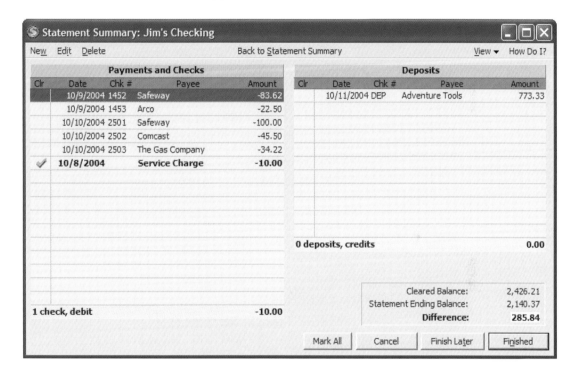

If you need to change a transaction (perhaps because you originally entered it incorrectly in the register), double-click the transaction in the Reconcile dialog to open the account register and edit it. To add a missing transaction, click the New (New Transaction) button in the Reconcile dialog to open the account register and make the addition.

balance accounts (cont.)

As you check off each transaction, Quicken updates the Difference figure in the lower-right corner of the dialog. Once you check off all the transactions, that figure should be zero. If it is, click the Finished (Finish) button.

Cleared Balance:	2,140.37
Statement Ending Balance:	2,140.37
Difference:	**0.00**

If the Difference amount is not zero after checking off all transactions, skip to correct differences on the next page to find out how to correct the problem.

If you balance successfully, the Reconciliation Complete dialog appears. On Windows, if you want to create a reconciliation report (you usually will not), click Yes. Otherwise, click No. In the account register, the transactions you checked off will be marked with an R in the Clr column.

correct differences

In the Reconcile dialog, if the Difference amount is not zero, it means that your account is not balancing for the current statement period. This usually occurs for one of two reasons: either a wrong number of payment or deposit items have been checked or some of the checked items have incorrect dollar amounts.

First you have to find the mistake. Begin by counting the number of credit items on your bank statement, and then count the number of deposits shown in the Reconcile dialog. If the number doesn't match, you've found the problem. Either add the deposit you forgot to enter into Quicken using the New (New Transaction) button, or uncheck a deposit that you marked in error.

If the problem isn't with credits, it is with the checks and payments. Compare the number of checks and payments on your bank statement against the number of debit items in the Reconcile dialog. It's possible that you may not have recorded an item in the register, or you might have duplicated a transaction, entered a payment as a deposit or a deposit as a payment, or marked an item cleared by mistake. You may have also missed adding bank service charges to your register that you'll find on your statement.

If the number of items is correct but the statement still doesn't balance, you have a problem with the dollar amount of one or more of your items. By hand or using a calculator, add up all the transactions shown under Payments and Checks, and compare the total with the total of debits on the statement. If the numbers don't match, you have a problem with the dollar amount of one or more of the debits. Compare each transaction on the statement with the corresponding entry under Payments and Checks until you find the culprit. If the debits are okay, check the dollar amounts of all the Deposits.

correct differences (cont.)

If the dollar amount of an unreconciled balance is small, you may decide that it's not worth the time it takes to track down the mistake. In that case, you can let Quicken enter a register adjustment, which will force your account to reconcile. If you click the Finished button in the Reconcile dialog while there is still a difference, Quicken will pop up the Adjust Balance dialog.

If you want Quicken to enter an account adjustment, click the Adjust button. If you want to take another whack at finding the mistake, click the Cancel button.

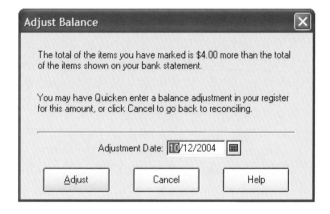

extra bits

balance accounts p. 86

- If you use online banking, Quicken's Auto-Reconcile can balance your accounts automatically, every time that you download transactions from your financial institutions. This saves you even more time. To turn on Auto-Reconcile on Windows on an account that has already been activated for online banking (see Chapter 5), choose Cash Flow > Reconcile. The Reconcile Online Account dialog opens. Make sure that Online Balance is selected, then check Auto reconcile after compare to register, then click OK. On the Mac, choose Quicken 2005 > Preferences, then click the Auto-Reconcile category. Check Enable Auto-Reconcile, then click OK.

correct differences p. 89

- The most common mistake you'll find in your registers is transposing two digits in data entry.
- If you're off by a small amount that is a round number, it's likely that you missed a bank service charge. Check your statement carefully for charges you don't normally see, such as those for check printing or using another bank's ATM.
- Using online banking makes balancing your checkbook and other accounts even easier, because you download your bank and credit card statement directly into Quicken's account registers. This eliminates most data entry errors.

7. manage your credit cards and mortgage

The most common forms of debt that people have are credit cards and the mortgage on their home. Naturally, Quicken can track both of these. Of the two, keeping on top of credit card debt is a key concern for many families. As purchases and interest charges mount, it's all too easy to get to the point where credit card debt becomes overwhelming.

One way to make sure that your credit card debt doesn't spin out of control is to track it carefully on a monthly basis. That means categorizing your card charges so that you know where you're spending your money and reconciling your credit card accounts to make sure that spending doesn't slip by unnoticed. In Chapter 8, you'll see how you can use Quicken's reports and graphs to get an even better view of your credit card spending.

For your home mortgage, you'll want to set up two accounts in Quicken: one showing the asset (your home's value) and the other tracking the liability (the mortgage on your home).

In this chapter, you'll learn how to use Quicken to manage your short-term debt such as credit cards, as well as keep track of your long-term debt, such as your mortgage.

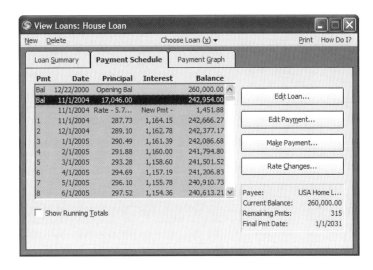

enter card charges

The best way to handle your credit cards in Quicken is to create a different account for each credit card. You'll enter each transaction into the account register, and you'll be able to see the current balance and reconcile the account with your credit card statement.

First, you'll need to create a credit card account for each of the credit cards that you want to track. See Chapter 2 if you need help creating the accounts.

Once you have your credit card accounts set up, you can enter transactions from your paper statement. Display the credit card account register by clicking the account in the Account Bar (Windows) or by choosing Lists > Registers > [Credit card account name] (Mac).

Enter the date, then press the Tab key to get to the Payee field (the Ref # field is usually not used; you might see something in it if you download your credit card statement). Enter the payee. Next, enter the charge amount.

Assign a category to the transaction by typing it into the Category field. Optionally, enter a memo about the transaction. Click Enter (Record).

make card payments

You usually don't need to enter payments to the credit card in the credit card register. When you make a payment to the credit card from your checking account, you will use a transfer category in the checking account register to show that money has flowed from the checking account to the credit card account, thereby decreasing the balance of the credit card account. Quicken automatically makes a corresponding entry in the credit card account. If you need more information about transfer categories, see transfer money in Chapter 4.

This $200 payment in the checking account register uses a transfer category for the destination of the transfer (the credit card account), which you can recognize because it is surrounded by square brackets ([]).

Payment amount

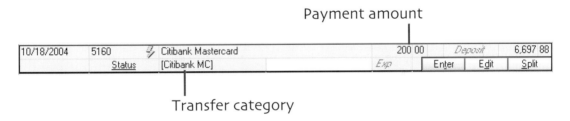

Transfer category

The automatic entry made in the credit card account shows the payment. The category field in the credit card account shows the transfer category for the account the payment came from, in this case the checking account.

Payment amount

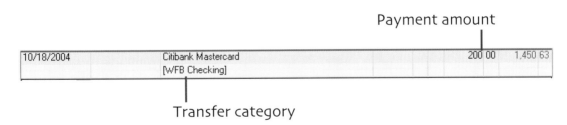

Transfer category

mortgage setup (Win)

When you set up a loan for money you are borrowing, such as the money you've borrowed for your home mortgage, Quicken sets up two accounts. The asset account tracks the value of your home. The liability account tracks the balance and payments of the mortgage. As you make loan payments, Quicken keeps track of the balance of the loan's principal, and of how much you have paid in interest. This last number is especially important, because interest on home loans is tax-deductible.

Quicken for Windows uses an assistant to help you set up your loan and asset accounts. Begin by choosing Property & Debt > Property & Debt Accounts > Add Account. The Quicken Account Setup Assistant appears, with a choice of different loan types. Click House (with or without Mortgage), then click Next.

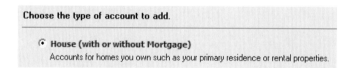

Give the account a name. This is the asset account, so you can use the choice that Quicken gives you (House), or you can use another descriptive name. Click Next. On the next screen, enter the date you bought the property, the purchase price you paid, and the current estimated value. You don't have to enter exact numbers here; you can change them later if needed. Click Next.

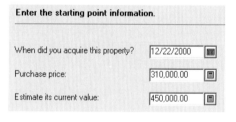

If there is a mortgage on the property, click Yes to create a liability account, then click Next.

The Edit Loan window appears, with the Opening Date already filled in (it is the same as the date you bought the property). Fill in the Opening Balance, the Original Length of the loan (typically 30 years for a home loan), the Compounding Period (that is how often interest is calculated; ask your lender if you're not sure), and how often you make payments. Click Next.

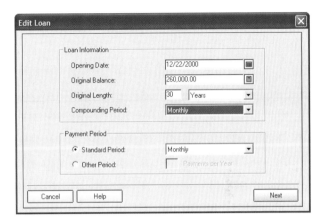

If you have a balloon payment, enter its information. Otherwise, from your latest mortgage statement, enter the loan's Current Balance and the as of date, the Payment Amount (add together both the Principal and Interest), the next payment date where it says due on, and the loan's Interest Rate. Click Done.

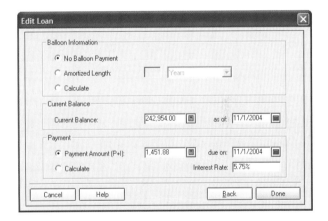

mortgage setup (Win)

The Edit Loan Payment window appears. In the Payment section, the Current Interest Rate and Principal and Interest fields will already be filled in. If you have other amounts in your monthly payment—for example, if you make monthly contributions to an escrow account for property taxes—click the Edit button. A Split Transaction window will appear. Enter as many line items as you need to account for the extra monthly amounts you pay, then click OK. You'll return to the Edit Loan Payment window, and the total of the line items you added in the Split Transaction window appears in the Other amounts in payment field. Quicken calculates the Full Payment amount.

In the Transaction section, choose the payment Type (Payment or Print Check), and enter the Payee. Check that the Next Payment Date and Category for Interest are correct, then click OK.

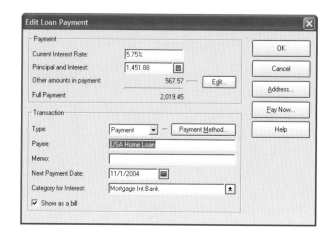

In the Account Bar, you can see that the asset (House) and liability (House Loan) accounts have been created. The asset account shows the current value of your home. The liability account, which is a negative number, shows how much you currently owe on your mortgage, and the total shows your home equity.

mortgage setup (Mac)

To set up your mortgage account, Quicken needs information about the terms of the loan and the lender. Then Quicken creates the loan payment schedule and liability account. As you make loan payments, Quicken keeps track of the balance of the loan's principal, and of how much you have paid in interest.

On the Mac, Quicken steps you through creating a loan with an assistant. Begin by choosing Lists > Loans. The Loans window appears.

Click the New button. The Loan Interview dialog appears.

Select the radio buttons in the Loan Interview dialog that are appropriate for the loan you're creating, then click Continue. A second Loan Interview dialog appears, asking if you want to set up the loan beginning with the first payment or with the next payment due. I suggest that you start with the first payment. You'll need to know your payment amount, the original amount of the loan, the date that you made the first payment, the total number of payments, and the annual interest rate. Click First, and then click Continue.

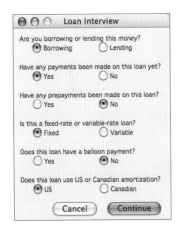

mortgage setup (Mac)

1 In the resulting Set Up Loan dialog, enter the name of your lender.

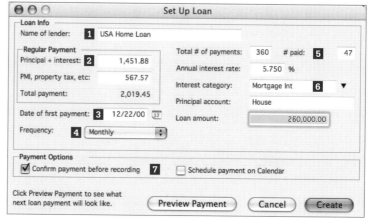

2 Enter the payment amounts. Enter the amount of your regular payment in the Principal + interest field. If you have one or more other amounts in your monthly payment—for example, if you make monthly contributions to an escrow account for property taxes—enter it in the PMI, property tax, etc. field.

3 Enter the date of your first payment.

4 Choose the frequency of the payment from the pop-up menu. Monthly is the default choice; change it if necessary.

5 Enter the Total # of payments. For example, for a 30-year mortgage, you'll have 360 payments. Quicken will calculate the number of payments that you have made since the first payment.

6 Enter the Annual interest rate, the interest expense category, and enter a name for the principal liability account that you'll use to track this loan.

Quicken pops up a dialog confirming that you want to create a new liability account linked to this loan. Click Yes. Enter the beginning loan amount in the Loan amount field.

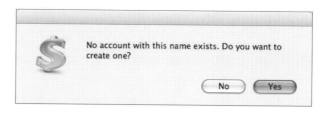

7 If you want to be automatically reminded about your loan payment, check Schedule payment on Calendar in the Payment Options section.

8 To make sure that everything looks good before you finish creating the loan, click the Preview Payment button to open the Preview Payment dialog. If the loan information looks good, click OK to return to the Set Up Loan dialog.

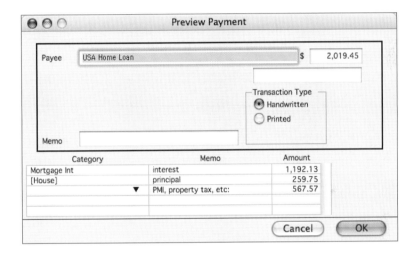

9 Click Create to save the loan information. The loan will appear in the Loans window.

make loan payments

To make a loan payment, you'll use the Loans window in Quicken for either Windows or Mac. The Loans window helps you make payments, and if you want to make an extra payment (such as an extra payment to go towards the loan's principal balance), you can do that, too.

On Windows, choose Property & Debt > Loans. The View Loans window appears.

The loan details are in the Loan Summary tab of the View Loans window. If you have more than one loan, you can switch between them with the Choose Loan menu at the top of the window.

Choose Loan menu

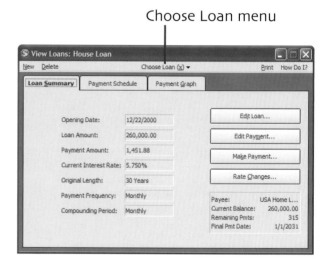

Click the Make Payment button. Quicken asks if this is a regular payment, or an extra payment. Click Regular or Extra.

Depending on which button you clicked, the Make Regular Payment or Make Extra Payment dialog appears. Aside from the name, the dialogs are identical, except that the regular payment amount is already filled in, and you must fill in the amount of an extra payment. Choose the account from which you want to make the payment from the Account to use pop-up menu, review the other information in the window, and click OK to record the payment.

On the Mac, open the account register for the bank account from which you will make the loan payment. Choose Lists > Loans. The Loans window appears.

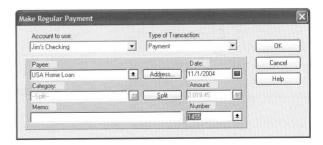

Select the loan for which you want to enter a payment and click the Use button, or simply double-click the loan's name. The Payment dialog appears.

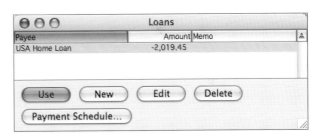

Enter any adjustments needed in the Payment dialog, then click OK. Quicken will enter the loan payment in the account register.

track your mortgage

Quicken automatically calculates the payment schedule for the mortgage, detailing the date, payment number, principal amount, interest amount, and running balance until the end of the loan.

To view the payment schedule on Windows, choose Property & Debt > Loans to open the View Loans window. If you have more than one loan, choose the one you want with the Choose Loan menu at the top of the window. Then click the Payment Schedule tab.

On the Mac, choose Lists > Loans to open the Loans window. Click to select the loan you want to view, and then click the Payment Schedule button. The payment schedule window appears.

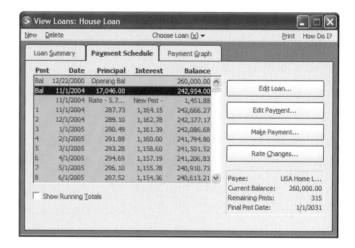

manage your credit cards and mortgage

extra bits

enter card charges p. 94

- You can save yourself virtually all of the data entry associated with a credit card account by enabling online access and downloading your credit card statement over the Internet. In almost all cases, you can download each month's statement from the credit card provider's web site. You can then reconcile the account without needing to refer to paper statements at all, and if you have signed up for online banking, you can send your credit card payments electronically. This is absolutely the best and easiest way to deal with your credit cards; I haven't written a paper check for a credit card payment in years.

- If you have credit cards that you use infrequently, it may not be worth even the minor trouble of setting them up in Quicken. For example, I have an old department store credit card that I rarely use. On those occasions when I do use it, I pay off the card's balance with a check or online payment from my checking account, and categorize that payment in the checking account register with the appropriate category for the purchase.

make card payments p. 95

- If you won't be paying off your credit card balance in full every month, consider adding a scheduled transaction that will remind you to make the card payment before your monthly due date. That will help you avoid those nasty late fees. Set the scheduled transaction up with a variable amount, and tell Quicken to remind you of the transaction, rather than enter it automatically in the register. Then you can edit the transaction to show the amount you will actually pay this month. See Chapter 4 for more information about scheduling transactions.

mortgage setup (Win) p. 96

- You use much the same procedure for setting up other kinds of loans as you do for your mortgage, except that you choose one of the other loan types (Vehicle or Liability) in the first step of the Quicken Account Setup Assistant. You can also set up a loan in the Loans window, which you can reach by choosing Property & Debt > Loans.

extra bits

mortgage setup (Mac) p. 99

- If you checked Schedule payment on Calendar in the Payment Options section of the Set Up Loan dialog, the Financial Calendar opens to allow you to schedule the payment.

make loan payments p. 102

- Loan payments are entered as split transactions. Open the split to see what portion went toward interest and what went to pay down the principal.

track your mortgage p. 104

- You can see the history of a loan by opening the liability account register for the loan.

- You can also get reports of your mortgage activity. See Chapter 8 for more information about reports.

manage your credit cards and mortgage

8. create reports and graphs

Quicken's reports and graphs are some of its most powerful tools, because they distill all your numbers and transactions into information that you can use to get a comprehensive picture of your finances. After using Quicken for just a few months, you'll have a good record of how much you are spending and where your money is going. If you have a bit too much credit card debt, you can easily see how much you are spending on credit card interest, which should give you the impetus to pay off those bills.

One of the best features of Quicken reports and graphs is that you can use them to look at your financial data in different ways. You can view your finances in as much or as little detail as you need, and you can pull out just the information that you want. For example, at tax time, I run a report to show all of my tax-deductible expenditures for the previous year, all neatly categorized and totaled. My accountant appreciates it, and because using the reports takes less of his time, it saves me money. The rest of the year, I use reports and graphs to track my income and expenses.

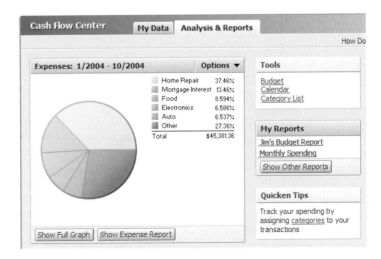

get EasyAnswers

Quicken provides a few different ways to get reports. A good way to find quick answers to your financial questions is through EasyAnswer reports, which answer basic questions such as "Where did I spend my money?" and "What are my investments worth?"

On Windows, choose Reports > EasyAnswer Reports and Graphs. The Reports and Graphs window appears, set to the EasyAnswer tab.

Report questions —

Expense category —

Report dates —

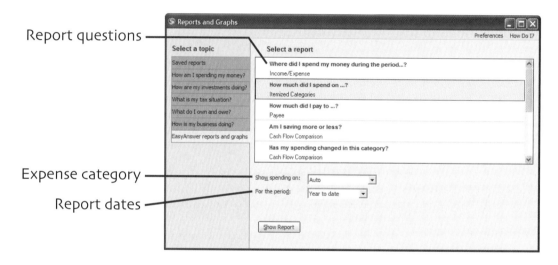

There are ten preconfigured reports in the form of basic questions in the window. Click to select one of them. Depending on which question you choose, the expense category and report dates pop-up menus may change. The report dates menu contains preset time periods for reports.

To get a report, click the report question you want answered, then choose the report date period from the pop-up menu. If the report you chose allows you to select a category, the expense category pop-up menu will appear. Choose the category you want. Click Show Report.

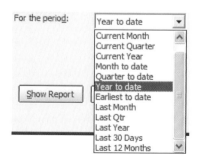

You can change the dates the report covers by choosing from the Date Range menu at the top of the report window. The Interval menu shows you subtotals for time periods; for example, you can see your expenses by Year, Month, Quarter, and so forth.

To get an EasyAnswer report on the Mac, click the Reporting tab, then click the Reports button in the toolbar. The Reports window appears. The report appears, set to the EasyAnswer tab.

Click to select the question you want answered, then choose the date range from the pop-up menu. If you picked a question that requires it, choose a category from the pop-up menu next to the question to narrow your report. Click Create. A new window appears with your selected report.

Interval pop-up menu

Customize button

Date Range pop-up menu

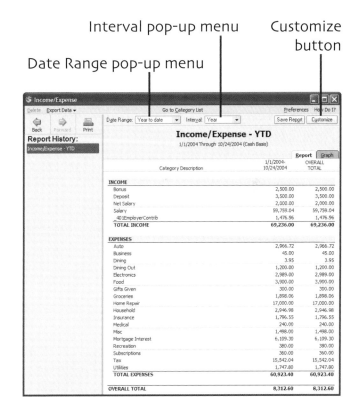

use standard reports

Standard reports give you information such as the details of transactions, net worth, and category transaction reports. Quicken comes with a large number of reports that are ready for you to run.

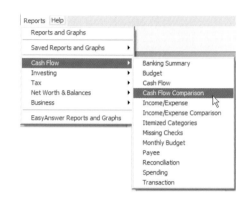

On Windows, select a standard report by choosing Reports > [report category] > [report name].

The report opens. You can change the dates the report covers by choosing from the Date Range menu at the top of the report window.

On the Mac, click the Reporting tab, then click the Reports button in the toolbar. The Reports window appears, set to the EasyAnswer tab. Click one of the other tabs (Standard, Business, Investment, or Memorized).

Category list ———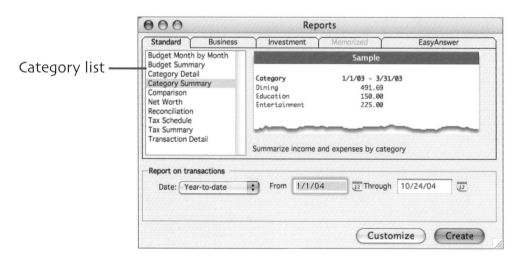

Click to select the report category from the category list. On the right side of the window, Quicken shows you a sample of the report you selected. Choose from the Date pop-up menu, or enter more specific dates in the From and Through fields. Then click Create. The report opens in a new window.

build custom reports

You can customize a report's details. This is useful when you want to include or exclude certain information. For example, I write books for a living, and I want to know how much money I make per book, and I want to exclude any other income. So I created a custom report that included income just from books. Because I had previously created a separate income category for each book, making the custom report was easy.

To customize a report on Windows, create a standard report of the type you want, then click the Customize button at the top of the report window. The Customize window appears.

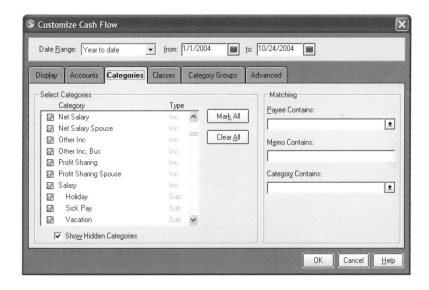

Depending on the kind of report you chose, the Customize window may look different than shown here. Click the different tabs in the Customize window and make choices to customize the report. For example, in the Categories tab of the Customize Cash Flow window shown, I can choose specific categories to include or exclude from the report by selecting or clearing categories in the category list. If I wanted to only include transactions with a particular payee, I would include that payee's name in the Payee Contains field. Experiment until you find the report settings you want, then click OK. The report that was already on your screen will change to match your custom settings.

create reports and graphs

build custom reports

To create a custom report on the Mac, open the Reports window, click to select a standard report of the type you want, then click the Customize button at the bottom of the Reports window. The Customize window appears; depending on the kind of report you chose the window may look different than shown here.

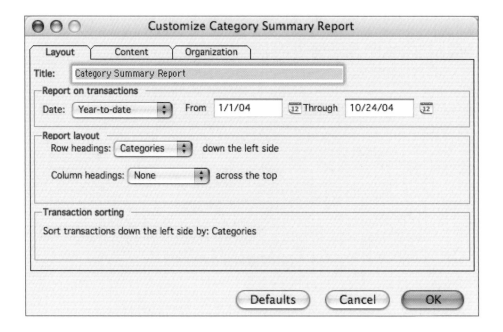

Click the different tabs in the Customize window and make choices to customize the report. Click OK to create the custom report.

save custom reports

Tweaking reports until they're just the way that you want them can take some effort, and it would be a waste of your time if you had to re-create a custom report every time. Instead, you can save custom report settings and reuse them. On Windows, these are called saved reports; on Mac, they are called memorized reports.

Creating saved reports on Windows is easy; when you close a custom report, Quicken automatically asks if you want to save it.

Click Save.

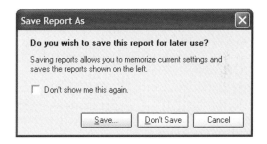

The Save Report dialog appears.

Give the report a name, and choose which of the financial centers you want to save it in. The custom report will appear in the My Reports section of the Analysis & Reports tab of the financial center you select. You can also access them in the Saved Reports and Graphs section of the Reports menu.

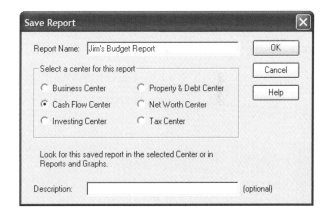

save custom reports (cont.)

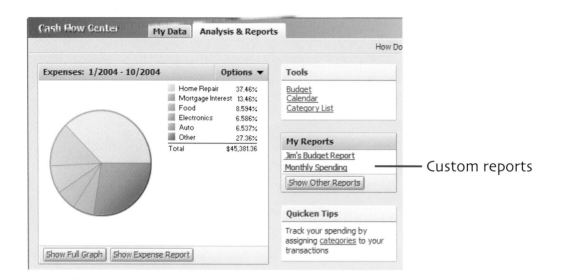

Custom reports

On the Mac, create a custom report, then choose Edit > Memorize. The Memorize Report Template dialog appears.

Enter the custom report name, and optionally add a description, then click Memorize. The report will be available for future use in the Memorized tab of the Reports window.

create graphs

When it comes to getting a good overview of your finances, reports are good, but graphs are better. Graphs can often illustrate relationships in your finances that numeric reports don't make clear. Quicken can display your financial data as bar graphs, line graphs, and pie charts to help you quickly analyze your income and expenses, develop budgets, and determine your net worth.

Graphs can also give you an important emotional boost, as I discovered while working to pay off my own consumer debt. I created a bar graph that showed how much debt I owed. Every month, as I made payments, I checked the graph to see how much the debt bar had shrunk. It felt great to see the downward trend as I worked towards my goal, and it felt even better the month that the bar finally hit the zero mark.

To get graphs on Windows, choose Reports > Reports and Graphs. The Reports and Graphs window appears. Click to choose the category that you want from the Select a topic list on the left side of the window, then click to select the particular report you want from the Select a report list. Not all reports have associated graphs; the ones that do have a Show Graph button at the bottom of the window.

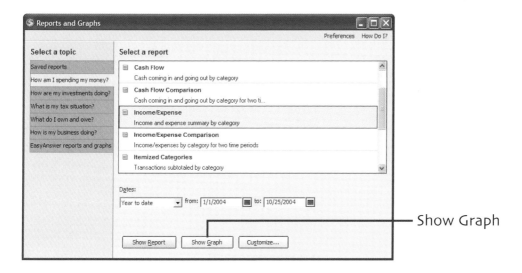

Show Graph

create graphs (cont.)

Choose the date range for the graph in the Dates section of the window, then click Show Graph. The graph appears in a new window. ──────

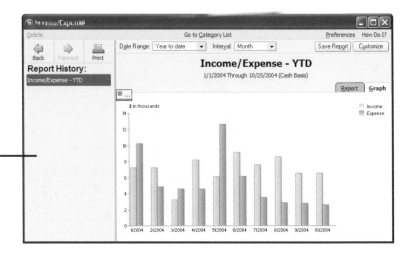

On the Mac, click the Reporting tab, then click the Graphs button in the toolbar. The Graphs window appears.

Click the tab (Standard, Memorized, or EasyAnswer) for the kind of graph you want, then click to select the graph. Click Create to open the window with a new graph.

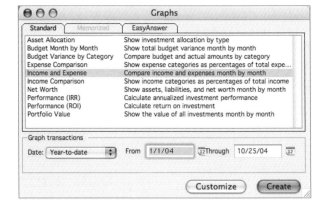

create reports and graphs

print reports or graphs

Sometimes you'll want to print the report or graph. In either case, begin by creating the report or graph that you want.

On Windows, click the Print button at the top of the report or graph window.

The Print dialog appears. Make any adjustments to the print job you desire, then click OK.

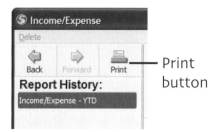

Print button

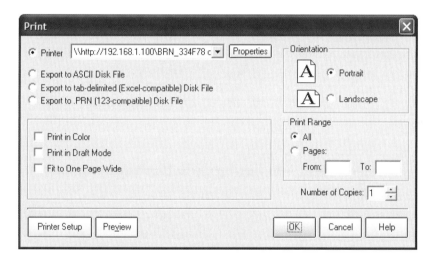

On the Mac, with the report or graph window open, choose File > Print Report or File > Print Graph (the menu item changes to match the kind of window you have open). The Print dialog appears. Click Print.

extra bits

use standard reports p. 110

- When creating reports, one of the options you have for setting the time period of a report is "year-to-date." This just means that it covers the time period from January 1 to today's date. Some reports also offer the option of "last year-to-date," which gives you a report including information from January 1 of last year to the corresponding date from last year that is the same as today's date. This is a great way to find out if your finances are better or worse off than they were at the same time one year ago.

- On almost all reports or graphs, you can use Quicken's Quick-Zoom feature to examine the information in your reports or graphs in greater detail. If you're viewing a report that summarizes the amounts from a category, you can double-click an amount and QuickZoom will take you to another report that shows more detail about the item you selected.

To use QuickZoom, create a report or graph, then move the cursor over one of the amounts in the report (or one of the graph segments) until the cursor turns into a magnifying glass.

EXPENSES	
Uncategorized	0.00
Auto	577.83
Business	0.00

Double-click the report amount or the graph segment. A new report or graph opens showing you details of the item you clicked.

save custom reports p. 113

- When you attempt to close a report that you have customized, Quicken will ask if you want to save the report. If you do many custom reports that you don't want to save, you can turn the message off by clicking the Don't show me this again button in the alert dialog.

create reports and graphs

9. set up and track investments

For the vast majority of us, the key to comfortable living in future years and a stress-free retirement is a solid and consistent savings and investment program. Quicken lets you update current market values and see whether you are earning or losing money on your investments.

Investments in Quicken are contained in a portfolio, which in turn can contain one or more securities. A security can be a single mutual fund, stocks, bonds, or a collection of investments that you have in a brokerage account.

In this chapter, you'll learn how to set up and add to an investment portfolio in Quicken, such as the kind of portfolio you would manage in an IRA or 401(k) account.

Holdings										Options ▼
Show: Value								As of: 11/4/2004		
Name	Quote/Price	Shares	Market Value	Cost Basis	Gain/Loss	Gain/Loss (%)	Day Gain/Loss	Day Change	Day Change (%)	
⊞ Altair Nanotechnologies	2.02	100	202.00	236.49	-34.49	-14.58	1.00	⬆ + 0.01	+0.50%	
⊞ Apple Computer	55.27	25	1,381.75	372.49	1,009.26	270.95	-1.00	⬇ - 0.04	-0.07%	
⊞ Cisco Systems	19.47	58	1,129.26	1,138.95	-9.69	-0.85	11.02	⬆ + 0.19	+0.99%	
⊞ Indevus Pharmaceuticals	6.33	200	1,266.00	821.49	444.51	54.11	-20.00	⬇ - 0.10	-1.56%	
⊞ JDS UNIPHASE CORP	3.13	150	469.50	1,375.44	-905.94	-65.87	0.00		0.00%	
⊞ Lucent	3.58	500	1,790.00	394.99	1,395.01	353.18	-15.00	⬇ - 0.03	-0.83%	
⊞ Pixar	80.99	15	1,214.85	965.37	249.48	25.84	-11.10	⬇ - 0.74	-0.91%	
⊞ S&P Mid Cap Spdr	112.95	15	1,694.25	1,343.49	350.76	26.11	16.50	⬆ + 1.10	+0.98%	
Cash			382.89	382.89						
Totals:			9,530.50	7,031.60	2,498.90	35.54	-18.58			

Online quotes by S&P Comstock, delayed at least 20 minutes. Updated 11/4/2004 at 11:50 am local time. Historical quotes by Iverson.

Download Historical Prices

how much detail?

Before you get started setting up your portfolio account, you need to decide how much investment history to include in your records. You have three options: enter a complete history, just this year's information, or your current investment holdings.

Of the three options, the complete history requires the most data entry, because you'll need to enter the initial purchase price for each security and all of the subsequent transactions. The benefit of this approach is that all of your reports are complete and Quicken can accurately calculate capital gains and losses. Because a large portion of the benefit of tracking your investments in Quicken is knowing how much money you have made or lost, this is the approach that I recommend.

If you have a financial institution that allows you to download information over the Internet directly into Quicken, much of your data entry will be eliminated. I highly recommend this. You'll know that your financial institution can download into Quicken because the name of the financial institution will appear during Quicken Account Setup.

Here are the pros and cons of the two methods of portfolio setup that I do not recommend. If you decide to enter just the current year's data, you'll enter the investment balances as of the end of last year and then enter all of the transactions for each security since the beginning of this year. The good thing about this method is that the information you need to find and enter is more recent and probably easier for you to obtain. Reports that deal with events from this year will be accurate, and if you sell a security, Quicken will be able to track which lots of the security you should sell to minimize or maximize your short-term capital gains. The downside of this method is that Quicken will not know the original cost of the security (called the cost basis), so you can't get accurate long-term capital gains or realized gain reports.

If you decide to enter just your current investment holdings, it will take the least amount of time, because all you have to do is enter information from your latest investment statement. The significant drawback is that data for this year and past years will be incomplete, and you won't be able to get reports for capital gains or realized gains.

set up and track investments

portfolio setup (Win)

To create a portfolio account on Windows, begin by choosing Investing > Investing Accounts > Add Account. The Quicken Account Setup window appears, asking you to specify the financial institution for the account.

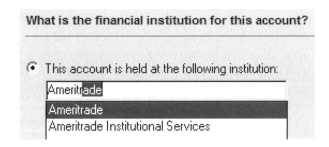

Type in the name of the financial institution. Quicken will try to find the institution in its internal financial institutions list and will enter matches as you type. Click Next when your financial institution appears. If Quicken is unfamiliar with your financial institution, you'll see one more screen that asks you to confirm the name you entered.

Next, you'll be asked if you want to set up your account online or manually. Make your choice, then click Next.

If you clicked Online and your financial institution is one of Quicken's download partners, the next screen you see will ask you to enter your account number and PIN that was provided to you by your financial institution.

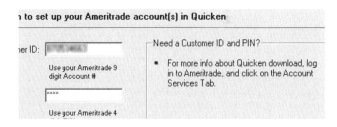

Enter the information, and click Next. Quicken connects to the Internet and downloads setup information about the account, then asks you to give the account a name. Do so, then click Next.

You'll see a summary screen with the information you entered. Click Done. Quicken will connect to your financial institution again to download transactions (most financial institutions keep the past 60–180 days online) and will confirm the account's proper setup in the Online Summary window. Click Done.

portfolio setup (Win)

The account will open, displaying the account holdings. Quicken makes placeholder entries for the current values of the securities in your account. Quicken does not download the cost basis for the holdings, so you should enter the transactions from your account statements that correspond to the placeholder entries, then delete the placeholders.

Value of the account's cash balance

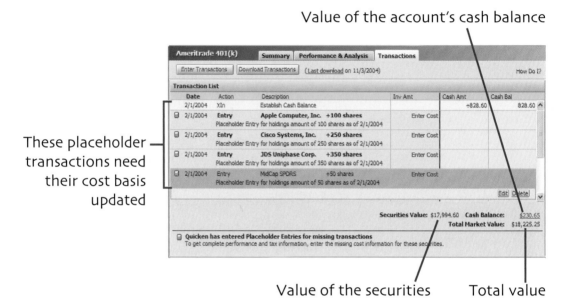

These placeholder transactions need their cost basis updated

Value of the securities   Total value

If you chose to set up the account manually, Quicken will ask you to specify the type of investment account (Standard Brokerage, IRA or Keogh, 401(k) or 403(b), or Single Mutual Fund). Choose the type you want, then click Next.

The next screen differs, depending on the type of investment account you chose, but it will ask you to provide a name and information related to the account. Enter the information, then click Next.

On the next screen, enter information about the cash balance in the account, taken from your latest statement or from the financial institution's Web site. Click Next.

Next, you should enter the ticker symbols of the securities in the account. Quicken will use these symbols to download security details and prices later.

If you don't know the ticker symbols, click the Ticker Symbol Lookup button, and your Web browser will open and allow you to find the symbol. Enter each ticker symbol and the name of the security, then click Next.

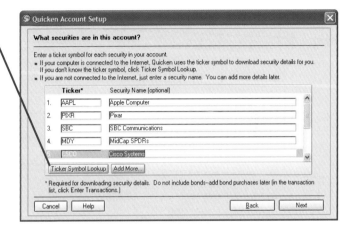

Quicken will connect to the Internet, confirm the symbols, and will then ask you to enter your current holdings for each security. Enter the number of shares you own for each security, and click the button to indicate if the security is a stock, mutual fund, or other security type. When you are done, click Next.

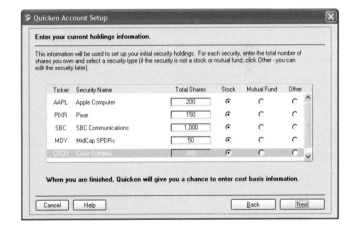

set up and track investments

portfolio setup (Win)

A summary screen appears, allowing you to check your work. If it is correct, click Done. If you made a mistake, click Back and fix the error. When you are done, the account's holdings screen appears, with the current information about the account. Once again, you should enter the cost basis for each security by clicking the Enter links in the Cost Basis column.

Enter links

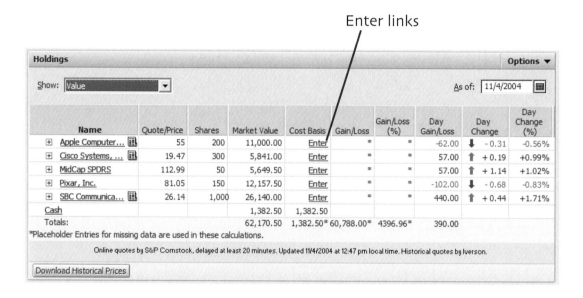

portfolio setup (Mac)

To create a portfolio account on the Mac, click the Investing tab in the toolbar, then choose File > New Account. The New Account Assistant window appears, asking you to specify the financial institution for the account.

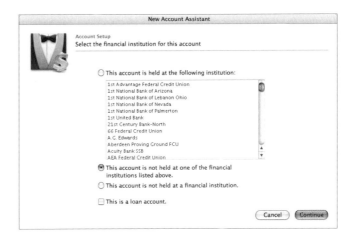

There are only a limited number of financial institutions supported on the Mac for online brokerage access; see page 132 for a list. If your institution is on the list, select it and click Continue. If your financial institution does not appear on the list, select This account is not held at one of the financial institutions listed above, and then click Continue.

On the next screen, in the Investments section, choose the kind of investment account you want to set up, then click Continue.

You're next asked to give the account a name. Type it into the Account name field, then click Continue.

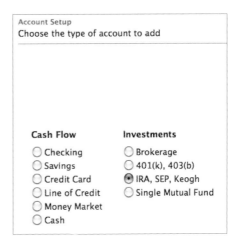

portfolio setup (Mac)

Enter the last statement date, then if the account has a cash balance, enter it in the Cash balance field. Click Continue.

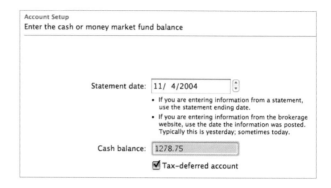

On the next screen, you'll enter your current holdings in this account. Click the Add button. A dialog will slide down from the top of the window. Enter the security name, its ticker symbol, the number of shares held, the purchase date, and the price per share when you bought it. Only the security name and the number of shares held are required at this time; you can go back and add the additional details later. Click OK. The information you added appears in the window. If you have more holdings to add, click the Add button again. Otherwise, click Continue.

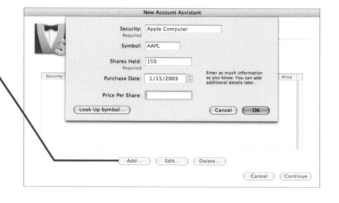

The register for the new Portfolio account opens.

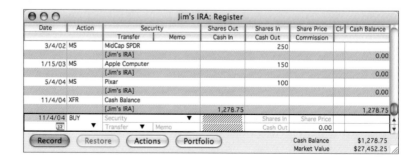

set up and track investments

use portfolio window

The Portfolio window is your main management tool for your investments. You can use it to see the overall value of your investments at a glance; sort your investments in different ways; see how much your investments are worth today, or at anytime in the past; and even track the prices of securities that you don't yet own, but wish to keep an eye on. The Portfolio window is an important tool for analyzing how well your investment strategy is working.

To view your Portfolio on Windows, click to select the investment account in the Account Bar, then click the Summary tab. In the default Value view, you'll see a list of the securities held in the account, along with the current price, the amount of shares owned, gains and losses, and so forth.

Show menu

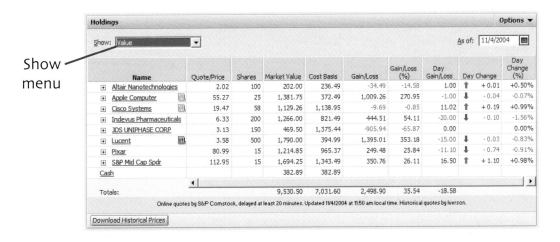

To see the performance of your portfolio, choose either Recent performance or Historic performance from the Show menu. The view changes to show you how well the investments have been doing.

Name	Market Value	Gain/Loss	Gain/Loss (%)	Gain/Loss 1-Month	Gain/Loss 1-Month (%)	Gain/Loss 3-Month (%)	Gain/Loss 12-Month (%)
Altair Nanotechnologies	202.00	-34.49	-14.58	20.00	10.99	68.33	N/A
Apple Computer	1,381.75	1,009.26	270.95	397.50	40.39	85.59	139.99

use portfolio window

You can also see a graph of your investment performance; click the Performance & Analysis tab of the Portfolio account.

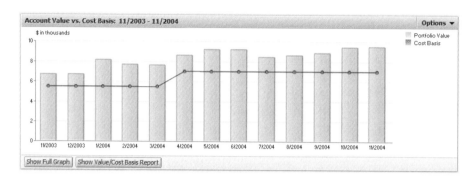

On the Mac, click the Investing tab on the toolbar, then click the Portfolio button. The Portfolio window appears.

Portfolio

Group by menu

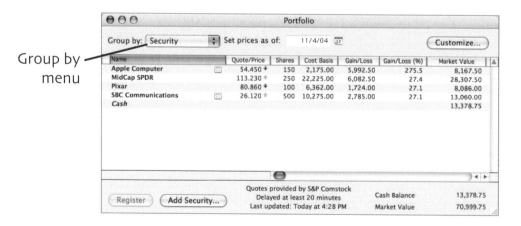

To change the Portfolio view, you can change the Group by pop-up menu. You can sort the contents of the window by Account (which lets you see the securities contained in multiple investment accounts); Security (which consolidates all of your securities in an alphabetical list view); Type (which shows the securities sorted by type, such as Bond, Mutual Fund, and Stock); or Asset Class (this sorts the securities by how large the companies or funds are).

view security details

Another way to work with the securities in your Portfolio window is to zoom in on individual securities to get more information. The security details include the setup information for the security; a graph of the security's performance; and a list of the transactions that you have made with that security.

To view security details on Windows, click the portfolio account in the Account Bar, then click the Summary tab. In the list of securities, the date of the security will be blue and underlined, indicating that it is a link. Click the link. The security detail window opens.

Security details —

Transaction history —

Your holdings —

Detailed quote information —

Price graph —

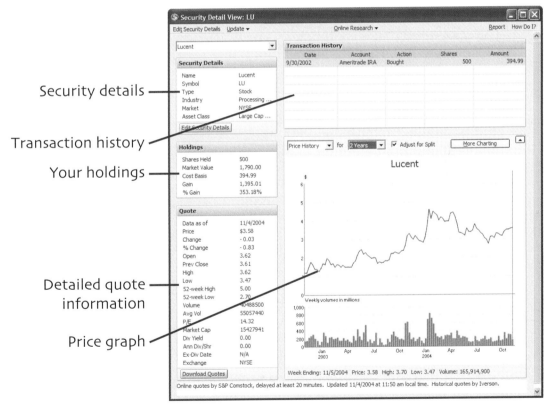

Security details in Windows

view security details

On the Mac, click the Investing tab on the toolbar, then click the Portfolio button on the toolbar. In the Portfolio window, double-click the name of the

security for which you want detail. The Security Detail window appears. Click the different tabs in the Security Detail window to see the Setup Info, Graph, Prices, or Transactions.

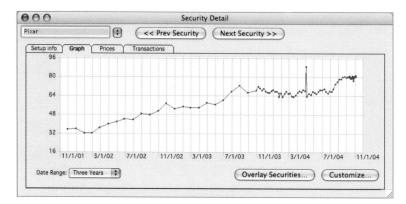

Security details in Macintosh

set up and track investments

download quotes

In order for your investment information to be up-to-date, you'll need to periodically download current security prices to your portfolio. Normally, downloading security prices will be just one of the tasks included when you do a One Step Update (see Chapter 5 for more on One Step Update), but it is also possible to get security price quotes without doing your other online activities.

To download security price quotes on Windows, choose Investing > Online Activities > Download Quotes. The One Step Update window appears, showing you the download progress. Your Portfolio will update to display the latest price quotes.

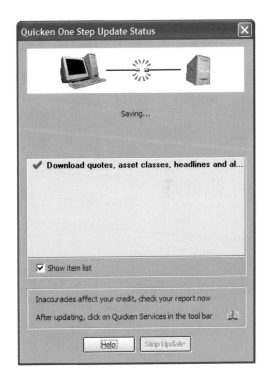

On the Mac, choose Online > Update Security Prices. The Quicken Quotes Progress window appears reporting the download progress.

The Portfolio window will update to display the latest price quotes.

extra bits

portfolio setup (Win) p. 121

- To see a list of all of the financial institutions that Quicken for Windows supports, choose Online > Participating Financial Institutions. A browser window opens with the list.

portfolio setup (Mac) p. 125

- To see a list of all of the financial institutions that Quicken for Macintosh supports, choose Online > Financial Institutions. The Financial Institutions window appears. To update the list with the latest information (new financial institutions are being added all the time), click the Update List button at the bottom of the window.

- Unfortunately, there are far fewer financial institutions that can download brokerage transactions directly into Quicken for Mac than can do so with Quicken for Windows. At press time, that list included 11 institutions: A.G. Edwards, Charles Schwab & Company, CSFB Private Client Services, Fidelity Investments, Harrisdirect, Morgan Keegan & Company, Northern Trust, RBC Dain Rauscher, TD Waterhouse, TIAA-CREF, and Wells Fargo Investments.

download quotes p. 131

- You can download prices as many times a day as you wish, but Quicken stores only one price per day, the last price you downloaded.

- Prices for stocks, options, and indexes are updated constantly during the business day, although the quotes you get online are delayed from real-time by about 20 minutes. Prices for mutual funds are updated only once per day at 6 p.m. Eastern time.

10. manage investments

After setting up your investment portfolio (see Chapter 9), you'll need to manage your investments on an ongoing basis. That means updating the share prices of your securities and making entries whenever you buy or sell an investment. You learned how to download security prices at the end of the last chapter, and this chapter will show you how to enter investment transactions in Quicken when you buy and sell securities. You'll also learn how to deal with transactions that aren't tied to a purchase or sale, such as when a security pays a dividend.

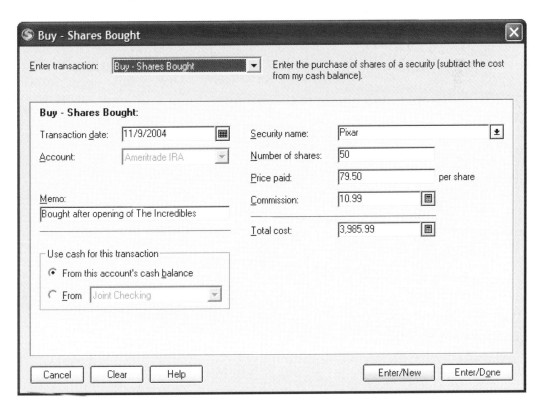

add transactions (Win)

Because entering security transactions can be a bit involved, Quicken uses special dialogs to walk you through the process. These dialogs ensure that you will enter all of the information that Quicken needs to properly track the transaction.

On Windows, begin by clicking to select the investment account in the Account Bar. Towards the top of the window, click Enter Transactions.

The Investment Transactions dialog appears. The contents of this dialog will change, depending on the investment action selected from the Enter transaction pop-up menu, and whether the account is a single mutual fund or a portfolio account. This example is for purchasing shares of a stock in a portfolio account. Of course, if you want another kind of transaction, you should choose it from the Enter transaction pop-up menu.

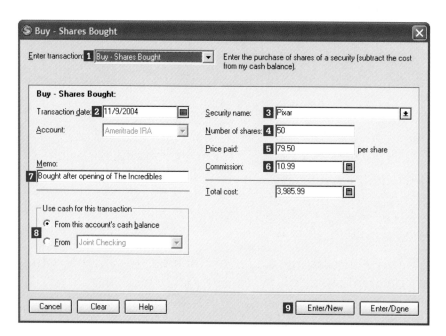

1 Choose Buy – Shares Bought from the investment transactions pop-up menu.

2 Enter the Transaction date.

3 Choose the security you want to purchase from the Security name pop-up menu. This menu lists all the securities you have previously bought. If you are buying a security that is new to your portfolio, click the Add New Security button at the bottom of the pop-up menu, and Quicken will walk you through a quick Wizard to add the new security.

Add New Security

4 Enter the number of shares you have bought in the Number of shares field.

5 Enter the price you paid per share in the Price paid field.

6 If you paid a broker commission, enter its dollar amount in the Commission field. Quicken calculates the cost of the transaction (number of shares times price per share plus commission) and places the result in the Total cost field.

7 If you want to add a memo, type it in the Memo field.

8 The money to pay for your purchase can either come from the cash balance in your portfolio account or from another Quicken account, such as your checking account. If it comes from the portfolio cash balance, in the Use cash for this transaction section, click From this account's cash balance. If the money comes from another account, click From, and then choose the account from the pop-up menu next to it.

9 If you want to save the current transaction and immediately enter another, click Enter/New. If you are done entering transactions, click Enter/Done. The investment transaction is saved, and it appears in the Transactions tab of the investment account.

add transactions (Mac)

On the Mac, you enter investment transactions using the Investment Actions window. This lists all of the possible investment transactions.

Begin by clicking the Investing tab on the toolbar, then clicking the Portfolio button, which opens the Portfolio window. If you instead want to do an investment action on a single mutual fund account, choose the account from the Registers pop-up menu on the toolbar, and its register will open.

Choose Activities > Investment Actions. The Investment Actions window appears. Double-click the investment action you want, and the associated action form appears.

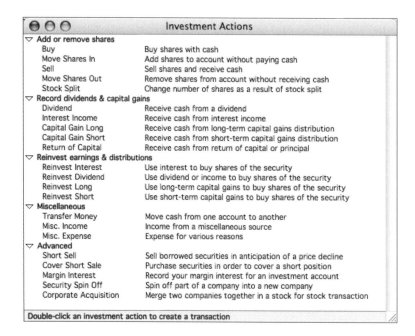

1 Choose the investment account from the Account pop-up menu.

2 Enter the transaction date.

3 Enter the number of shares you bought.

4 Choose the security you want to purchase from the pop-up menu next to Of. This menu lists all the securities you have previously bought. If you are buying a security that is new to your portfolio, Quicken will walk you through a quick Wizard to add the new security.

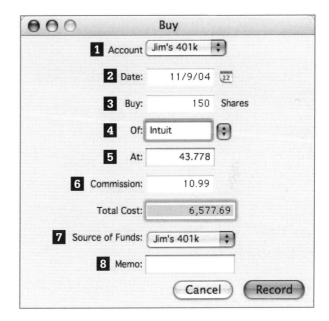

5 Enter the share price in the At field.

6 Enter the Commission amount. Quicken calculates the Total Cost.

7 Use the Source of Funds pop-up menu to specify where the money for the purchase is coming from.

8 If you like, add a Memo.

9 Click Record to save your transaction.

deal with dividends

There are many transactions that can occur in your investment accounts that are not the result of buying or selling shares of securities with cash. The most common are dividends in a portfolio account and capital gains distributions and reinvestments in single mutual fund accounts.

To enter these transactions manually, you will use the investment action forms again. On Windows, select the investment account in the Account Bar, click the Transactions tab, then click Enter Transactions. In the investment actions dialog, choose the kind of transaction you need to enter, then fill out the dialog.

On the Mac, choose Activities > Investment Actions. The Investment Actions window appears. Double-click the investment action you want, and the associated action form appears. Fill out the form, and click Record.

If your financial institution supports it, downloading investment transactions gives you many of the same benefits as online banking, namely less manual entry, better accuracy, and a significant time savings.

To download investment transactions on Windows, click the One Step Update button in the toolbar, then choose the accounts that you want to update in the One Step Update dialog, then click Update Now. Quicken will go online, connect to your financial institutions, and download any transactions that are available.

Accounts that have downloaded investment transactions that need to be reviewed will be flagged in the Account Bar.

Flag —— ⚑ Ameritrade IRA   9,638.55

Click the flag to open the account and review your transaction. On the Transactions tab of the account, the bottom half of the window will show the downloaded transactions. Click to select a transaction, and Accept and Delete buttons will appear below the transaction. If the transaction is OK, click Accept. The transaction will appear in the transaction list.

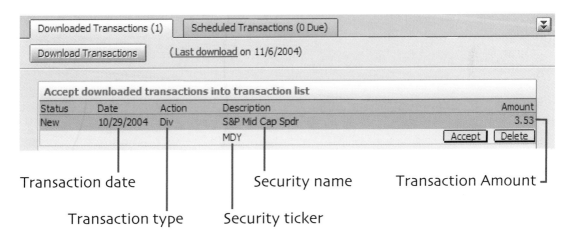

On the Mac, begin downloading investment transactions by clicking the Download button in the Investing section of the toolbar. The Download Transactions window appears. Choose the investment account you want from the pop-up menu at the top the window, then click the Get Online Data button. Quicken goes online and downloads the transactions, which are displayed in the Download Transactions window. Click the Accept button to add the downloaded items to your register.

manage investments **139**

extra bits

add transactions (Win) p. 134

- You'll find explanations of the more exotic investment actions found in the Enter transaction pop-up menu, such as short selling, in the Quicken User Guide.

- The column at the right edge of a single mutual fund account register and a portfolio account register differs. In a portfolio account, the column shows the running Cash Balance in the account. Mutual fund accounts don't have cash balances, so the column is called Share Balance, and shows a running total of the accumulated shares in the account.

add transactions (Mac) p. 136

- When you're selling a security, if you leave the Destination of Funds field blank, Quicken credits the proceeds of the sale to the Portfolio account, which increases the cash balance in the account. This doesn't work for single mutual fund accounts, because such accounts can't have a cash balance.

- The number of investment transactions available in a mutual fund account is smaller than the transactions available in a portfolio account, because a portfolio account provides a wider array of investment options. For example, you can short sell a security in a portfolio account, but you can't short sell a mutual fund.

deal with dividends p. 138

- Unlike online banking, online investment transactions through Quicken are a one-way trip; you can enter transactions in Quicken by downloading them, but you can't use Quicken to create new transactions, such as buying or selling securities. For that, you'll need to use your online broker's Web site, or even talk to your broker on the telephone.

- You enable an investment account for online transactions in the same way that you online enable any other account. If you need help, see Chapter 5.

manage investments

index

index

index

index